生产系统建模与仿真

Modeling and Simulation of Production System

（双语版）

罗亚波　著

华中科技大学出版社
中国·武汉

内 容 简 介

"生产系统建模与仿真"是工业工程专业的一门主干课程,既涉及较深的数学理论知识,又涉及在生产运作领域的应用方法。在武汉理工大学"十三五"规划教材项目的支持下,笔者整理该课程十余年的教学积累,撰写了这一本双语版教材。全书可分为三大部分:第1章至第4章为生产系统建模基础理论,介绍了复杂系统的主要特征、系统建模基础、生产系统优化模型、生产系统中的概率问题;第5章至第8章为生产系统求解方法,介绍了典型的传统优化方法与先进仿生算法的原理及其在生产系统求解中的应用方法;第9章介绍了生产系统建模与仿真课程设计的内容,是对前两部分所学理论与方法的一次综合实践。

本书可以作为工业工程专业本科生和研究生教学用书,也可以作为管理学科相关专业的教材,并为企业生产管理人员提供参考。

图书在版编目(CIP)数据

生产系统建模与仿真=Modeling and Simulation of Production System:英、汉/罗亚波著. —武汉:华中科技大学出版社,2020.8
ISBN 978-7-5680-6217-6

Ⅰ.①生… Ⅱ.①罗… Ⅲ.①生产管理-系统建模-高等学校-教材-英、汉 ②生产管理-系统仿真-高等学校-教材-英、汉 Ⅳ.①F273-39

中国版本图书馆 CIP 数据核字(2020)第 145272 号

生产系统建模与仿真(双语版) 罗亚波 著
Shengchan Xitong Jianmo yu Fangzhen(Shuangyu Ban)

策划编辑:张少奇
责任编辑:罗 雪
封面设计:刘 婷
责任监印:周治超
出版发行:华中科技大学出版社(中国·武汉)   电话:(027)81321913
　　　　　武汉市东湖新技术开发区华工科技园　　邮编:430223
录　　排:武汉三月禾文化传播有限公司
印　　刷:湖北新华印务有限公司
开　　本:787mm×1092mm 1/16
印　　张:15
字　　数:383 千字
版　　次:2020 年 8 月第 1 版第 1 次印刷
定　　价:45.80 元

本书若有印装质量问题,请向出版社营销中心调换
全国免费服务热线:400-6679-118 竭诚为您服务
版权所有　侵权必究

前　言

工业工程(industrial engineering,IE)是在科学管理的基础上发展起来的一门应用性工程专业学科。美国工业工程师学会(AIIE)早在1955年,就提出了对工业工程的定义:"工业工程是对人、物料、设备、能源和信息等所组成的集成系统,进行设计、改善和实施的一门学科,它综合运用数学、物理和社会科学的专门知识和技术,结合工程分析和设计的原理与方法,对该系统所取得的成果进行确认、预测和评价。"

同时,工业工程专业的教育体系,在发达国家也已比较成熟,已经依据不同的专业背景,形成了很多独具特色的工业工程专业,如:美国普渡大学的工业工程专业以农业为背景,美国密歇根大学的工业工程专业则是以制造业为背景。总体而言,以美国、日本为代表的发达国家,已经形成了与其工业发展水平相应的成熟的工业工程教育体系。

相比较而言,工业工程教育在中国则还处于初级阶段。直至20世纪90年代初期,中国才在部分重点大学首批建立了工业工程专业。随着中国工业的发展,企业对工业工程的专业需求也日趋急迫,早期的工业工程专业毕业生出现了供不应求的局面。相应地,近十余年来,中国大部分大学开设了工业工程专业,工业工程专业已经成为中国发展最快的专业之一。

由于工业工程专业教育在中国尚处于初级阶段,教材的撰写还缺乏可借鉴的经验;同时,一些课程涉及的理论与实践问题较深,需要以长期的研究工作为基础。因此,与我国工业发展阶段相适应的专业教材,目前还比较欠缺。

"生产系统建模与仿真"是工业工程专业的一门主干课程,既涉及较深的数学理论知识,如排队论、系统建模、优化理论、仿真方法等;又涉及在生产运作领域的应用问题,如生产系统布局优化、作业车间调度问题等。目前,国内关于该课程的成熟的教材还很少。

多年来,笔者主讲课程"生产系统建模与仿真",并依托国家自然科学基金(51875430、51375357、50705072)、湖北省杰出青年人才基金、武汉市青年科技晨光计划等基金项目,在相关领域开展了长期的研究工作。本书就是通过整理该课程的教案,并结合多年来在该领域的研究工作撰写而成的。

全书主要内容如下。

第1章,绪论:在介绍生产系统的特征、分类、演化历史的基础上,着重阐述了对生产系统进行建模与仿真的必要性与目标。

第2章,系统建模基础:介绍了与复杂系统相关的基本概念和基础知识,如系统的概念、系统建模的一般步骤、NP-Hard问题与NPC问题等,解析了具有代表意义的三类系统建模方法。

第3章，生产系统优化模型：在系统建模的基础上，具体阐述了以生产系统为对象的建模方法，分别介绍了单机调度模型、并行机调度模型、独立作业系统调度模型，初步阐述了作业车间调度问题的相关概念。

第4章，生产系统中的概率问题：在介绍概率论、排队论的基本概念和理论的基础上，通过实例阐述了概率分析方法、排队论在生产系统建模中的应用。

第5章，基于复合形法的生产系统求解方法：首先结合实例，介绍了传统优化方法——复合形法的基本思想和一般步骤，然后阐述了复合形法在作业车间调度优化中的应用。

第6章，遗传算法及其在生产调度中的应用：首先介绍了遗传算法的基本原理与实现方法，然后以车间布局优化、装箱问题为例，阐述了遗传算法在生产系统建模与优化中的应用，最后详细阐述了如何应用遗传算法解决车间调度问题。

第7章，蚁群算法及其在生产系统优化中的应用：首先介绍了蚁群算法的基本原理，然后以车间调度问题、零件配送路径规划问题为实例，详细阐述了蚁群算法在生产系统建模与优化中的应用。

第8章，生产线平衡理论与方法：分别以流水线和混流生产线为例，在阐述生产线平衡的基本概念与原理的基础上，结合实例，详解了生产线平衡的建模理论与求解方法。

第9章，生产系统建模与仿真课程设计：首先描述了课程设计任务，然后以小规模和中等规模作业车间调度问题为例，阐述了课程设计任务的解决方法和步骤，最后详解了采用作业车间调度优化系统进行的车间调度问题求解实验。

研究生余晗琳、张凯鹏、郝海强参与了本书的撰写与编辑工作，在此一并表示感谢！

本教材获批武汉理工大学"十三五"规划教材。通过本书，读者既可以系统学习建模、优化与仿真理论，又可以了解这些理论在生产系统设计中的应用方法。本书可以作为工业工程专业本科生和研究生教学用书，也可以作为管理学科相关专业的教材，并为企业生产管理人员提供参考。

当然，一本成熟的教材，需要经历长时间的教学互动磨合和积累，《生产系统建模与仿真》也不例外。我们将在今后的教学实践中，进一步完善该教材，并恳请国内外同仁多提宝贵意见。

罗亚波

2020年3月20日

于武汉理工大学

目　　录

第 1 章　绪论 …………………………………………………………………… (1)
　1.1　生产系统的特征 …………………………………………………………… (1)
　1.2　生产系统的分类 …………………………………………………………… (1)
　1.3　生产系统的演化历史 ……………………………………………………… (2)
　1.4　生产系统建模与仿真的必要性与目标 …………………………………… (3)

第 2 章　系统建模基础 ………………………………………………………… (5)
　2.1　系统的概念 ………………………………………………………………… (5)
　2.2　系统建模的一般方法 ……………………………………………………… (6)
　2.3　NPC 问题与 NP-Hard 问题 ……………………………………………… (8)
　2.4　三类系统建模问题实例解析 ……………………………………………… (12)

第 3 章　生产系统优化模型 …………………………………………………… (16)
　3.1　生产系统建模概论 ………………………………………………………… (16)
　3.2　单机调度模型 ……………………………………………………………… (17)
　3.3　并行机调度模型 …………………………………………………………… (18)
　3.4　独立作业系统调度模型 …………………………………………………… (19)
　3.5　作业车间调度问题 ………………………………………………………… (22)

第 4 章　生产系统中的概率问题 ……………………………………………… (26)
　4.1　概率分析方法的应用概论 ………………………………………………… (26)
　4.2　概率论的几个基本概念及其应用 ………………………………………… (27)
　4.3　中心极限定理及其应用 …………………………………………………… (31)
　4.4　队列特征分析 ……………………………………………………………… (33)
　4.5　小结 ………………………………………………………………………… (37)

第 5 章　基于复合形法的生产系统求解方法 ………………………………… (38)
　5.1　复合形法的基本思想和一般步骤 ………………………………………… (38)
　5.2　复合形法求解实例 ………………………………………………………… (41)
　5.3　复合形法在作业车间调度优化中的应用 ………………………………… (45)

第 6 章　遗传算法及其在生产调度中的应用 …………………………………………… (51)
6.1　遗传算法的形成和发展 ……………………………………………………… (51)
6.2　遗传算法基础 ………………………………………………………………… (52)
6.3　遗传算法应用实例——车间设备布局优化 ………………………………… (55)
6.4　遗传算法应用实例——装箱问题 …………………………………………… (59)
6.5　遗传算法求解作业车间调度问题 …………………………………………… (60)
6.6　小结 …………………………………………………………………………… (62)

第 7 章　蚁群算法及其在生产系统优化中的应用 …………………………………… (63)
7.1　蚁群算法概述 ………………………………………………………………… (63)
7.2　蚁群算法的基本原理 ………………………………………………………… (64)
7.3　蚁群算法求解实例 …………………………………………………………… (70)
7.4　小结 …………………………………………………………………………… (74)

第 8 章　生产线平衡理论与方法 ………………………………………………………… (75)
8.1　生产流水线优化方法 ………………………………………………………… (75)
8.2　混流生产线平衡 ……………………………………………………………… (85)

第 9 章　生产系统建模与仿真课程设计 ………………………………………………… (91)
9.1　课程设计任务描述 …………………………………………………………… (91)
9.2　小规模作业车间调度问题求解示例 ………………………………………… (91)
9.3　中等规模作业车间调度问题求解示例 ……………………………………… (95)
9.4　小结 …………………………………………………………………………… (102)

参考文献 …………………………………………………………………………………… (103)

第 1 章 绪 论

1.1 生产系统的特征

生产系统是指由人、生产原料、生产工具共同组成的能将生产原料转换为产品的系统。由一个人、简单工具和原料,就可以组成一个手工作坊式的简单生产系统。包含复杂工作流、物质流、信息流和复杂约束关系的大型现代化车间,则是复杂生产系统。无论是简单系统还是复杂系统,生产系统都具有以下典型特征。

(1) 生产系统具备人、生产原料、生产工具三要素。人是生产系统的主导要素,通过劳动来控制生产原料或操作生产工具,从而达到将生产原料转换为产品的目标。

(2) 生产系统具有层次性。当生产系统达到一定的复杂度,为了使系统更有效地运作,系统内将形成具有专有目标功能的子系统,如资源规划系统、质量控制系统、物流控制系统、库存管理系统等,以实现逐层控制和独立控制。

(3) 生产系统是一个信息处理系统。生产系统包含各类信息流,如:人工信息、原料信息、设备状态信息、生产计划信息。这些信息流之间具有关联特征,如何有效处理这些信息流,是生产系统的重要内容。

(4) 生产系统是劳动转化系统。无论是体力密集型还是科技密集型生产系统,其内容都是将人类脑力或体力劳动融入生产系统,并通过产品体现出其价值。

(5) 生产系统是知识转化系统。无论是简单生产系统还是复杂生产系统,其运作过程都是以人类的知识为基础的。没有知识作为基础,原料无法最终转换为有使用价值的产品。

随着人类社会的发展、科技水平的提升,生产系统包含越来越多的科技知识和越来越复杂的信息流。当生产系统复杂到一定程度的时候,对生产系统进行合理的优化,就成了提升生产系统效率的必然途径。对生产系统进行建模与仿真的目的,就是实现生产系统的优化。

1.2 生产系统的分类

从不同的视角,生产系统有不同的分类方法,如:从工业特点的视角,可分为连续性生产系统和离散性生产系统;从生产计划的来源,可分为订货式生产系统和存货式生产系统;从生产系统组织形式的视角,可分为作业车间系统、流水车间系统、生产线三大类。一般依据生产系统不同的组织形式进行建模、优化与仿真。

（1）作业车间(job shop)系统。作业车间系统是通用加工系统,没有固定的流程和专业化产品生产的目标,其运作过程以作业任务为单位,生产设备具有通用性。一般的普通加工车间就是典型的作业车间系统,可以描述为:有 i 个待加工工件,每个工件的加工任务由若干相互关联的工序组成,将这些工序合理地分配到 m 类 n 台设备进行加工,并在满足工序之间复杂关联约束关系的前提下,使作业系统效率最高。

（2）流水车间(flow shop)系统。流水车间系统一般是专用制造系统,主要用于处理标准化、流程化、连续的物流。作业人员和作业工具对每批生产任务进行同样的操作,生产固定的产品。流水车间一般是大批量生产车间或具有连续生产布局的车间,车间以标准化生产流程为依据进行布局。流程标准化的工业车间,如装配、喷涂、化工等车间,是流水车间系统的典型例子。

（3）生产线(production line)。生产线是以生产固定产品或零部件为目标,并围绕该目标组织固定的设备和专业人员而形成的生产系统。生产线的种类较多:按生产对象分为产品生产线和零部件生产线;按节奏快慢分为流水生产线和非流水生产线;按自动化程度分为自动化生产线、半自动化生产线和非自动化生产线。与流水车间系统相比,生产线具有更显著的固化特征、更高的专业化程度和更明确的产品生产特征。

1.3　生产系统的演化历史

从第一次工业革命之前的工场手工业时代,到方兴未艾的以智能化生产为目标的工业4.0时代,生产系统经历了漫长的演化过程。

（1）第一次工业革命之前,即工场手工业时代。16～18世纪是西欧封建社会解体并开始向资本主义过渡的时期,工场手工业通过长期的发展,带来日益发达的劳动分工,生产工具不断改进,生产日趋专门化,同时也培养了一大批有熟练技术的工人。这一时期是在生产工具和劳动分工的发展达到一定程度时产生的,为第一次工业革命的发生及工场手工业向机器大工业过渡,创造了必要的物质技术条件。工场手工业时代的生产系统主要有以下两种形式。

① 分散的手工工场:商人仅将原料提供给众多的小手工业者进行加工,生产分散进行,手工业者仍保存着形式上的经济独立地位。

② 集中的手工工场:商人对手工业者的控制进一步加强,他们不仅供应手工业生产的原料,还供应生产工具等。这就使手工业者彻底地从属于商人,变成了一无所有的雇佣劳动者。商人将这些劳动者集中在大型作坊中,共同协作进行生产活动。

（2）工业1.0,即机械制造时代,通过水力和蒸汽机实现工厂机械化,大幅度解放了体力劳动,时间大概是18世纪60年代至19世纪中期,其标志是蒸汽机的出现与应用。从社会关系来说,工业革命使依附于落后生产方式的自耕农阶级消失了,工业资产阶级和工业无产阶级形成和壮大起来。在机械制造时代,生产系统的形式由工场制转变为工厂制,其主要特点是:

① 以蒸汽机为主要生产动力,机械动力替代了人工劳动,生产效率大大提高;

② 形成了规模化生产,生产、销售实行专业化分工,市场范围迅速扩大;

③ 形成了较为完整的管理系统,按产品或工艺分成了生产车间、工段和班组,出现了职能化组织结构;

④ 经济社会从以农业、手工业为基础转型到以工业、机械制造带动经济发展的新模式。

(3) 工业 2.0,即电气化与自动化时代,在劳动分工基础上采用电力驱动产品大规模生产,一定程度上实现了生产自动化,时间是 19 世纪 70 年代至 20 世纪初,其标志是电力的广泛应用,用电力取代蒸汽动力驱动机器,从此零部件生产与产品装配实现分工,工业进入大规模生产时代。因为有了电力,生产活动进入了由继电器、电气自动化控制机械设备生产的时代,从而在一定程度上实现了自动化,开创了产品批量生产的高效新模式。工业 2.0 的实现,更大程度地解放了生产过程中的体力劳动。

著名的福特生产流水线便是在这一时期出现的。在此生产系统内,流水线把一个重复的过程分为若干个子过程,每个子过程可以和其他子过程并行运作,从而使得产品的生产工序被分割成若干个环节,工人间的分工更为细致,产品的质量和产量大幅度提高,促进了生产工艺过程和产品的标准化。福特生产流水线的出现,大幅度降低了汽车生产成本,使汽车工业迅速成为美国的一大支柱产业。

(4) 工业 3.0,即电子信息化时代,在升级工业 2.0 的基础上,广泛应用电子与信息技术,使制造过程自动化控制程度进一步大幅度提高,使生产效率、良品率、分工合作效率、机械设备寿命都得到了前所未有的提升。电子信息时代从 20 世纪 70 年代开始并一直延续至今,其显著标志是计算机和互联网的出现。自此,机器能够逐步替代人类作业,不仅接管了相当比例的体力劳动,还接管了部分脑力劳动。

丰田生产方式(TOYOTA production system,TPS)就出现于工业 3.0 时代,生产系统的特征由大规模流水线生产逐渐过渡到精益生产。TPS 是丰田公司通用的制造方法,其基本思想是"彻底杜绝浪费",通过生产的整体化,追求产品制造的合理性及品质至上的成本节约。精益生产的核心,即关于生产计划、控制和库存管理的基本思想,对丰富和发展现代生产管理理论具有重要作用。

(5) 工业 4.0,即智能化时代,是由德国政府在《德国 2020 高技术战略》中所提出的十大未来项目之一。该项目旨在提升制造业的智能化水平,建立具有适应性、资源高效率及基因工程学的智慧工厂。当然,由于智能技术的发展还处于初级阶段,因此工业 4.0 目前也还处于概念描述和技术攻关的初级阶段。

1.4 生产系统建模与仿真的必要性与目标

随着生产系统日益复杂,对生产系统进行优化以提升其运作效率,就显得尤为重要。而生产系统建模与仿真,是实现系统优化的手段。即使是看似简单的生产系统,例如小规模的并行机系统,优化前后的差异也非常大。

并行机问题可以描述如下:有 n 个任务在时间点 0 处可以开始加工,有 m 台设备可以加工这些任务,一般来说,任务数 n 大于设备数 m,调度目标是使所有任务的总加工时间最小。

假设现有待加工工件 A1、A2、A3、A4 和两台相同的可用设备 M1、M2。对并行机问题来说,工件可以被分配至任意一台设备上进行加工。若四个工件在设备上的加工时间(单位:min)分别是 4、8、6、10,即使假定每台设备上必须分配两个工件进行加工,也可以得到完工时间不同的以下三种配置方式：

$$M1(A1,A2),M2(A3,A4)$$
$$M1(A1,A3),M2(A2,A4)$$
$$M1(A1,A4),M2(A2,A3)$$

相应的甘特图如图1-1所示。通过甘特图可知，以上三种配置方式对应的总加工时间（单位：min）分别是16、18、14，其中的最优配置方案是M1(A1,A4)，M2(A2,A3)。而如果没有每台设备上必须分配两个工件的假定，则配置方案更多，其中最劣方案是四个工件都分配在一台设备上，完工时间为28 min。可以发现，在并行机问题中，对于任务的不同分配方式，系统效率各不相同，在本案例中，最优解和最差解之间的效率有100%的差异。

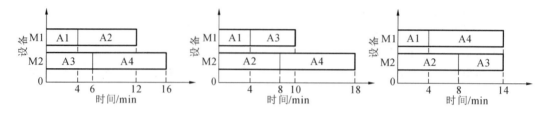

图1-1 并行机问题实例甘特图

再如生产线平衡问题，若某工厂生产一种零部件，其加工过程共有四道工序，记为P1、P2、P3、P4。已知生产该零部件四道工序的作业时间（单位：min）分别为5、3、2、1，瓶颈工序为P1。若为该流水线上的每道工序各设置一个工位，则流水线的生产节拍为5 min，设备利用率（设备利用率＝(设备实际运行时间/设备等待时间)×100%）为47%，生产线平衡率为55%。而若将流水线上各工序配置的工位数量进行适当调整和改进，如工序P1配置三个工位，工序P2配置两个工位，工序P3配置两个工位，工序P4配置一个工位，则流水线的生产节拍约为1.67 min，设备利用率为77.4%，生产线平衡率为82.3%。由此可以看出，在生产线平衡问题中，对于不同的工位配置方式，生产线效率有很大的差异。

从以上简单案例可以看出，即使对于元素很少的简单生产系统而言，优化前后的生产效率也大相径庭。随着技术的发展、工业化的不断升级，生产系统日趋复杂，表现为生产系统中的元素大幅度增多，元素之间的相互关联显著增强，元素之间的耦合关系更加复杂。这使得生产系统成为元素耦合较强的复杂系统，如果不对其进行优化设计，则很容易陷入低效运作，导致高昂的生产运作成本。

生产系统建模与仿真的方法和目标是：基于数学理论对生产系统进行数学建模，采用先进的优化方法对模型进行优化，通过仿真手段对生产系统的设计方案进行运行过程模拟和结果验证，从而为验证或改善设计方案提供参考，最终达到优化生产系统、提升生产系统运作效率的目标。

第 2 章　系统建模基础

2.1　系统的概念

1. 系统的定义

英文中系统"system"一词来源于古希腊文"systema",后者意为部分组成的整体。一般系统论的创始人贝塔朗菲(Ludwig Von Bertalanffy)将系统定义为:系统是相互联系、相互作用的诸元素的综合体。这个定义强调了元素间的相互作用,以及系统对元素的整合作用。中国科学家钱学森认为:系统是由相互作用、相互依赖的若干组成部分结合而成的具有特定功能的有机整体,而且这个有机整体又是它从属的更大系统的组成部分。可以说,一群有相互关联的个体组成的集合就称为系统。

可以这样对系统的定义进行数学描述:如果对象集 S 满足条件

① S 中至少包含两个不同元素;

② S 中的元素按一定方式存在相互联系;

那么称 S 为一个系统,S 中的元素为系统的组成部分。

系统具备以下三个特性:

(1) 多元性,系统是多样性的统一,差异性的统一;

(2) 相关性,系统不存在孤立元素组分,所有元素或组分相互依存,相互作用,相互制约;

(3) 整体性,系统是所有元素构成的复合统一整体。

满足以上数学描述,并具备以上三个特征的有机整体,就可以作为系统来进行建模和分析。

2. 系统的分类

按照形成和运行特征划分,系统可以分为以下三类。

(1) 自然系统:系统内的个体按自然法则存在或演变,产生或形成一种群体的自然现象与特征。自然系统的典型特征是自组织性,即系统高度自治,并且通过自组织的方式协调运行,如生态平衡系统、生命机体系统、天体系统、物质微观结构系统等就是典型的自然系统。人脑属于自然系统,是迄今我们所知道的最复杂的系统。

(2) 人工系统:系统内的个体根据人为的、预先编排好的规则或计划好的方向运作,以实现或得到系统内各个体不能单独实现的功能、性能与结果。人工系统的典型特征是设计性,即系统是以设计为基础而产生的,并且依据设计的规则协调运行,如产品组件系统、自动控制系统、计算机系统、液压系统、教育系统、医疗系统等,都是典型的人工系统。

(3) 复合系统:复合系统是自然系统和人工系统的组合,既具有一定的设计特征,又具有显著的自组织特征,如社会系统、交通系统、生产系统、经济系统等。这些系统在形成和运行过程中,经过了人为的设计,但是,系统所包含的元素存在复杂关联特征,使得系统在运行与演化过程中,并不能完全在人为设计的控制之内,而是具有自组织特征,这就形成了复合系统。

3. 系统概念的理解

可以从三个方面理解系统的概念。

(1) 系统是由若干要素组成的。这些要素可能是一些个体、元件、零件,也可能其本身就是一个系统。如运算器、控制器、存储器、输入和输出设备组成了计算机的硬件系统,而硬件系统又是计算机系统的一个子系统。

(2) 系统有一定的结构。一个系统是其构成要素的集合,这些要素相互联系,相互制约。系统内部各要素之间相对稳定的联系方式、组织秩序及失控关系的内在表现形式,就是系统的结构。例如钟表是由齿轮、发条、指针等零部件按一定的方式装配而成的,但一堆齿轮、发条、指针随意放在一起却不能构成钟表;人体由各个器官组成,但各器官简单拼凑在一起不能成为一个有行为能力的人。

(3) 系统有一定的功能,或者说系统要有一定的目的性。系统的功能是指系统在与外部环境相互联系和相互作用中表现出来的性质、能力和功能。例如信息系统的功能是进行信息的收集、传递、储存、加工、维护和使用,辅助决策者进行决策,帮助企业实现目标。

2.2 系统建模的一般方法

系统建模,就是对现实世界中的某一特定系统,根据问题的求解目标和约束条件,抽象出可以通过数学或软件方法求解的仿真与优化模型。凡是用模型描述系统的因果关系或相互关系的过程都属于建模,因描述的关系各异,所以实现这一过程的手段和方法也是多种多样的。可以通过对系统本身运动规律的分析,根据事物的机理来建模,也可以通过对系统的实验或统计数据的处理,并根据关于系统的已有知识和经验来建模。

1. 系统建模的作用

系统建模主要用于三个方面。

(1) 分析和设计实际系统。例如,工程界在分析设计一个新系统时,通常先进行数学仿真和物理仿真实验,最后再到现场做实物实验。用数学仿真来分析和设计一个实际系统时,必须有一个描述系统特征的模型。对于许多复杂的工业控制过程,建模往往是最为关键和最为困难的任务。

(2) 预测或预报实际系统的某些状态的未来发展趋势。例如,根据以往的测量数据建立气象变化的数学模型,用于预报未来的气象。

(3) 对系统实行最优控制。只有先建立一个能表征系统特征的数学模型,才能在数学模型的基础上,根据极大值原理、动态规划、反馈、解耦、极点配置、自组织、自适应和智能控制等方法,设计各种各样的控制器或控制律,从而实现系统优化。

对于同一个实际系统,人们可以根据不同的用途和目的建立不同的模型。因为既不可能也没必要把实际系统的所有细节都列举出来,所以建立的任何模型都只是实际系统原型的简化。如果在简化模型中能保留系统原型的一些本质特征,那么就可认为模型与系统原型是相似的,是可以用来描述原系统的。因此,实际建模时,必须在模型的简化与分析结果的准确性之间做出适当的折中。

2. 系统建模流程

系统建模的一般流程如图 2-1 所示。

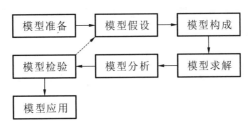

图 2-1 系统建模的一般流程

(1) 模型准备。首先要了解问题的实际背景,明确题目的要求,然后搜集各种必要的信息。

(2) 模型假设。在明确建模目的、掌握必要资料的基础之上,通过对资料的分析与计算,找出起主导作用的因素,经过必要的精炼、简化之后,提出若干符合客观实际的假设,使问题的主要特征凸显出来,忽略问题的次要方面。一般来说,一个实际问题不经过简化假设,就很难转换成数学问题。假设不合理或过于简单,会导致模型失效;假设过分详细,则会大幅度提升建模复杂度,使建模和求解工作都很难进行。因此,模型假设,是在简化与可行之间的折中,其目标是在求解正确性的前提下,尽可能简化模型、高效求解。

(3) 模型构成。根据所作的假设及事物之间的联系,利用适当的数学工具去刻画各变量之间的关系,建立相应的数学结构,把问题转化为数学问题。

(4) 模型求解。利用已知的数学方法来求解上一步所得到的数学问题,这时往往还要做出进一步的简化或假设。在难以得出解析时,可以借助计算机通过迭代搜索的方式求出数值解。

(5) 模型分析。对模型解答进行数学上的分析,有时要根据问题的性质分析变量间的依赖关系或稳定状况,有时要根据所得结果给出数学上的预报,有时则可能要给出数学上的最优决策或控制,不论哪种情况,常常都需要进行误差分析、模型对数据的稳定性或灵敏性分析等。

(6) 模型检验。分析所得结果的实际意义,与实际情况进行比较,看理论分析是否符合实际。如果结果不够理想,应该修改、补充假设或重新建模,有些模型需要经过几次反复的修改,才能不断完善。

(7) 模型应用。所建立的模型必须在实际中应用才能得到验证和产生效益,在应用中不断改进和完善。应用的方式取决于问题的性质和建模的目的。

3. 系统建模步骤

系统建模的一般步骤如下。

1) 抽象设计变量

通过调研,对所研究的系统有全面、深入的了解,然后将问题进行抽象和分离,从错综复杂的问题中分离出能反映问题特征的研究对象,对系统进行尽可能详细的描述。

2) 构造目标函数

目标表示仿真要回答的问题,以及系统方案的说明,明确系统的范围与环境。一般来说,仿真目标不同,所建立的模型及所需采集的数据也不同。目标函数(objective function)是指所关心的目标(某一变量)与相关的因素(某些变量)的函数关系。

3) 构造约束条件

从纯数学的角度讲,存在无约束问题,但是在工程实际中,任何一个模型几乎都是有限制条件的。这些限制条件在建模过程中称为约束条件。只有满足所有约束条件的建模方案才可以作为用于求解的模型。

4) 设计求解方法

建立完整的数学模型,只是系统建模的第一步,更重要的是,采用何种方法来求解数学模型,从而得到满足约束条件的优化解。求解方法有传统优化方法和仿生方法,根据问题的特性,可以选择不同的方法进行模型求解。

2.3 NPC 问题与 NP-Hard 问题

2.3.1 系统复杂性的概念及其基本特征

复杂系统(complex system)是由许多平级要素构成的网络,这些组分通过使用一些既定的规则井然有序地处理外界复杂的信息,自身可以通过学习和记忆从而做出更好的决策,并不断完善系统以应对更复杂的信息。复杂系统具有一定的规模,是不断进化的系统,如生物的大脑、细胞、社会总体及生态系统等。每个复杂系统内部都有多个子系统,这些子系统之间相互联系、相互作用,影响着最终的决策。

一般认为复杂系统具有以下特征。

1) 非线性

非线性表明整个系统不是由简单的组分堆砌而成的,而是各组分有机地结合在一起,即整个系统远大于各组分之和,每一个子系统及部分子系统之和也不能代表系统整体,它们只能是该系统的一部分。

这就表明非线性是复杂系统的前提,是必要条件。

2) 动态性

动态性说明系统是活的,是持续进化的,是远离平衡态的。随着时间的迁移,在自身因素和外界环境的共同影响下,系统不断调节自身以适应环境的变化,通过自组织的作用,向更有序的方向发展和改进。

3) 开放性

开放性表明系统是开放的,与外部环境是相互关联、相互作用的,不断地与外界进行信息与物质的交换并及时做出反馈,只有在这种交换前提下,系统才能得到长足的发展。

4) 积累效应(初值敏感性)

积累效应说明在系统初期的决策会对整个系统的发展产生巨大的影响,也就是人们常说的"蝴蝶效应"。当系统在起始状态时发生了微小的变化,那么随着时间的迁移和系统不断的演化,这种微小的变化就会慢慢积累并逐步放大,最终会对系统的决策产生巨大的影响。这种敏感性的存在,不利于对整个系统做出精准的预测。

5) 分形性(结构自相似性)

系统中的各组分以一定的方式与系统整体相关联,同时系统中的各组分之间也会存在自相似性。这为我们研究认识系统整体与各组分提供了思路。

6) 自组织性

自组织性表明每一个子系统或者每一个组分各司其职,并在此条件下互相保持着一定的联系,所有的行为是自发组织起来的。这就表明了当一个系统的自组织性越强,那么这个系统进化和适应新的外界环境的速度就越快。

综上所述,一个复杂系统内部有很多相互联系有机结合的子系统,具有能独立完成相关功能的动态体系,是一个开放的具有自组织性和自相似性的非线性系统。

正如当身体受伤时,人体的自我治愈并不是杂乱无章的,而是各组织、细胞按照相关的步骤严格执行的:身体受伤→血小板迅速抵达伤口止血并凝固→人体内的免疫系统发挥体液免疫和细胞免疫功能,抵御外来细菌病毒的侵害→相关细胞组织自我修复治愈→伤口愈合。即使当前世界科技已经得到了长足的发展,可是人们还是无法创造出像大脑那样聪明的机器,因为人脑中有成百上千亿个脑细胞,而每一个脑细胞所发挥的作用相当于世界上较为先进的计算机,这种脑细胞之间的相互联系会导致制造复杂度呈几何倍数飞速增加,所要面对的难题也是无法想象的。我们身边充满了复杂系统。

2.3.2 P、NP、NPC、NP-Hard 问题

1. 基本概念

1) 时间复杂度(time complexity)

时间复杂度定性描述了一个算法运行所需的时间。它表明随着问题规模的扩大,由于解空间的爆炸,求解该问题的时间也越长。它用于衡量一个算法求得最优解所需的时间的多少。时间复杂度常用符号 O 表示。算法的时间复杂度一般可以分为两种级别:

(1) 多项式级的复杂度,如 $O(1)$、$O(n\log_2 n)$ 等;

(2) 非多项式级的复杂度,如 $O(n!)$、$O(a^n)$ 等。计算机往往不能计算这种时间复杂度。

如冒泡排序法,它是一种相对简单的排序方法,它的规则是对需要排序的数列进行若干次遍历,每一次遍历时,都会按照从前往后这个顺序依次比较相邻两个数的大小,如果前面的数比后面的数大,则交换它们所处的位置。这样,在第一次遍历后,该数列中最大的数字就会处于这个数列的末尾,第二次遍历之后,第二大的数字就会排在倒数第二的位置上,以此类推,就可以得知,在进行最后一次遍历后,最小的数字就会被放置在数列的首项。这样一来,整个数列会按照从小到大的顺序有序排列。

假设该数列中有 N 个数,遍历一遍的时间复杂度为 $O(N)$,因为要遍历 $(N-1)!$ 次,因此冒泡算法的时间复杂度为 $O(n^2)$。

2) 约化(reducibility)

若可寻找到一个变化法则,对任意一个问题 A 的输入,可以按照这个法则相应地将其变换成问题 B 的输入,使两个问题的输出结果相同,那么就可以说,问题 A 可以约化为问题 B。简单地说,问题 A 可以约化为问题 B 的含义是可以用问题 B 的解法去求解问题 A,也可以说,问题 A 是问题 B 的一种特殊情况;同时也告诉了我们一个直观的信息,即问题 B 的时间

复杂度大于或者等于问题 A 的时间复杂度。

约化具有传递性，即如果问题 A 可以约化为问题 B，问题 B 可以约化为问题 C，那么问题 A 也可以约化为问题 C。

2. P、NP、NPC、NP-Hard 问题的定义

1) P 问题

P(polynomial)问题指计算起来很快的问题。

如果一个问题在多项式时间复杂度内可以寻找到解决算法，那么这个问题就是 P 问题，也就是说其算法的时间复杂度是多项式级的。

比如从 N 个数中找到最小值，可以采用相邻两个数轮番比较的形式，首先将第一个数和第二个数进行大小比较，再选择较小的数和第三个数进行比较，以此类推，只需要进行($N-1$)次比较就可以得到最终的答案；或者将 N 个数从小到大进行排序，可以采用冒泡排序法来求解，如果运气好，这 N 个数一开始就是从小到大排列的，这样不用进行任何操作就可以得到结果，而最糟糕的情况就是这 N 个数的初始排序是从大到小的，这时我们可以采用别的方法进行求解。

这类问题可以使用穷举法来进行求解。

2) NP 问题

NP(non-deterministic polynomial)问题是指存在多项式算法能够解决的非决定性问题，即可以在多项式时间复杂度内猜到一个解的问题。

如求某图中任意两点之间是否有一条小于 50 个单位长度的路线，在已知问题存在解的前提下，随便选择一条路线，如果算出来的路径总长小于 50 个单位长度，那么便猜到了一个可行解，也就是说在运气足够好的情况下，可以在多项式时间复杂度内来求解该问题。

还有一类问题是将一个比较大的数分解成两个数的乘积，这类问题一般都没有办法很快地求解，但是任意给两个数，我们可以验证这两个数的乘积是不是等于已知数。例如，我们很难在较短的时间内找到两个数的乘积等于 94743，但是若给出 99 和 957 这两个数，我们可以在非常短的时间内验证这两个数的乘积等于 94743。

这样就可以推断出所有的 P 问题都是 NP 问题，因为 P 问题能在多项式时间复杂度内解决，因此必能在多项式时间复杂度内验证每一个解。

NP 问题计算起来不一定很快，但可以非常快地验证每一个答案正确与否。

3) NPC 问题

NPC(non-deterministic polynomial complete)问题是在 P 问题与 NP 问题上的一个重大进展，它是 NP 问题的一个子集。如果所有 NP 问题都可以在多项式时间复杂度内约化(polynomial-time reducibility)成某个 NP 问题，则该 NP 问题称为 NPC 问题。

判定一个问题是否为 NPC 问题，需要依据以下两个条件：

(1) 这个问题是 NP 问题；

(2) 所有的 NP 问题都可以约化得到这个问题。

如果满足上述两个条件，即可判定一个问题是 NPC 问题。

旅行商问题(traveling salesman problem)是典型的 NPC 问题，同时也是数学领域著名的问题之一。该问题所描述的是一个旅行商人要拜访 N 座城市，所选的路径应满足每个城市只能拜访一次，而且最后要回到刚开始出发的城市。路径的选择目标是要使该路径的路程为所有可行路径中的最小值。由于该问题的可行解是所有顶点的全排列，并且随着顶点数目的增加,会产生解组合的爆炸,因此这种复杂度是计算机接受不了的。如假设有20座城市,则有19!种排列方式,若计算机每秒可以排列1亿次,则也需要38.4年。

0-1背包问题是一种组合优化的NPC问题,它指的是在每种物品只使用一次的情况下,给定N个重量分别为$W_1,W_2,\cdots,W_N$,价值分别为$V_1,V_2,\cdots,V_N$的物品和一个容量为C的背包,所要求的目标是在不超过背包总容量的前提下,使得装入背包内的物品总价值最大。这类问题的求解思路是在不同的排列组合中寻求这些物品中最有价值的一个子集。

对于NPC问题,没有有效的多项式算法,只能用指数级甚至阶乘级时间复杂度的算法进行求解。

4) NP-Hard问题

NP-Hard问题,顾名思义,就是比所有的NP问题都难以求解的问题。该类问题只需满足NPC问题的第二个条件,并不一定要满足第一条,即NP-Hard问题比NPC问题更为广泛,并且其中不全是NP问题。

NP-Hard问题与NPC问题一样难以找到多项式时间复杂度算法,因为它不一定是NP问题。即便NPC问题找到了多项式级算法,NP-Hard问题也可能无法得到多项式级算法。由于NP-Hard问题放宽了限定条件,因此这类问题的时间复杂度更高,更难进行求解。

如数字分区问题,对该问题的描述是能否将一个给定的正整数多重集合S分为其内所有元素之和相等的两个集合S_1和S_2。这个问题被称为最简单的NP-Hard问题,同时它也是NPC问题。假设给定一个集合$S=\{1,2,1,2,1,3\}$,则存在一个子集$S_1=\{2,3\}$和另一个子集$S_2=\{1,2,1,1\}$完全划分了集合S,并且其内的所有元素之和相等;同时也可以找到子集$S_1=\{1,3,1\}$和$S_2=\{2,1,2\}$,为该问题的另一组解。

在中国棋手柯洁0∶3输给AlphaGo之后,人们认识到了人工智能的强大。实际上围棋本身是一种复杂的数学游戏,围棋的棋盘一般为19×19的,一共有361个点可以放置棋子,每一个落子点存在着黑子、白子或者空白这三种可能,所以整张棋盘上最终的落子情况有1083种可能;但实际下棋中会有先后顺序,并且每个棋子之间存在着联系,整个复杂度远远要比这个数字大。所以要研究出一种围棋必胜的下法这个问题也属于NP-Hard问题。

NPC问题与NP-Hard问题的区别是:验证一个问题是不是NP-Hard问题时,不需要验证该问题是不是NP问题;但验证一个问题是不是NPC问题时,该问题首先得是NP问题才行。由此便可以知道NPC问题是NP-Hard问题的一个子集。

P、NP、NPC、NP-Hard问题的关系文氏图如图2-2所示。

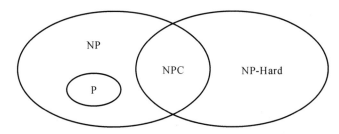

图2-2 P、NP、NPC、NP-Hard问题的关系文氏图

2.4 三类系统建模问题实例解析

1. 第一类问题:填充问题

例 2-1 从 n 个装有面粉、大米、谷物等不同密度物质的布袋中,选择一部分装入容积为 V 的麻袋,其中,第 i 个布袋质量为 W_i,体积为 V_i。问:如何选装可使装入物质量总和最大?

解 求 X_i(设计变量)。物理意义:$X_i=0$ 表示第 i 个布袋不被选装,$X_i=1$ 表示第 i 个布袋被选装。

$$\max \sum_{i=1}^{n} W_i X_i$$

s.t.
$$\sum_{i=1}^{n} V_i X_i \leqslant V$$
$$X_i = 0 \text{ 或 } 1$$

求解得到 $X_i(i=1,2,\cdots,n)$,即得到选装方案。

例 2-2 货运飞机有前舱、中舱、后舱三个货舱,能装载四类可任意形状包装的粉末状货物,为保持飞行平衡,货舱装入重量的分配必须与限重成比例,如表 2-1 所示。各类货物的总质量、单位体积及单位利润如表 2-2 所示。

表 2-1 货舱重量配比与容积

飞机货舱	前舱	中舱	后舱
限重/t	10	16	8
容积/m³	6800	8700	5300

表 2-2 货物属性

货物	总质量/t	单位体积/(m³/t)	单位利润/(元/t)
A1	18	480	3100
A2	15	650	3800
A3	23	580	3500
A4	12	390	2850

问:如何设计装载方案,能使获利最大?

解 求 x_{ij}。物理含义:设计变量 x_{ij} 的值表示第 i 种货物装入第 j 舱($j=1$,2,3 分别表示前舱、中舱、后舱)的质量。

$$\max Z = 3100(x_{11}+x_{12}+x_{13}) + 3800(x_{21}+x_{22}+x_{23}) + 3500(x_{31}+x_{32}+x_{33}) + 2850(x_{41}+x_{42}+x_{43})$$

s.t. 货重约束:

$$x_{11}+x_{12}+x_{13} \leqslant 18$$

$$x_{21} + x_{22} + x_{23} \leqslant 15$$
$$x_{31} + x_{32} + x_{33} \leqslant 23$$
$$x_{41} + x_{42} + x_{43} \leqslant 12$$

限重约束：
$$x_{11} + x_{21} + x_{31} + x_{41} \leqslant 10$$
$$x_{12} + x_{22} + x_{32} + x_{42} \leqslant 16$$
$$x_{13} + x_{23} + x_{33} + x_{43} \leqslant 8$$

容积约束：
$$480\, x_{11} + 650\, x_{21} + 580\, x_{31} + 390\, x_{41} \leqslant 6800$$
$$480\, x_{12} + 650\, x_{22} + 580\, x_{32} + 390\, x_{42} \leqslant 8700$$
$$480\, x_{13} + 650\, x_{23} + 580\, x_{33} + 390\, x_{43} \leqslant 5300$$

平衡约束：
$$\frac{x_{11} + x_{21} + x_{31} + x_{41}}{10} = \frac{x_{12} + x_{22} + x_{32} + x_{42}}{16} = \frac{x_{13} + x_{23} + x_{33} + x_{43}}{8}$$

物理含义：max Z 表示方案的最大利润。

2. 第二类问题：配置问题

例 2-3 某车间每天可获得 50 个毛坯，车间里有两类加工设备甲、乙，它们可将毛坯分别加工成零件 A1、A2。以 1 个毛坯为原料，甲、乙两类设备所耗加工时间和所得零件数量如下：

甲耗 12 小时加工 3 个 A1，每个利润 24 元；

乙耗 8 小时加工 4 个 A2，每个利润 16 元。

即

甲每小时获利 6 元，每毛坯获利 72 元；

乙每小时获利 8 元，每毛坯获利 64 元。

所有工人每天总工作时间为 480 小时，设备甲每天加工零件总数最大为 100。问：如何制订生产计划，使每天利润最大？

解 求 x_1，x_2。物理含义：用 x_1 个毛坯生产 A1，用 x_2 个毛坯生产 A2。

$$\max Z = 3 \times 24 \times x_1 + 4 \times 16 \times x_2$$

s. t.
$$x_1 + x_2 \leqslant 50$$
$$12\, x_1 + 8\, x_2 \leqslant 480$$
$$3\, x_1 \leqslant 100$$
$$x_1 \geqslant 0, x_2 \geqslant 0$$

物理含义：max Z 表示最大利润。

例 2-4 有甲、乙、丙、丁四个居民区和 A、B、C 三个水库。各居民区的基本用水量为 30、70、10、10，必须得到保证。A、B、C 每天固定供水量为 50、60、50。除基本供水量外，四个居民区最多可额外申请用量为 50、70、20、40。其中四个居民区的用水量与三个水库的供水量的单位为吨。各水库与居民区之间的运输成本如表 2-3 所示。

表 2-3　水库与居民区之间的运输成本　　　　　　　　　　　　　　（单位：元）

水库与居民区	甲	乙	丙	丁
A	160	130	220	170
B	140	130	190	150
C	190	200	230	/

问：怎样设计方案使供水获利最大？

解　由于水成本是相同的，不同的是运输成本，因此，可将获利最大的问题转化为运输成本最小的问题。

求 x_{ij}。物理含义：x_{ij} 表示第 i 个水库向 j 个居民区的送水量，$i=1,2,3$ 分别对应 A、B、C，$j=1,2,3,4$ 分别对应甲、乙、丙、丁。

$$\min Z = 160 x_{11} + 130 x_{12} + 220 x_{13} + 170 x_{14} + 140 x_{21} + 130 x_{22} + 190 x_{23} + 150 x_{24} \\ + 190 x_{31} + 200 x_{32} + 230 x_{33}$$

s. t.
$$x_{11} + x_{12} + x_{13} + x_{14} = 50$$
$$x_{21} + x_{22} + x_{23} + x_{24} = 60$$
$$x_{31} + x_{32} + x_{33} = 50$$
$$30 \leqslant x_{11} + x_{21} + x_{31} \leqslant 80$$
$$70 \leqslant x_{12} + x_{22} + x_{32} \leqslant 140$$
$$10 \leqslant x_{13} + x_{23} + x_{33} \leqslant 30$$
$$10 \leqslant x_{14} + x_{24} \leqslant 50$$

例 2-5　某汽车厂生产小型、中型、大型三类汽车，各类汽车的制造资源消耗与每月制造资源供给量如表 2-4 所示，试制订每月的生产计划，使利润最大。

表 2-4　汽车制造资源状况

每台汽车	小型	中型	大型	月供给
钢材/t	1.5	3	5	600
制造时间/min	280	250	400	60000
利润/万元	2	3	4	—

解　求 x_1、x_2、x_3。物理含义：大型、中型、小型三类汽车的生产计划分别为 x_1、x_2、x_3。

$$\max Z = 2 x_1 + 3 x_2 + 4 x_3$$

s. t.
$$1.5 x_1 + 3 x_2 + 5 x_3 \leqslant 600$$
$$280 x_1 + 250 x_2 + 400 x_3 \leqslant 60000$$
$$x_1, x_2, x_3 \geqslant 0$$

3. 第三类问题：裁切问题

例 2-6　某钢管厂原料钢管的长度均为 19 m，现有一客户需要 50 根 4 m、20 根 6 m、15 根 8 m 的钢管。问：如何下料最节省？

解 首先,列出所有切割模式,如表 2-5 所示。

表 2-5 所有切割模式

钢管	4 m/根	6 m/根	8 m/根	余料/m
1	4	0	0	3
2	3	1	0	1
3	2	0	1	3
4	1	2	0	3
5	1	1	1	1
6	0	3	0	1
7	0	0	2	3

设计变量 X_i,表示按第 i 种模式切割的钢管根数。

可以分别按以下两个目标来确定决策目标。

① 决策目标:余量最少。

$$\min Z_1 = 3x_1 + x_2 + 3x_3 + 3x_4 + x_5 + x_6 + 3x_7$$

s.t.
$$4x_1 + 3x_2 + 2x_3 + x_4 + x_5 \geqslant 50$$
$$x_2 + 2x_4 + x_5 + 3x_6 \geqslant 20$$
$$x_3 + x_5 + 2x_7 \geqslant 15$$

② 决策目标:使用原材料根数最少。

$$\min Z_2 = x_1 + x_2 + x_3 + x_4 + x_5 + x_6 + x_7$$

s.t.
$$4x_1 + 3x_2 + 2x_3 + x_4 + x_5 \geqslant 50$$
$$x_2 + 2x_4 + x_5 + 3x_6 \geqslant 20$$
$$x_3 + x_5 + 2x_7 \geqslant 15$$

第 3 章 生产系统优化模型

3.1 生产系统建模概论

3.1.1 生产系统建模发展历程

由于早期的生产模式主要是手工作坊模式,组成生产系统的元素很少,元素间的关系简单,因此还没有上升到系统的高度。1776 年,第一台有实用价值的蒸汽机诞生,标志着工业化时代的来临。20 世纪 70 年代左右,柔性制造系统(flexible manufacturing system,FMS)出现,使得生产系统的复杂度大幅度提升,对生产系统进行建模与优化的必要性也凸显出来。

1976 年,日本 FANUC 公司展出了由加工中心和工业机器人组成的柔性制造单元(FMC),为发展 FMS 提供了重要的设备形式。随着时间的推移,FMS 在技术上和数量上都有较大发展,进入实用阶段,以由 3~5 台设备组成的 FMS 为最多,但也有规模更庞大的系统投入使用。1982 年,日本 FANUC 公司建成自动化电机加工车间,该车间由 60 个柔性制造单元(包括 50 个工业机器人)和 1 个立体仓库组成,另有 2 台自动引导车传送毛坯和工件;此外还有 1 个无人化电机装配车间,它们都能连续 24 小时运转。这种自动化和无人化车间,是向实现计算机集成的自动化工厂迈出的重要一步。与此同时,还出现了若干仅具有 FMS 基本特征,但自动化程度不是很完善的经济型 FMS,使 FMS 的设计思想和技术成就得到普及应用。FMS 的出现和发展,使得制造系统具有更高的灵活性和不确定性,对制造系统进行建模以实现预测和优化,变得日益重要。可以说,FMS 促进了生产系统建模技术的产生和发展。

生产系统建模技术的发展与数学科学的发展是相辅相成的。排队论于 20 世纪 50 年代渐渐发展起来,60 年代开始零星地用于描述制造系统的某些问题,在 70 年代和 80 年代以排队论方法分析 FMS 颇为盛行。从 20 世纪 70 年代末起,数学规划开始用于制造系统建模,人们用整数规划解决 FMS 中的任务分派问题,用动态规划解决 FMS 运行中的不确定性问题。

Petri 网理论是 Petri 在 20 世纪 60 年代初提出来的,它适用于分析非同步并发系统(asynchronous concurrent system)。20 世纪 70 年代,它开始被用于计算机系统分析。其用于制造系统建模始于 20 世纪 80 年代初期,也主要是针对 FMS。

从 20 世纪 80 年代开始,人们尝试建立计算机集成制造系统(computer integrated manufacture system,CIMS)。CIMS 一般应覆盖制造活动主要环节的建模工作,如设计、工艺、生产计划、加工、装配、销售等环节的建模。它不仅包含物流自动化,还涉及信息自动化问题,因此其建模复杂度可想而知。

随着科技的发展,生产系统变得日益复杂,逐步成为一个包含制造理论、制造技术、制造过程、制造资源和组织体系等元素的复杂工程系统。工程和研究人员对这样复杂的系统的建模开展了大量卓有成效的工作,如生产系统结构描述模型、系统运行管理模型、系统分析模型、系统设计实施模型、系统生产计划调度模型等。新的数学方法也被应用于生产系统建模与求解,如遗传算法、蚁群算法、粒子群算法等启发式算法或元启发式算法等。

当然,生产系统建模还是一个正在发展中的领域,方兴未艾。随着生产系统的日趋复杂,生产系统建模方法也在不断完善。

3.1.2 基本概念

对生产系统的优化程度进行评价,涉及以下概念。

交货期(due date):工件应该交货的时刻。

空置时间(idle time):设备已启动,但未运行加工任务的空转时间。

完工时间(completion time):最后一道工序加工结束的时间。

释放时间(release time)或到达时间(arrival time):工件可以开始加工的时间。

加工时间(processing time):工件处于被加工状态的时间。

等待时间(waiting time):工件第 $k-1$ 道工序结束到第 k 道工序开始的时间差。

流程时间(flow time):数值上等于完工时间与到达时间之差,还等于加工时间与等待时间之和。

延期时间(tardiness):延期时间=max{0,完工时间-交货期}。

超前时间(earliness):超前时间= max{0,交货期-完工时间}。

3.2 单机调度模型

单机调度问题,即在满足某些约束条件的前提下,将 n 项任务{$J_1, J_2, \cdots, J_n$}进行合理排序,分配到一台设备上依次进行加工,以使得某些指标达到最优。其中,设计变量为任务的排序方案。约束条件包括:

①交货期约束:每一项任务都有其交货期;
②设备独占约束:一台设备在某一时刻只能处理一项任务;
③加工连续性约束:单项任务只能一次连续完成,不能分割成多时间段任务进行加工。

约束条件可分为硬约束和软约束。硬约束是指必须满足的约束,如设备独占约束、加工连续性约束等。不满足硬约束的解是不可行解。软约束则是不用必须严格满足的约束,是可以在不同程度上满足的约束,软约束的满足程度影响目标的优化程度,因此,软约束往往被转换为优化目标来进行表达。如果交货期并不要求被刚性满足,而是可以通过市场方式进行柔性满足,如通过经济补偿换取交货期延迟,则交货期约束可以看作软约束。

优化目标包括完工时间最短、延期成本最低、总成本最低等。由于存在临时库存成本,任务并不一定提前越早完成越好,在很多情况下,任务"刚好"在交货期完成,往往总成本最小。

以如下案例来介绍单机调度优化模型的建模方法。

有 5 项加工任务,从 0 时刻开始,都处于可加工状态,其中,第 i 项任务所需要的加工时间为 t_i,交货期为 d_i。求 n 项任务的最优加工顺序,使得所有任务完工超前时间总和最小。

可以采用二维矩阵来表达排序,如 5 项任务的排序为 (4,2,3,5,1),则采用二维矩阵 S 进行表达:

$$S = \begin{bmatrix} 0 & 0 & 0 & 1 & 0 \\ 0 & 1 & 0 & 0 & 0 \\ 0 & 0 & 1 & 0 & 0 \\ 0 & 0 & 0 & 0 & 1 \\ 1 & 0 & 0 & 0 & 0 \end{bmatrix}$$

其中,$s_{14}=1$ 表示排序第一的为编号为 4 的任务,其他依此类推。

则设计变量为 s_{ij},当 j 任务排序为 i 时,$s_{ij}=1$;否则,$s_{ij}=0$。

优化目标为

$$\min \sum_{k=1}^{5} \left(\sum_{j=1}^{5} s_{kj} d_j - \sum_{i=1}^{k} \sum_{j=1}^{5} s_{ij} t_j \right)$$

约束条件为

$$\sum_{i=1}^{k} \sum_{j=1}^{5} s_{ij} t_j \leqslant \sum_{j=1}^{5} s_{kj} d_j$$

$$k=1,2,\cdots,5;s_{ij}=0 \text{ 或 } 1;i=1,2,\cdots,5;j=1,2,\cdots,5$$

如果可以通过议价补偿延期时间,则交货期变为软约束,可以从总成本最小的角度构造目标函数。

3.3 并行机调度模型

并行机调度问题描述:设有 n 项独立的任务,由 m 台相同的机器进行加工处理,任务 i 所需的处理时间为 T_i,每项任务都可以在任何一台机器上完成,每项任务只能一次性连续加工完成,寻找最优分配和排序方案,使得该加工系统效率最高。并行机调度模型分为以下两种情况。

1) 无交货期约束

无交货期约束的情况下,问题比较简单,一般以完工时间最短为优化目标,可以将任务按加工时间由长到短排序,再以顺序折返的方式分配给 m 台机器。例如:设 $m=3,n=8$,8 项任务的加工时间(单位:min)分别为 15、7、12、3、9、10、16、9,则排序为

S7,S1,S3,S6,S5,S8,S2,S4

则在 3 台机器上的分配与排序为

M1:S7,S8,S2,机器完工时间为 32 min

M2:S1,S5,S4,机器完工时间为 27 min

M3:S3,S6,机器完工时间为 22 min

相应的任务完工时间为 32 min。

2) 有交货期约束

基于并行机调度问题的一般描述,增加交货期约束:第 i 项任务的交货期为 D_i。设机器

台数为 m,任务数量为 n,则设计变量为

$$x_{ij}, i=1,2,\cdots,m; j=1,2,\cdots,n$$

含义:x_{ij} 的值为第 i 台机器上排序为 j 的任务的编号,如 $x_{23}=6$,表示第 2 台机器上加工排序为 3 的任务编号为 6。每台机器最后一项排序任务后剩余的设计变量均赋值 0,D_{i0} 设置为正无穷大。

目标函数:

$$\min \max(\sum_{j=1}^{n} Sx_{1j}, \sum_{j=1}^{n} Sx_{2j}, \cdots, \sum_{j=1}^{n} Sx_{mj})$$

约束条件:

$$\sum_{j=1}^{n} Sx_{ij} \leqslant Dx_{ij}, \quad i=1,2,\cdots,m$$

以上目标函数即为最大最小化问题,即使所有机器中的最大完工时间最小化。

3.4 独立作业系统调度模型

单机调度问题和并行机调度问题的共同点是单项任务可以在一台设备上一次性连续加工完成。如果单项任务包含多道涉及不同设备的加工工序,则该调度问题就是作业系统调度问题。如果在该系统中,不同任务的加工流程相同,加工结果相似,形成一条小型的流水线,则该系统为独立作业系统。Johnson 模型就是典型的独立作业系统模型。

20 世纪 50 年代,随着工业化的发展,制造系统的复杂度显著提升,对制造系统进行优化也逐步得到了重视。美国伊利诺伊大学厄巴纳-香槟分校(University of Illinois at Urbana-Champaign)的博士研究生 Johnson Selmer Martin,在其博士论文中对数学规划问题进行了深入研究,并于 1954 年在学术期刊 *Transactions of the American Mathematical Society* 上发表了论文 *On the representations of an integer as the sum of products of integers*,提出了 Johnson 算法。该论文是关于作业调度的第一篇学术论文,对后期关于调度问题的研究产生了深远影响。

Johnson 算法针对在由 2 台设备 M1 和 M2 组成的流水线上完成 n 个相似作业的问题,提出了实用的调度规则。以图 3-1 为例,介绍 Johnson 算法的基本思想和步骤。

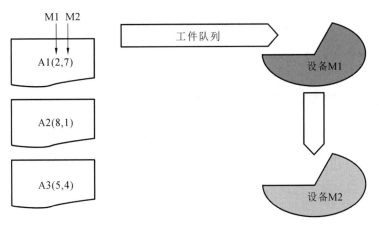

图 3-1 Johnson 算法案例

图 3-1 所示的是一个包含 3 个工件、2 台设备的作业系统，每个工件依次经过 M1、M2 两台设备进行两道工序的加工，每个工件两道工序所需加工时间如图 3-1 所示。如何对工件排序，使系统获得最高效率呢？这一看似简单的问题，包含 6 个排序方案，并对应不同的完工时间。图 3-2 分别描述了 3 种方案及其对应的甘特图，图 3-3 描述了另外 3 种方案对应的完工时间。可以看出，6 种方案中，完工时间最长为 24 min，最优解为第 2 种方案，对应的完工时间为 16 min，这反映了对排序进行优化的必要性。

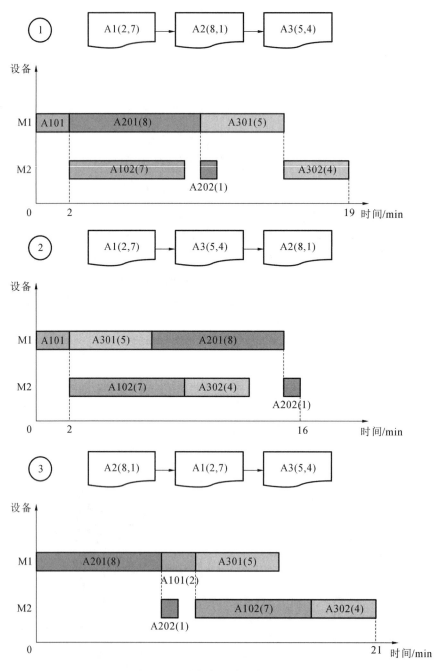

图 3-2 三种方案及其对应的甘特图

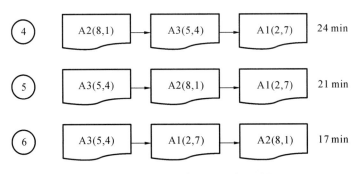

图 3-3 另外三种方案对应的完工时间

对于以上只有 3 个工件的例子,可用枚举法找出最优解。但由于排序问题多为 NPC 问题,随着规模的增加,解空间呈几何级数增长,如同样的条件下,将工件增加到 7 个,则将有 5040 个可行解,工件仅仅增加了 4 个,解的规模则扩大为 840 倍。因此,对于更多工件的情况,难以用枚举法求解。Johnson 对这类问题进行深入研究后,归纳出了一种可行的通用算法,称为 Johnson 算法或 Johnson 规则。

以 7 个工件的案例来介绍 Johnson 算法的步骤,7 个工件的两道工序的加工时间(单位:min)如图 3-4 所示。

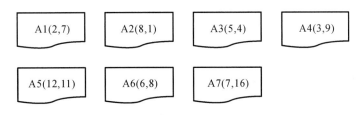

图 3-4 7 个工件的两道工序的加工时间

步骤一:建立三元组表。如表 3-1 所示,将 7 个工件的工件号作为表格第一列,两道工序中加工时间较短的工序的加工时间作为表格第二列,加工时间较短的工序对应的设备号作为表格的第三列。

表 3-1 三元组表

工件号	加工时间/min	设备号
1	2	1
2	1	2
3	4	2
4	3	1
5	11	2
6	6	1
7	7	1

步骤二:三元组表重排序。如表 3-2 所示,以加工时间这一列数值由小到大为依据,对表格的行进行重排序。

表 3-2 重排序的三元组表

工件号	加工时间/min	设备号
2	1	2
1	2	1
4	2	1
3	4	2
6	6	1
7	7	1
5	11	2

步骤三：依据设备号由两端向中间填充。如图 3-5 所示，当设备号为 1 时，由左边向中间填充工件号，当设备号为 2 时，由右边向中间填充工件号，填充完成后得到的排序即为最优解。

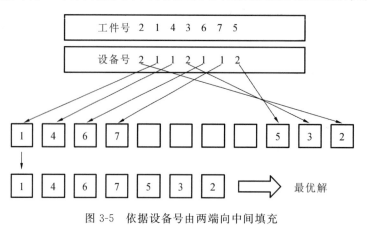

图 3-5 依据设备号由两端向中间填充

3.5 作业车间调度问题

1. 作业车间调度问题基本概念

作业车间调度问题（job shop scheduling problem，JSSP）：将 n 项独立的加工任务，分配到 m 台设备进行加工，每一项独立加工任务都包含可能存在先后关系的多道加工工序，每一道加工工序只能在功能匹配的设备上完成，制订调度方案，使得该系统某些指标，如完工时间、超前时间或延期时间等最优。

图 3-6 所示是一个由 4 项独立任务组成的任务集，每一任务包含若干存在并行或串行关系的工序，如 106 与 107 是串行关系，二者又和 108 形成并行关系。该作业系统中有 A、B、C 三类设备，工序对应分配的设备类型及加工时间如工序上方的字符所示，如工序 101 只能分配到 A 类设备，加工时间为 10 分钟。假定 A、B、C 三类设备分别有 2、3、2 台，编号为 A1、A2、B1、B2、B3、C1、C2，这就构成了由 4 项共包含 33 道具有关联属性工序的独立任务、3 类共 7 台设备组成的作业车间系统。求解该系统调度问题，就是要在满足各种约束条件的前提下，将这 33 道工序合理地分配到这 7 台设备上，使得某项指标达到最优。

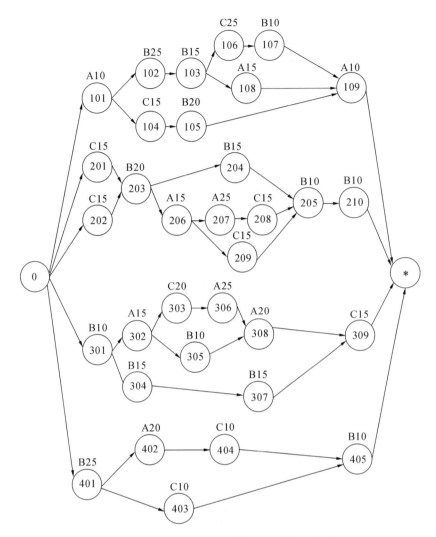

图 3-6 作业车间系统中的任务关联关系实例

对于作业车间系统,定义如下概念。

(1) 前序工序:在一项任务中,某些工序之间存在串行关系,某一工序必须在另一些工序完成后才能启动加工,那么,另一些必须首先完成且完成后此工序就能启动加工的工序,即为此工序的前序工序。如图 3-6 所示,102 是 103 的前序工序,107、108 是 109 的前序工序,但 106 不是 109 的前序工序。

(2) 前续工序:当某一设备被安排了一系列待加工工序后,工序会形成一个串行队列,在队列排序中,排在某工序前的一个工序,称为此工序的前续工序。

(3) 串行关联约束:任一工序必须在其前序工序完成后才能启动加工。由此形成的约束,定义为串行关联约束。作业系统的解必须满足串行关联约束。

(4) 加工属性约束:将工序分配到某一设备,设备的加工类型必须与工序的加工属性相匹配,如图 3-6 中的工序 201 必须分配到 C 类设备上进行加工。

(5) 任务独占约束:由于加工工件的不可分性,任何工件上不能有两道工序同时进行加工,即任一任务同一时间至多只能有一道工序处于加工状态。

(6) 设备独占约束:由于设备的不可分性,任一设备上在同一时间只能有一道工序处于加工状态,即任一设备上的加工工序的加工状态不能出现时间上的重叠。

(7) 排序模式:工序被分配到某一设备后,在设备上的排序规则称为排序模式。排工顺序与排序模式,共同决定了工序在设备上的顺序。

2. 作业关系图、作业关系表、甘特图

JSSP 的优化模型将在第 4 章进行详细介绍。这里首先介绍能描述 JSSP 属性的作业关系图、作业关系表和甘特图的表达方法。

作业关系图即表达作业属性及作业之间串行或并行关系的连接图。图 3-6 即为一个作业关系图。可以看出,作业关系图包含作业编号、加工属性、加工时间、作业关联关系等要素。如图 3-6 中的工序 109,需要在 A 类设备上完成加工,加工时间为 10 min,前序工序为 107、108、105。作业关系图清楚地表达了 JSSP 的约束条件。

作业关系表是表达 JSSP 属性的另一种方法,如编号为 1 的工件,其对应的作业关系表如表 3-3 所示。依据作业关系表,可以反过来绘制作业关系图,并且一一对应。

表 3-3 作业关系表

工件号	工序号	设备类型	加工时间/min	前序工序
1	101	A	10	—
1	102	B	25	101
1	103	B	15	102
1	104	C	15	101
1	105	B	20	104
1	106	C	25	103
1	107	B	10	106
1	108	A	15	103
1	109	A	10	107、108、105

甘特图是表达工序及设备调度方案的图,如图 3-7 所示是甘特图示例。在甘特图中,用矩形条表达一道工序,矩形条长度表达工序的加工时间,矩形条首末端表达工序的加工起止时间,矩形条所处的高度表达所使用的加工设备。可以从甘特图中一目了然:是否满足各种约束条件、设备利用率、完工时间、调度方案的优化程度等。

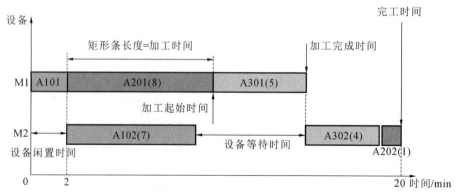

图 3-7 甘特图示例

作业车间调度问题是 NP-Hard 问题，一直是调度领域研究的热点问题，目前一般采用启发式算法或元启发式算法求解，但求解主要从经验和实用性出发，在有限时间内得到可接受的解。迄今为止，并没有一种方法在数学上被严格证明是肯定能求解作业车间调度问题的，实际上，目前的任何一种方法，都不一定能得到最优解，甚至即使得到了可接受的解，也不能度量其与最优解之间的差距。近年来，国内外虽然取得了一些研究成果，但主要集中在关联关系简单的小规模问题上，研究还处于初级阶段，还有很长的路要走。

第4章 生产系统中的概率问题

4.1 概率分析方法的应用概论

工业工程是对人、物料、设备、能源和信息等所组成的集成系统,进行设计、改善和实施的一门学科,它综合运用数学、物理和社会科学的专门知识和技术,结合工程分析和设计的原理与方法,对系统进行确认、预测和评价。工业工程的核心目标是提升效率,而提升效率的重要手段是优化方法。通过优化方法,能实现资源的高效配置,从而提升效率。在优化方法的应用过程中,存在一些不确定因素,这些不确定因素使得概率分析非常有必要,概率分析也为优化方法的应用提供了数值依据。

其一,概率分析能通过对风险的预测来优化成本的配置。风险分析是概率分析的重要内容之一,是通过研究各种不确定因素发生的概率分布及其对项目经济效益指标的影响,从而对项目可行性和风险性及方案优劣做出判断的一种分析方法。风险分析常用于对大中型项目的评估和决策之中。例如,通过对产品的不同部件进行失效概率分析,从而计算不同部件的合理的保修期;又如,对大型工程项目的各个环节进行风险分析,从而为不同环节配置不同的但更为合理的保险额度。这些都是通过概率分析来实现成本的优化配置的途径。

其二,通过概率分析,能发现一些潜在的问题。例如:如果某一台设备的事故率远远高于其他设备,我们就有理由质疑这台设备存在设计缺陷,重新对这台设备进行检查和鉴定,而不是仅仅加强对工人的安全培训;如果某一路段事故率非常高,我们就有理由怀疑这一路段存在安全隐患,从而对这一路段进行详细考察,而不是仅仅提升司机的安全驾驶意识。这些显著偏离正常概率范畴的特性概率,称为偏执概率。偏执概率对于潜在问题的发现有重要价值。

其三,通过概率分析,能对资源配置进行有效的优化。超市收银台的开放数量设置,是一个典型的例子。由于超市中顾客数量是动态的,在不同的时间段顾客数量显著不同,那么,如果收银台开放数量保持恒定不变,则在顾客比较少的时段,人力资源会严重闲置。因此,通过对每天各时间段的顾客数据进行分析,可以拟合出不同时间段的顾客数量期望值,然后根据顾客数量的期望值和收银台队列长度的期望值,可以计算出不同时间段收银台的开放数量,从而优化人力资源的配置。在生产系统设计中,这种以概率分析为依据的优化配置也很普遍,例如:根据设备的统计数据,配置维修人员岗位数;根据全年订单的统计数据,确定不同时间段轮休的额度;根据历年的订单状况,确定扩大再生产的规模;等等。

概率论本身就是数学学科的重要组成部分,涉及内容很多,而且系统性很强,在本书中不专门介绍这一数学学科。本章对概率论的基本概念都一带而过，重点介绍生产系统建模与仿真中应用得比较多的概率理论与方法，主要包括中心极限定理、二项分布、正态分布、排队论等内容。

4.2 概率论的几个基本概念及其应用

4.2.1 概率密度函数

分布函数为连续函数的随机变量称为连续型随机变量。连续型随机变量往往通过其概率密度函数直观描述，概率密度函数的定义如下：

若 $P\{a \leqslant x \leqslant b\} = \int_a^b f(x) \mathrm{d}x$，则 $f(x)$ 是连续型随机变量 X 的概率密度函数。

由定义知道，概率密度函数 $f(x)$ 具有以下性质：

(1) 非负性，$f(x) \geqslant 0, \forall x \in (-\infty, +\infty)$；

(2) 规范性，$\int_{-\infty}^{+\infty} f(x) = 1$；

(3) 对于任意实数 $a, b(a \leqslant b), P\{a \leqslant x \leqslant b\} = \int_a^b f(x) \mathrm{d}x$；

(4) 若 $f(x)$ 在 x 处连续，则 $F'(x) = f(x)$。

正态分布是最常见的概率分布形式之一，其概率密度函数的表达式为

$$f(x) = \frac{1}{\sigma \sqrt{2\pi}} \mathrm{e}^{-\frac{(x-\mu)^2}{2\sigma^2}}, -\infty < x < +\infty \tag{4-1}$$

正态分布的数学期望 μ 为位置参数，决定了分布的位置；其标准差 σ 为尺度参数，决定了分布的幅度。

在生产制造中，我们常常采取正态分布去研究一些成品、原材料和机器等的质量规律，因为生产中每个工作站及每条生产线上的工序质量波动具有统计规律性，所以可以通过数理统计方法对一个生产系统进行预估评价。

例 4-1 如某工位是以最终成品的不合格品数作为质量指标，所采用的方法是抽样调查。在总体中抽取 8 个样本容量为 200 的样本进行质检，发现每个样本中的不合格品件数分别为 8、3、4、1、5、0、7、6。已知允许样本的不合格品件数为 9，试对该工位的工序能力进行分析。

解 每个样本中不合格品率平均值为

$$\overline{p} = \frac{8+3+4+1+5+0+6+7}{8 \times 200} = 0.02125(件)$$

任意容量为 200 的样本的不合格品数期望值为

$$\mu = n\overline{p} = 200 \times 0.02125 = 4.25(件)$$

该工位的工序能力为

$$C_\mathrm{p} = \frac{\mathrm{TU} - \mu}{3\sigma} = \frac{9 - 4.25}{3 \times \sqrt{4.25 \times (1 - 0.02125)}} = 0.754$$

其中，C_p 表示一道工序的工序能力，TU 表示样本中所允许的不合格产品的件数。工序能力的判定标准如表 4-1 所示。

表 4-1 工序能力判定标准

C_p	工序级别	判断结论
$C_p > 1.67$	特级	工序能力过分充裕
$1.67 \geqslant C_p > 1.33$	A 级	工序能力充分
$1.33 \geqslant C_p > 1.00$	B 级	工序能力合格，但不太充分
$1.00 \geqslant C_p > 0.67$	C 级	工序能力不足
$C_p \leqslant 0.67$	D 级	工序能力严重不足

由此可知，该工位的工序能力不足。

4.2.2 期望与方差

在一些实际问题和理论问题中，人们感兴趣于那些能描述随机变量某一部分特征的常数。例如：一个篮球队中上场比赛的运动员的身高是一个随机变量，人们常常关心的是上场运动员的平均身高；一个城市中一户家庭拥有的汽车辆数是一个随机变量，在考察城市交通状况时，人们关心户均拥有汽车的辆数；评价棉花的质量时，既需要注意纤维的平均长度，又需要注意纤维长度与平均长度的偏离程度，平均长度较大，偏离程度较小，棉花的质量就较好。这些描述随机变量的常数就是期望与方差。

在概率论和统计学中，一个离散型随机变量的期望值是试验中每次可能结果的概率乘以其结果的总和。换句话说，期望值是随机试验在同样的机会下重复多次的结果计算出的等同"期望"的平均值。或者说，期望值表示的是一个随机试验的可能结果的平均值，并不一定等于随机试验的任何一个结果。

例如，当某公司在购买某一零件时，希望所购买的零件的不合格品数尽可能少或者没有不合格品。现在已知三家生产该零件的厂商，每生产 1000 个该零件时，各家厂商的合格品率分别是 95.7%，99%，97%，所以根据期望的定义，就可以计算出这三家厂商每生产 1000 个该零件时合格品数的平均值分别为 957、990、970。这样该公司就可以进行决策，选择购买第二家厂商的零件。

方差是各个数据与平均值之差的平方的平均数，用来度量随机变量和其数学期望之间的偏离程度。在许多实际问题中，研究随机变量和均值之间的偏离程度有着很重要的意义。容易发现，$E(|X-E(X)|)$ 能有效度量随机变量 X 与其均值 $E(X)$ 的偏离程度，但由于带有绝对值，运算不方便，因此通常用 $E((X-E(X))^2)$ 表示，也就是方差。一般用下面的公式进行计算：

$$D(X) = E(X^2) - [E(X)]^2$$

正态分布方差：

$$D(X) = \sigma^2$$

二项分布方差：

$$D(X) = np(1-p)$$

式中：n 是某事件（随机变量）发生的次数，p 是该事件发生的概率。

比如在各种制造企业的车间生产中，对所生产的产品进行质量控制所使用的方法是 6σ 管理，即利用方差的定义及原理，将最终产品的质量分布控制在 $\pm 3\sigma$ 中。

例 4-2 某一生产制造商的质检部门对其生产的零件采用抽样调查进行统计，将不符合标准的零件统称为缺陷产品，在全面检查后，进行缺陷数目统计并标注，所得出的结果如表 4-2 所示，求缺陷数控制图的上下界限。

表 4-2 缺陷数控制图数据表

样本号	1	2	3	4	5	6	7	8	9	10	合计
缺陷数/件	5	7	4	6	9	8	3	6	4	3	55

解 每个样本缺陷数平均值为

$$\bar{c} = \frac{\sum c}{k} = \frac{55}{10} = 5.5（件）$$

缺陷数控制图的上下界限为

$$\text{UCL} = \bar{c} + 3\sqrt{\bar{c}} = 5.5 + 3\sqrt{5.5} = 12.53（件）$$
$$\text{CL} = \bar{c} = 5.5（件）$$
$$\text{LCL} = \bar{c} - 3\sqrt{\bar{c}} = 5.5 - 3\sqrt{5.5} = -1.53 = 0（用 0 代替负值）$$

其中：UCL 表示上界限，CL 表示中心线，LCL 表示下界限。

4.2.3 分布函数

对于一个非离散型随机变量 X 来说，它可能取的值不能被一一列举出来，于是它就不能像离散型随机变量那样可以用分布律来描述。另外，我们通常所遇到的非离散型随机变量取任一指定的实数值的概率都等于 0，因此我们关心的也不再是它取某个特定值的概率，比如测量的误差 0.05 mm，元件的寿命 1251.3 h 或是排队请求服务的时间等，我们感兴趣的是这类随机变量的取值落在某个区间的概率，即 $P\{x_1 < X \leqslant x_2\}$。

定义：设 X 是一个随机变量，x 是任意实数，函数 $F(x) = P\{X \leqslant x\}$ 称为 X 的分布函数。其含义如下。

(1) 若将 X 看作数轴上随机点的坐标，则分布函数 $F(x)$ 的值就表示 X 落在区间 $(-\infty, x]$ 的概率。

(2) 对任意实数 $x_1, x_2 (x_1 < x_2)$，随机点落在区间 $(x_1, x_2]$ 的概率 $P\{x_1 < X \leqslant x_2\} = P\{X \leqslant x_2\} - P\{X \leqslant x_1\} = F(x_2) - F(x_1)$。

(3) 随机变量的分布函数是一个普通的函数，它完整地描述了随机变量的统计规律性。通过它，人们就可以利用数学分析的方法来全面研究随机变量。

分布函数的性质如下：

① 非负有界性，$0 \leqslant F(x) \leqslant 1$；
② 单调不减性，对任意的 $x_1 < x_2$，有 $F(x_1) \leqslant F(x_2)$；
③ 右连续性，$F(x+0) = F(x)$。

如等可能地在数轴上的有界区间 $[a, b]$ 上投点，记 X 为落点的位置（数轴上的坐标），

求随机变量 X 的分布函数,则分为以下几种情况。

(1) 当 $x<a$ 时,$\{X\leqslant x\}$ 是不可能事件,于是 $F(x)=P\{X\leqslant x\}=0$。

(2) 当 $a\leqslant x\leqslant b$ 时,由于 $\{X\leqslant x\}=\{a\leqslant X\leqslant x\}$ 且 $[a,x]\subset[a,b]$,因此由几何概率可知 $F(x)=P\{X\leqslant x\}=P\{a\leqslant X\leqslant x\}=\dfrac{x-a}{b-a}$。

(3) 当 $x>b$ 时,由于 $\{X\leqslant x\}=\{a\leqslant x\leqslant b\}$,因此 $F(x)=P\{X\leqslant x\}=P\{a\leqslant X\leqslant b\}=\dfrac{b-a}{b-a}=1$。

综上所述,X 的分布函数为

$$F(x)=\begin{cases}0, & x<a \\ \dfrac{x-a}{b-a}, & a\leqslant x\leqslant b \\ 1, & x>b\end{cases}$$

对于正态分布而言,因为 $X\sim N(\mu,\sigma^2)$,$f(x)=\dfrac{1}{\sigma\sqrt{2\pi}}\mathrm{e}^{-\frac{(x-\mu)^2}{2\sigma^2}}$,所以

$$F(x)=\dfrac{1}{\sigma\sqrt{2\pi}}\int_{-\infty}^{x}\mathrm{e}^{-\frac{(x-\mu)^2}{2\sigma^2}},\ -\infty<x<+\infty$$

其中,$\mu=0,\sigma=1$ 的正态分布称为标准正态分布,表达式为

$$\Phi(x)=\dfrac{1}{\sqrt{2\pi}}\int_{-\infty}^{x}\mathrm{e}^{-\frac{t^2}{2}}\mathrm{d}t$$

$\Phi(x)$ 具有以下重要性质:

$$\Phi(x)=1-\Phi(-x)$$

该性质在生产系统中的应用是根据产品的合格率计算不合格品率。

例 4-3 某磨床车间加工一轴类零件,所要求外径的标准为 $\phi 20_{0}^{+0.05}$ mm。在对一批零件进行抽样检查后得出 $\bar{d}=20.025$ mm,已知这道工序的工序能力 $C_p=0.8$,试计算不合格品率。

解 因为所生产零件尺寸的分布中心与标准中心重合,所以先计算合格品率:

$$\begin{aligned}P\{\text{TL}\leqslant X\leqslant \text{TU}\}&=\Phi\left(\dfrac{T}{2\sigma}\right)-\Phi\left(-\dfrac{T}{2\sigma}\right)\\&=\Phi(3C_p)-\Phi(-3C_p)\\&=1-2\Phi(-3C_p)\\&=1-2\Phi(-2.4)\end{aligned}$$

(注:TL 表示公差带下限,TU 表示公差带上限。)

所以不合格品率为

$$P=1-P\{\text{TL}\leqslant X\leqslant \text{TU}\}=2\Phi(-2.4)$$

查正态分布表可知 $\Phi(-2.4)=0.008198$,所以

$$P=2\times 0.008198\times 100\%=1.640\%$$

4.3 中心极限定理及其应用

4.3.1 伯努利试验与二项分布

随机试验中某事件是否发生，试验的可能结果只有相互对立的两个，这种只有两个可能结果的试验称为伯努利试验。例如：投掷硬币哪一面朝上的试验结果只能是"正"和"反"之一；投掷六面骰子，结果大于或等于 5 为"成功"，否则为"失败"，则结果只可能为"成功"和"失败"之一。

伯努利试验有两个特点：

(1) 对立性，每次试验的结果只能是对立事件中的一个，要么出现 A，要么出现非 A；

(2) 独立性，每次试验的结果互不影响，且各次试验中事件 A 出现的概率都相等，设为 p，非 A 事件出现的概率为 $q=1-p$。

由于现实中，往往统计意义更值得关注，如对于超市而言，并不会关心某人某时段是否来购物，而是关心某时段会有大约多少人来购物，从而优化不同时段开放收银台的数量。因此，进行多次伯努利试验，某一结果发生次数的总和，是更值得关注的数值。重复进行 n 次伯努利试验，就形成了一个伯努利过程(Bernoulli process)，也称为 n 重伯努利试验，例如抛硬币 100 次，就是一个 100 重伯努利试验。设在一次试验中事件 A 发生的概率为 $p(0<p<1)$，则在 n 重伯努利试验中事件 A 恰好发生 k 次的概率为 $P_n(k)=C_n^k p^k q^{n-k}$，$q=1-p(k=0,1,2,\cdots,n)$。

二项分布：进行 m 次 n 重伯努利试验，某一结果在一次 n 重伯努利试验中出现的次数所形成的概率分布称为二项分布。

例 4-4 在某一车间内有 4 台设备加工相同的零件，每台设备的加工是相互独立的，在任意时间段停工的概率均为 0.3。求在一次观察中恰好有 2 台设备停机的概率。

解 因为该车间有 4 台设备，所以该观察可视为 4 重伯努利试验，$n=4$，$p=0.3$，则恰好有 2 台设备停机的概率为

$$P\{x=2\} = C_4^2 \times 0.3^2 \times 0.7^2 = \frac{8}{27}$$

例 4-5 在成品仓库中对 100 个零件进行质量抽检，已知这 100 个零件里有 30 件废品和 70 件合格产品，现从中有放回地抽取 5 次，每次只取出一件产品。试求：(1)取出的 5 件产品中有 2 件废品的概率；(2)取出的 5 件产品中至少有 2 件是废品的概率。

解 取到废品的概率为 0.3，5 次抽取相互独立，故该抽取可视为 5 重伯努利试验。

设 x 为取到废品的次数，则

$$P\{x=k\} = C_5^k \times 0.3^k \times 0.7^{5-k}, k=0,1,2,3,4,5$$

(1) $P\{x=2\} = C_5^2 \times 0.3^2 \times 0.7^3 = 0.3087$

(2) $P\{x \geqslant 2\} = 1 - P\{x<2\} = 1 - P\{x=0\} - P\{x=1\}$

$$= 1 - C_5^0 \times 0.3^0 \times 0.7^5 - C_5^1 \times 0.3 \times 0.7^4 \approx 0.4718$$

根据以上定义和示例可以看出，现实中的多数情况，如某一时段超市的顾客总数、某一季节雨天的总数等都服从二项分布。

4.3.2 正态分布

正态分布最早是在求二项分布的渐近公式过程中得到的，它是二项分布的极限分布。正态分布又名高斯分布（Gaussian distribution），是一个在数学、物理及工程等领域都非常重要的概率分布，在统计学的许多方面有着重大的影响。若随机变量 X 服从一个数学期望为 μ、方差为 σ^2 的高斯分布，记为 $N(\mu,\sigma^2)$，则其分布为正态分布，期望值 μ 决定了其概率密度函数的位置，标准差 σ 决定了分布的幅度。因其概率密度函数曲线呈钟形，因此人们又经常称之为钟形曲线。我们通常所说的标准正态分布是 $\mu=0,\sigma=1$ 的正态分布。

正态分布 $N(\mu,\sigma^2)$ 的概率密度函数 $f(x)$ 曲线如图 4-1 所示。

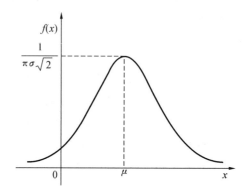

图 4-1　正态分布概率密度函数曲线

正态分布曲线的特征如图 4-2 所示，描述如下：

（1）关于直线 $x=\mu$ 对称；

（2）在 $x=\mu$ 处达到最大值；

（3）在 $x=\mu\pm\sigma$ 处有拐点；

（4）$x\rightarrow\infty$ 时曲线以 x 轴为渐近线；

（5）固定 σ 改变 μ，则曲线沿 x 轴平移而不改变形状；

（6）固定 μ 改变 σ，则当 σ 很小时，曲线的形状与尖塔相似，当 σ 的值增大时，曲线趋于平坦。

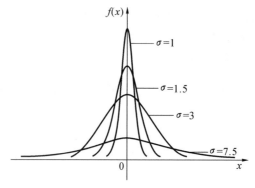

图 4-2　正态分布曲线的特征

4.3.3 中心极限定理

中心极限定理(central limit theorem):如果一个随机变量是很多随机变量之和,而其中每一个随机变量对总和产生不大的影响,那么,这一总和在自变量范围内近似地服从正态分布。

中心极限定理是概率论中用来描述满足一定条件的一系列随机变量之和的概率分布的极限的定理。这一定理是数理统计学和误差分析的理论基础,指出了大量随机变量近似服从正态分布的条件。在自然界与生产中,一些现象受到许多相互独立的随机因素的影响,如果每个因素所产生的影响都很微小,则总的影响可以看作近似服从正态分布。中心极限定理就是从数学上证明了这一理论。

4.3.4 应用实例

例 4-6 某车间有 200 台设备,假设每台设备汇报维修请求的概率是 0.6,问至少有多少个维修人员在岗,才能使所有请求得到及时响应的概率为 99.9%。

解 数学模型:该问题可以转换为 $n=200$ 的伯努利试验,服从 $p=0.6$ 的二项分布,即 $X \sim B(200,0.6)$,近似服从正态分布。

求解策略:假设有 a 个维修人员在岗,则同时汇报请求的数量小于或等于 a 时,所有请求都能得到及时处理,同时汇报请求的数量小于或等于 a 的概率为

$$F(a) - F(0) = \Phi\left(\frac{a-\mu}{\sigma}\right) - \Phi\left(\frac{0-\mu}{\sigma}\right)$$

$$\mu = E(x) = 200 \times 0.6 = 120$$

$$\sigma = \sqrt{D(X)} = \sqrt{np(1-p)}$$
$$= \sqrt{200 \times 0.6 \times 0.4} = \sqrt{48}$$

则

$$\Phi\left(\frac{a-120}{\sqrt{48}}\right) - \Phi\left(\frac{-120}{\sqrt{48}}\right) = 0.999$$

查正态分布表得 $a=142$,即 142 个维修人员在岗,可以满足响应要求。

4.4 队列特征分析

4.4.1 排队系统基本概念

排队系统包含以下基本元素。

1) 输入过程

输入过程指服务请求按怎样的规律到达排队系统的过程。

(1) 请求总体数量,又称输入源。输入源可以是有限的,也可以是无限的。

(2) 请求到达的形式。这是描述请求是怎样来到系统的,是单个到达还是成批到达。

(3) 请求的概率分布,或称请求相继到达的时间间隔分布。

2) 服务台

服务台可以从以下三个方面来描述。

（1）服务台数量及构成形式：从数量上说，服务台有单台和多台之分；从构成形式上看，有单队单服务台式、单队多服务台并联式、多队多服务台并联式、单队多服务台串联式等。

（2）服务方式：指在某一时刻接受服务的顾客数，有单个服务和成批服务两种。

（3）服务时间的分布：在多数情况下，对某一个顾客的服务时间是一随机变量，与顾客到达的时间间隔分布一样，服务时间的分布有定长分布、负指数分布、埃尔朗分布等。

根据以上基本元素，排队系统按照队列特征，可以分为单队单台、单队多台和多队多台三类，如图4-3所示；按照服务特征，可以分为等服务时间队列和随机服务时间队列两类。因此，排队系统就有单队单台等服务时间队列、单队单台随机服务时间队列、单队多台等服务时间队列、单队多台随机服务时间队列、多队多台等服务时间队列、多队多台随机服务时间队列六种类型。

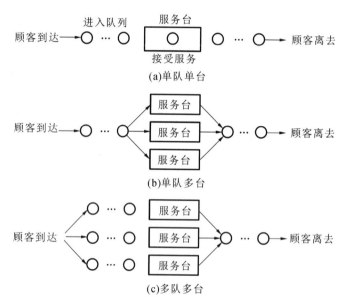

图4-3 排队系统按照队列特征分类

分析排队系统时所涉及的常用概念如下。

L：平均队长，即稳态系统任一时刻请求数的期望值。

L_q：平均等待队长，即稳态系统任一时刻等待服务的请求数的期望值。

W：平均逗留时间，即在任一时刻进入稳态系统的请求逗留时间的期望值。

W_q：平均等待时间，即在任一时刻进入稳态系统的请求等待时间的期望值。

λ：请求到达的平均速率，即单位时间内平均到达的请求数。

$1/\lambda$：平均到达时间间隔。

μ：平均服务速率，即单位时间内服务完毕的请求数。

$1/\mu$：平均服务时间。

s：系统中服务台的个数。

ρ：服务强度，即每个服务台单位时间内的平均服务时间，一般 $\rho=\lambda/(s\mu)$。

N：稳态系统任一时刻的状态（即系统中所有请求数）。

U：任一请求在稳态系统中的逗留时间。

Q:任一请求在稳态系统中的等待时间。

$P_n = P\{N=n\}$:状态概率,系统中有 n 项任务的概率;特别当 $n=0$ 时,$P_n = P_0$,即系统所有服务台全部空闲的概率。

λ_e:有效平均到达率,指单位时间内到达服务系统(包括未进入系统)的概率。

4.4.2 等服务时间队列特征分析

等服务时间队列中,服务台对每一个请求的服务时间相等或近似相等,如地铁刷卡检票系统、同类产品包装系统等。等服务时间的特征计算方法如下:

队列长度期望值=同时汇报服务的期望值-在岗人数;

任务等待时间期望值=队列长度期望值×单位服务时间;

服务空闲率=服务人员空闲数期望值/服务人员总数;

服务利用率=1-服务空闲率。

4.4.3 随机服务时间队列分析

1. 队列因素

随机服务时间队列对不同请求的服务时间可能有较大的差异,如超市收银系统队列,顾客购买的商品数量不同,服务时间也有较大差异;银行服务队列,顾客所申请的业务不同,服务时间也有较大差异。以下因素影响随机服务时间队列的特性。

(1) 任务因素。

① 平均到达间隔时间:$T_0 = \dfrac{T}{n}$。

② 平均到达速率:$\lambda = \dfrac{1}{T_0} = \dfrac{n}{T}$。

③ 到达时间间隔的分布函数:$A_0(t) = 1 - F(t)$。

(2) 服务因素。

① 平均服务时间:$T_S = \dfrac{T}{n_S}$。

② 平均服务速度:$\mu = \dfrac{1}{T_S} = \dfrac{n_S}{T}$。

③ 服务时间的分布函数:$A_S(t) = 1 - F_S(t)$。

④ 业务量强度:$u = \dfrac{\lambda}{\mu} = \dfrac{n}{n_S}$。

⑤ 服务强度:$\rho = \dfrac{\lambda}{\mu}$。

其中,下标"S"表示系统。

2. 特征分析

(1) 状态概率:系统中有 n 项任务的概率为 $P_n = (1-\rho)\rho^n$。

(2) 任务的期望值:$L_S = \sum\limits_{n=0}^{\infty} n P_n = \sum\limits_{n=0}^{\infty} n(1-\rho)\rho^n = \dfrac{\rho}{1-\rho} = \dfrac{\lambda}{\mu-\lambda}$。

(3) 平均等待任务数:$L_q = \dfrac{\rho\lambda}{\mu-\lambda}$。

(4) 任务等待时间的期望值：$W_q = \dfrac{\rho}{\mu - \lambda}$。

例 4-7 某加工中心为任务队列提供服务，任务平均到达速率为 2.1 项/h，完成任务的平均时间为 0.4 h/项，试分析该系统的性能指标。

解 （1）基本因素：
$$\lambda = 2.1(项/h), T_s = 0.4(h), \mu = \frac{1}{0.4} = 2.5(项/h)$$

（2）服务强度：
$$\rho = \frac{\lambda}{\mu} = 0.84$$

（3）系统期望值：
$$L_s = \frac{2.1}{2.5 - 2.1} = 5.25$$

（4）平均等待队长：
$$L_q = \rho L_s = 0.84 \times 5.25 = 4.41$$

（5）平均等待时间：
$$W_q = \frac{0.84}{2.5 - 2.1} = 2.1(h)$$

例 4-8 在一条生产线上，采用传送链对半成品进行搬运输送，已知该供给系统服务于一台加工设备，这台加工设备上有一名操作工人，系统中预先设定的到达该工位半成品的速度为 4 min/件，该操作工人的加工速度为 3 min/件。试求：(1) 该操作工人的利用率；(2) 平均等待的半成品数目；(3) 操作工人平均加工的半成品数；(4) 半成品平均等待时间；(5) 半成品在系统中的平均逗留时间。

解 （1）该操作工人的利用率：
$$\rho = \frac{\lambda}{\mu} = \frac{15}{20} = 75\%$$

（2）平均等待的半成品数目：
$$\bar{n}_L = \frac{\lambda^2}{\mu \times (\mu - \lambda)} = \frac{15^2}{20 \times (20 - 15)} = 2.25(件)$$

（3）操作工人平均加工的半成品数：
$$\bar{n}_S = \frac{\lambda}{\mu - \lambda} = \frac{15}{20 - 15} = 3(件)$$

（4）半成品平均等待时间：
$$\bar{t}_L = \frac{\lambda}{\mu \times (\mu - \lambda)} = \frac{15}{20 \times (20 - 15)} = 0.15(h)$$

（5）半成品在系统中的平均逗留时间：
$$\bar{t}_S = \frac{1}{\mu - \lambda} = \frac{1}{20 - 15} = 0.2(h)$$

4.5 小　　结

　　由于生产系统具有不确定因素,因此概率分析是生产系统建模与仿真的重要手段之一。本章首先介绍了概率理论的一些基本概念;然后详细介绍了伯努利试验、二项分布、正态分布、中心极限定理等原理,并通过典型的例子,讲解了这些理论在生产系统分析中的应用;最后,初步介绍了排队论的一些概念和基本理论,并用例子说明了随机服务时间队列的一般求解方法。

第 5 章 基于复合形法的生产系统求解方法

5.1 复合形法的基本思想和一般步骤

复合形法是求解约束最优化问题的直接方法之一,它的基本思想是先在可行域内构造具有 n_1 个顶点的初始复合形,经过对该复合形各顶点的目标函数值进行比较,找到目标函数值最大的顶点,即最坏点,然后通过一系列的计算,求出目标函数值有所下降的可行的新点,并用此点代替原先的最坏点,形成新的复合形,从而逐步使复合形顶点向最优解收敛。

在求解一般的只有不等式约束的最优化问题时,复合形法的主要求解步骤如图 5-1 所示。

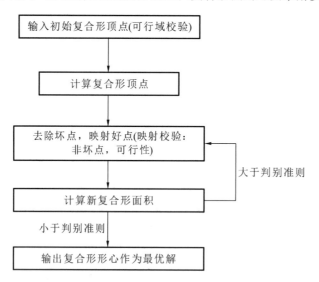

图 5-1 复合形法的步骤

(1) 初始化,即在可行域内构造复合形的 n_1 个顶点。如果优化问题的变量个数为 n,一般按式(5-1)取 n_1 的值:

$$n+1 \leqslant n_1 \leqslant 2n \tag{5-1}$$

初始顶点可以由设计者决定或由随机函数产生。首先,输入一个可行的初始点 X_1(每个顶点包括 n 个变量);然后,产生其余的 n_1-1 个点,其中点 $X_{(k+1),i}$ 通过式(5-2)产生:

$$X_{(k+1),i} = a_i + r_i(b_i - a_i), i = 1, 2, \cdots, n \tag{5-2}$$

式中:$X_{(k+1),i}$ 是 X_{k+1} 的第 i 个分量;a_i 和 b_i 分别是 $X_{(k+1),i}$ 的下限和上限;r_i 为(0,1)区间内均

匀分布的随机数。根据式(5-2)计算得到的 n_1-1 个随机点不一定都在可行域内,因此要设法将非可行点移到可行域内。如果 X_{k+1} 满足条件,则继续产生下一个顶点;否则,先求前 k 个顶点的形心 X_C：

$$X_C = \frac{1}{k}\sum_{j=1}^{k} X_j \tag{5-3}$$

再将 X_{k+1} 沿 X_{k+1} 与 X_C 的连线向形心缩小一半,即

$$X_{k+1} = X_C + 0.5(X_{k+1} - X_C) \tag{5-4}$$

如果此时 X_{k+1} 仍然为不可行点,再按式(5-4)计算,使其继续向形心移动,直到 X_{k+1} 为可行点为止。显然,只要形心可行,点 X_{k+1} 一定可以移到可行域内。随即产生的 n_1-1 个点经过这样的处理后,全部成为可行点,并构成初始复合形。

此种方法完全适用于可行域是凸集的情况。如果可行域为非凸集,形心可能不在可行域内,则上述方法可能失败。此时可以通过改变设计变量的下限和上限值,重新产生各顶点。

(2) 计算复合形各顶点的函数值。

$$f_j = f(X_j), j = 1,2,\cdots,n_1 \tag{5-5}$$

(3) 比较其大小,求出最坏点 X_H、最好点 X_B 及次坏点 X_G,最坏点是使目标函数值最大的点,最好点是使目标函数值最小的点。

$$X_H : F(X_H) = \max(f_j | j = 1,2,\cdots,n_1)$$
$$X_B : F(X_B) = \min(f_j | j = 1,2,\cdots,n_1)$$
$$X_G : F(X_G) = \max(f_j | j = 1,2,\cdots,n_1, j \neq H)$$

式中:H 表示最坏点对应的 j 值

(4) 判断迭代的终止条件。给定迭代终止收敛精度 ε,以目标函数值的标准差作为判断的基准,当标准差 σ 小于或等于 ε 时,迭代完成,约束最优解为 $X^* = X_B, f(X^*) = f(X_B)$。若标准差大于 ε,则转步骤(5)。终止条件的判断式为

$$\sigma = \left[\frac{1}{n_1-1}\sum_{j=1}^{n_1}(f_j - \overline{f})^2\right]^{\frac{1}{2}} \leqslant \varepsilon \tag{5-6}$$

式中:$\overline{f}$ 为 n_1 个点的平均目标函数值,即

$$\overline{f} = \frac{1}{n_1}\sum_{j=1}^{n_1} f_j \tag{5-7}$$

(5) 求去掉最坏点 X_H 后所有点的形心 X_C。

$$X_C = \frac{1}{n_1-1}\sum_{j=1, j\neq H}^{n_1} X_j \tag{5-8}$$

求解后,判断形心 X_C 是否可行,若为可行点,则转步骤(6);若为非可行点,则重新设定设计变量的下限和上限值,即令

$$a = X_B, b = X_C$$

然后转步骤(1),重新构造初始复合形。

(6) 求映射点 X^R。依据经验,从最坏点 X_H 向形心 X_C 映射的方向,目标函数值下降的可能性更大。以形心 X_C 为中心,将最坏点 X_H 按一定比例进行映射,有较大可能找到一个比最坏点 X_H 的目标函数值小的新点 X^R,X^R 称为映射点。

$$X^R = X_C + \alpha(X_C - X_H) \tag{5-9}$$

式中:α 是映射系数,$\alpha > 0$,一般取 $1.2 \sim 1.5$。

(7) 验证映射点 X^R 是否是可行点。若映射点 X^R 不是可行点,则令 $\alpha=\alpha/2$,转步骤(6)重新计算映射点 X^R,直至可行为止。

(8) 计算映射点 X^R 的目标函数值 $f(X^R)$,如果 $f(X^R)<f(X_H)$,则用映射点 X^R 代替最坏点 X_H,完成一次迭代,构成新的复合形,转步骤(3);如果 $f(X^R)\geqslant f(X_H)$,转步骤(9)。

(9) 若 $\alpha\geqslant\mu$(μ 为预先给定的一个小正数),则令 $\alpha=\alpha/2$,转到步骤(6)重新计算映射点 X^R。若 $\alpha<\mu$,则用次坏点 X_G 代替最坏点 X_H,转步骤(5)。

复合形法流程图如图 5-2 所示。

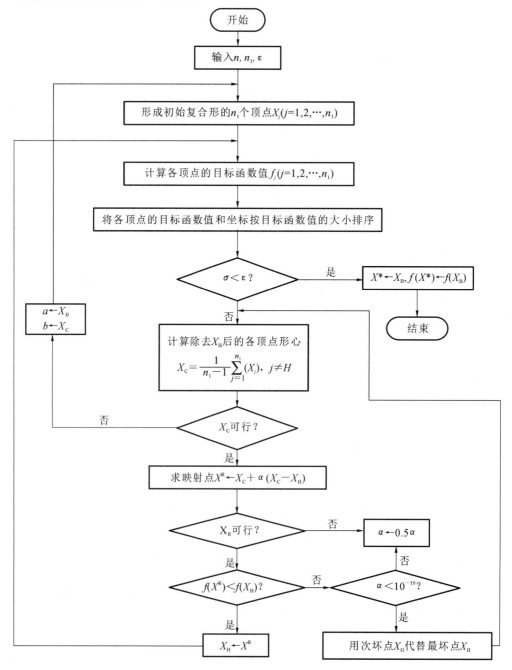

图 5-2 复合形法流程图

5.2 复合形法求解实例

例 5-1 求 x_1, x_2。
$$\min f(X) = 4x_1 - x_2^2 - 12$$
s.t.
$$D: g_1(X) = 25 - x_1^2 - x_2^2 \geqslant 0$$
$$x \in D \subset R^n$$
$$g_2(X) = x_1 \geqslant 0$$
$$g_3(X) = x_2 \geqslant 0$$

要求形成两个新复合形。初始复合形的三个顶点为
$$X_1 = [2 \quad 1]^T, X_2 = [4 \quad 1]^T, X_3 = [3 \quad 3]^T$$

解 （1）校验初始复合形各顶点的可行性。

对于 X_1，有
$$g_1(X_1) = 25 - 2^2 - 1^2 = 20 > 0$$
$$g_2(X_1) = 2 > 0$$
$$g_3(X_1) = 1 > 0$$

所以 X_1 是可行点，同理可验证 X_2, X_3 均是可行点。

（2）计算初始复合形各顶点的目标函数值。
$$f(X_1) = 4 \times 2 - 1^2 - 12 = -5$$
$$f(X_2) = 4 \times 4 - 1^2 - 12 = 3$$
$$f(X_3) = 4 \times 3 - 3^2 - 12 = -9$$

所以，坏点 $X_H = X_2$，好点 $X_B = X_3$。

（3）计算去掉坏点 X_H 后其余各顶点的形心 X_C。
$$X_C = \frac{1}{n_1 - 1} \sum_{j=1, j \neq H}^{n_1} X_j$$
$$= \frac{1}{3-1} \times ([2 \quad 1]^T + [3 \quad 3]^T)$$
$$= [2.5 \quad 2]^T, j \neq 2$$

（4）将形心 X_C 代入约束条件，验证其是否可行。
$$g_1(X_C) = 25 - 2.5^2 - 2^2 = 14.75 > 0$$
$$g_2(X_C) = 2.5 > 0$$
$$g_3(X_C) = 2 > 0$$

可知，X_C 满足约束条件，是可行点。

（5）取映射系数 $\alpha = 1.3$，计算映射点 X^R。
$$X^R = X_C + \alpha(X_C - X_H)$$
$$= [2.5 \quad 2]^T + 1.3 \times ([2.5 \quad 2]^T - [4 \quad 1]^T)$$
$$= [0.55 \quad 3.3]^T$$

（6）将映射点 X^R 代入约束条件，检验其是否可行。

$$g_1(X^R) = 25 - 0.55^2 - 3.3^2 = 13.8075 > 0$$
$$g_2(X^R) = 0.55 > 0$$
$$g_3(X^R) = 3.3 > 0$$

可知,X^R满足约束条件,是可行点。

(7) 计算映射点的目标函数值 $f(X^R)$。
$$f(X^R) = 4 \times 0.55 - 3.3^2 - 12 = -20.69 < f(X_H) = f(X_2) = 3$$

所以用映射点 X^R 取代坏点 X_H,构成第一个新的复合形,它的三个顶点是
$$X_1 = [2 \quad 1]^T, X_2 = [0.55 \quad 3.3]^T, X_3 = [3 \quad 3]^T$$

(8) 计算第一个新的复合形各顶点的目标函数值。
$$f(X_1) = 4 \times 2 - 1^2 - 12 = -5$$
$$f(X_2) = 4 \times 0.55 - 3.3^2 - 12 = -20.69$$
$$f(X_3) = 4 \times 3 - 3^2 - 12 = -9$$

所以,坏点 $X_H = X_1$,好点 $X_B = X_2$。

(9) 计算去掉坏点 X_H 后其余各顶点的几何中心点 X_C。
$$X_C = \frac{1}{n_1 - 1} \sum_{j=1, j \neq H}^{n_1} X_j$$
$$= \frac{1}{3-1} \times ([0.55 \quad 3.3]^T + [3 \quad 3]^T)$$
$$= [1.775 \quad 3.15]^T, j \neq 1$$

(10) 将形心 X_C 代入约束条件,验证其是否可行。
$$g_1(X_C) = 25 - 1.775^2 - 3.15^2 = 11.926875 > 0$$
$$g_2(X_C) = 1.775 > 0$$
$$g_3(X_C) = 3.15 > 0$$

可知,X_C 满足约束条件,是可行点。

(11) 取映射系数 $\alpha = 1.3$,计算映射点 X^R。
$$X^R = X_C + \alpha(X_C - X_H)$$
$$= [1.775 \quad 3.15]^T + 1.3 \times ([1.775 \quad 3.15]^T - [2 \quad 1]^T)$$
$$= [1.4825 \quad 5.945]^T$$

(12) 将映射点 X^R 代入约束条件,检验其是否可行。
$$g_1(X^R) = 25 - 1.4825^2 - 5.945^2 = -12.540831 < 0$$
$$g_2(X^R) = 1.4825 > 0$$
$$g_3(X^R) = 5.945 > 0$$

可知,X^R 不满足所有约束条件,不是可行点,将映射系数减半,即令 $\alpha = 0.65$,再重新计算映射点 X^R。
$$X^R = X_C + \alpha(X_C - X_H)$$
$$= [1.775 \quad 3.15]^T + 0.65 \times ([1.775 \quad 3.15]^T - [2 \quad 1]^T)$$
$$= [1.6287 \quad 4.5475]^T$$

(13) 再将映射点 X^R 代入约束条件,检验其是否可行。
$$g_1(X^R) = 25 - 1.62875^2 - 4.5475^2 = 1.667413 > 0$$
$$g_2(X^R) = 1.62875 > 0$$

$$g_3(X^R) = 4.5475 > 0$$

可知，X^R 满足约束条件，是可行点。

(14) 计算映射点 X^R 的目标函数值 $f(X^R)$。

$$f(X^R) = 4 \times 1.62875 - 4.5475^2 - 12 = -26.1648 < f(X_H) = f(X_1) = -5$$

所以用映射点 X^R 取代坏点 X_H，构成第二个新的复合形，它的三个顶点是

$$X_1 = [1.62875 \quad 4.5475]^T, \quad X_2 = [0.55 \quad 3.3]^T, \quad X_3 = [3 \quad 3]^T$$

(15) 计算第二个新的复合形各顶点的目标函数值。

$$f(X_1) = 4 \times 1.62875 - 4.5475^2 - 12 = -26.163392$$
$$f(X_2) = 4 \times 0.55 - 3.3^2 - 12 = -20.69$$
$$f(X_3) = 4 \times 3 - 3^2 - 12 = -9$$

所以，坏点 $X_H = X_3$，好点 $X_B = X_1$。

(16) 经过两次迭代计算，获得的优化结果是 $X^* = X_1 = [1.62875 \quad 4.5475]^T$，且对应的目标函数值为 $f(X^*) = f(X_1) = -26.163392$。

例 5-2 求 x_1, x_2

$$\min f(X) = 60 - 10x_1 - 4x_2 + x_1^2 + x_2^2 - x_1 x_2, X \subset D \subset R^2$$

s.t. $\quad D: g(X) = -x_1 - x_2 + 11 \geqslant 0$
$$0 \leqslant x_1 \leqslant 6$$
$$0 \leqslant x_2 \leqslant 8$$

解 (1) 产生初始复合形的各顶点。本例是具有两个设计变量的非线性规划问题，取复合形顶点的数目为 $n_1 = 2n = 2 \times 2 = 4$，采取人为选点的方法产生初始复合形的全部顶点，即选取下列四点作为初始复合形顶点：

$$X_1 = [1 \quad 5.5]^T, \quad X_2 = [1 \quad 4]^T$$
$$X_3 = [2 \quad 6.4]^T, \quad X_4 = [3 \quad 3.5]^T$$

(2) 形成初始复合形，求出各顶点的目标函数值，并找出坏点 X_H 和好点 X_B。各顶点的函数值为

$$f(X_1) = 53.75, \quad f(X_2) = 47$$
$$f(X_3) = 46.56, \quad f(X_4) = 26.75$$

所以，坏点 $X_H = X_1$，好点 $X_B = X_4$。

(3) 计算除去坏点 X_H 后其余各点的形心 X_C。

$$X_C = \frac{1}{n_1 - 1} \sum_{j=1, j \neq H}^{n_1} X_j$$
$$= \frac{1}{4-1} \times ([1 \quad 4]^T + [2 \quad 6.4]^T + [3 \quad 3.5]^T)$$
$$= [2 \quad 4.63]^T, \quad j \neq 1$$

(4) 将形心 X_C 代入约束条件，验证其是否可行。由于 $g(X_C) = 4.37 > 0$，且 $0 < 2 < 6$，$0 < 4.63 < 8$，因此 X_C 为可行点。

(5) 取映射系数 $\alpha = 1.3$，计算映射点 X^R。

$$X^R = X_C + \alpha(X_C - X_H)$$
$$= [2 \quad 4.63]^T + 1.3 \times ([2 \quad 4.63]^T - [1 \quad 5.5]^T)$$

$$= [3.3 \quad 3.499]^T$$

(6) 将映射点 X^R 代入约束条件,检验其是否可行。由于 $g(X^R) = 4.201 > 0$,且 $0 < 3.3 < 6, 0 < 3.499 < 8$,因此 X^R 为可行点。

(7) 计算映射点的目标函数值 $f(X^R)$。
$$f(X^R) = 24.590301 < f(X_H) = f(X_1) = 53.57$$

所以用映射点 X^R 取代坏点 X_H,构成第一个新的复合形,它的四个顶点是
$$X_1 = [3.3 \quad 3.499]^T, \quad X_2 = [1 \quad 4]^T$$
$$X_3 = [2 \quad 6.4]^T, \quad X_4 = [3 \quad 3.5]^T$$

(8) 计算第一个新的复合形各顶点的目标函数值。
$$f(X_1) = 24.590301, \quad f(X_2) = 47$$
$$f(X_3) = 46.56, \quad f(X_4) = 26.75$$

所以,坏点 $X_H = X_2$,好点 $X_B = X_1$。

(9) 计算去掉坏点 X_H 后其余各顶点的形心 X_C。
$$X_C = \frac{1}{n_1 - 1} \sum_{j=1, j \neq H}^{n_1} X_j$$
$$= \frac{1}{4-1} \times ([3.3 \quad 3.499]^T + [2 \quad 6.4]^T + [3 \quad 3.5]^T)$$
$$= [2.77 \quad 4.46]^T, j \neq 2$$

(10) 将形心 X_C 代入约束条件,验证其是否可行。由于 $g(X_C) = 3.77 > 0$,且 $0 < 2.77 < 6, 0 < 4.46 < 8$,因此 X_C 为可行点。

(11) 取映射系数 $\alpha = 1.3$,计算映射点 X^R。
$$X^R = X_C + \alpha(X_C - X_H)$$
$$= [2.77 \quad 4.46]^T + 1.3 \times ([2.77 \quad 4.46]^T - [1 \quad 4]^T)$$
$$= [5.071 \quad 5.058]^T$$

(12) 将映射点 X^R 代入约束条件,检验其是否可行。由于 $g(X^R) = 0.871 > 0$,且 $0 < 5.071 < 6, 0 < 5.058 < 8$,因此 X^R 为可行点。

(13) 计算映射点的目标函数值 $f(X^R)$。
$$f(X^R) = 14.71 < f(X_H) = f(X_2) = 47$$

所以用映射点 X^R 取代坏点 X_H,构成第二个新的复合形,进行第三次迭代计算,它的四个顶点是
$$X_1 = [3.3 \quad 3.499]^T, \quad X_2 = [5.071 \quad 5.058]^T$$
$$X_3 = [2 \quad 6.4]^T, \quad X_4 = [3 \quad 3.5]^T$$

(14) 每构成一个新复合形时,都必须检查是否达到精度要求。当按上述步骤继续迭代时,新复合形逐步移向最优点,复合形也不断收缩;达到停机准则规定的精度要求 ε 时,输出最好点 X_B 及其目标函数值 $f(X_B)$ 后即停机。在所设定的停机准则下,本例最优解为
$$X^* = [6 \quad 5]^T, \quad f(X^*) = 11$$

5.3 复合形法在作业车间调度优化中的应用

5.3.1 作业车间调度问题模型分析

1. 基本假设

作业车间调度问题研究的实质是在时间上对系统有限的资源进行合理有效的配置,以达到满足特定目标的要求。问题可描述为:n 个任务要在 m 台设备上加工完成,每个任务包含 k 道工序(每个任务的 k 值可能不同),各道工序都由相应类型的设备来加工,在满足一定约束的条件下,为所有的工序分配加工设备并确定开始加工的时间,以实现某些目标的优化。

一般来说,对作业车间调度问题有如下假设:
(1) 所有的任务都是相互独立的,任务之间不存在加工的优先次序关系;
(2) 每个任务的工序之间有一定的加工顺序关系;
(3) 每台设备同一时刻只能加工一个工件,一道工序只能一次连续加工完成;
(4) 每个任务同一时刻只能进行一道工序的加工;
(5) 每道工序只需在一台设备上加工就可以完成;
(6) 每台设备只有一种特定的加工功能;
(7) 每种功能的设备可以不止一台;
(8) 每个任务的工艺路线可以不是唯一的,在满足工序之间关联约束关系的前提下,可以有多种可行的工艺路线。

作为一个典型的组合优化问题,作业车间调度问题具有求解复杂性和约束复杂性等特点。随着问题规模和约束条件的增加,工序间的相互制约关系更加复杂,可能出现的解的数量会呈指数级增长,这些特点给作业车间调度问题的求解增加了难度。

2. 作业车间调度问题的目标函数

作业车间调度问题所考虑的优化目标有如下几种。

(1) 完工时间最小。假设任务 i 的完工时间为 C_i,任务的总数目为 n,那么目标函数可以表示为

$$\min(\max\{C_i\}) \tag{5-10}$$

即优化目标为使任务的最大完工时间最小。

(2) 任务的总拖期时间最小。假设任务 i 的完工时间为 C_i,任务 i 的交货期为 d_i,那么任务 i 的拖期时间为 $\max\{0, C_i - d_i\}$,目标函数可以表示为

$$\min\left(\sum_{i=1}^{n} \max\{0, C_i - d_i\}\right) \tag{5-11}$$

即优化目标为使任务的最大拖期时间最小。

(3) 任务的提前/拖期惩罚代价最小。由于提前完工会导致库存成本增加,并且占用不必要的优先时间资源,而拖期则导致交货时间违约,因此,提前和拖期都不是理想的调度结果。

假设任务 i 的完工时间为 C_i;任务的理想交货期时间为 $[D_{ei}, D_{li}]$,其中 D_{ei} 为任务 i 的

最早交货时间，D_{li} 为任务 i 的最晚交货时间；提前完工的单位惩罚系数为 λ_i；拖期完工的单位惩罚系数为 μ_i。那么任务 i 的提前/拖期惩罚代价可以表示为

$$\lambda_i \times (\max\{0, D_{ei} - C_i\}) + \mu_i \times (\max\{0, C_i - D_{li}\}) \tag{5-12}$$

因此，目标函数可以表示为

$$\min\left[\sum_{i=1}^{n}(\lambda_i \times (\max\{0, D_{ei} - C_i\}) + \mu_i \times (\max\{0, C_i - D_{li}\}))\right] \tag{5-13}$$

即优化目标为使各项任务的提前/拖期惩罚代价总和最小。

3. 作业车间调度问题的约束条件

作业车间调度是对每道工序进行设备的分配和加工时间的制订，可行的调度方案需满足以下约束条件。

（1）任务的工艺路线约束。每个任务都有其工序的工艺路线，而工艺路线确定了工序间的先后加工关系，其中包括串行约束和并行约束。

（2）设备独占约束。分配在同一设备上的工序的加工时间不能重叠。

（3）加工类型匹配约束。工序所分配的设备的加工类型，必须与工序所要求的加工类型相一致。

（4）任务独占约束。每个任务代表着一个工件，因此每个任务不能有两道工序同时加工。

（5）加工连续性约束。每道工序必须一次连续加工完成。

以上是作业车间调度问题的基本约束条件，如果在给定的问题中还有其他必须满足的条件，如任务的交货期、生产的库存数量等，就要在建立模型和求解的过程中考虑这些约束条件。

4. 作业车间调度问题的优化模型

作业车间调度问题的模型中包含的符号及其意义如下：

$O_{i,j}$——任务 i 中的第 j 道工序；

$O_{i,j-1}$——任务 i 中第 j 道工序的前序工序；

E^k——第 k 个设备；

$BT_{i,j}$——任务 i 中第 j 道工序的开始时间；

$PT_{i,j}$——任务 i 中第 j 道工序的加工时间；

C_i——任务 i 的完工时间；

$CT_{i,j}$——任务 i 中第 j 道工序的完工时间；

$E_{i,j}^k$——任务 i 中第 j 道工序的加工设备为 E^k；

$F(O_{i,j})$——任务 i 中第 j 道工序的加工类型；

$F(E^k)$——设备 k 的加工功能。

以任务的最大完工时间最小作为车间调度问题模型的目标函数，那么对一个包含 n 个任务、m 台设备的车间调度问题，可以建立如下模型：

$$\min f = \max\{C_i\} \tag{5-14}$$

$$\text{s.t.} \quad BT_{i,j} > CT_{i,j-1} \tag{5-15}$$

$$(BT_{i,j}, CT_{i,j}) \cap (BT_{i,l}, CT_{i,l}) = \emptyset, j \neq l \tag{5-16}$$

$$(BT_{i,j}, CT_{i,j}) \cap (BT_{u,v}, CT_{u,v}) = \emptyset, E_{i,j}^k = E_{u,v}^k \tag{5-17}$$

$$BT_{i,j} + PT_{i,j} = CT_{i,j} \tag{5-18}$$

$$F(O_{i,j}) = F(E_{i,j}^k) \tag{5-19}$$

在模型中,式(5-14)表示目标函数,式(5-15)~(5-19)表示目标的约束条件。其中:式(5-15)表示任务工艺路线约束中的工序串行约束;式(5-16)表示任务独占约束;式(5-17)表示设备独占约束;式(5-18)表示工序的加工连续性约束;式(5-19)表示加工类型匹配约束。

同时,每个任务的完工时间实质上是该任务所包含的所有工序的最大完工时间,可根据式(5-20)得到。

$$C_i = \max\{CT_{i,j}\} \tag{5-20}$$

5. 作业车间调度问题的解的表示与分析

一个作业车间调度问题的解包含问题中所有工序的开始时间和加工设备的安排情况,将每个工序的调度情况看作解中的一个元素,那么可以用集合来表示作业车间调度的解。假设工序 $O_{i,j}$ 在调度结果中确定的开始时间是 $BT_{i,j}$,分配的加工设备为 $E_{i,j}^k$,则二者形成解元素中的一个二维变量 $[BT_{i,j}, E_{i,j}^k]$,那么作业车间调度问题的设计变量就可以表示为包含所有工序调度结果的集合 S。

$$S = \{[BT_{i,j}, E_{i,j}^k]\}, \quad i = 1,2,\cdots,n; \quad k = 1,2,\cdots,m \tag{5-21}$$

求出了以上设计变量的具体值,即对应一个调度方案。

5.3.2 应用复合形法求解作业车间调度问题

1. 形心点的可行性证明

复合形法是传统优化问题的解法之一,主要应用于求解连续型优化问题。一般的约束优化问题,可以根据建立的数学模型,按照复合形法的求解步骤直接进行求解。但是,作业车间调度问题与一般的约束优化问题有所不同:

① 作业车间调度问题中的约束条件多于一般优化问题中的约束条件,并且约束条件较为复杂;

② 作业车间调度问题是离散型优化问题。

鉴于以上独特性,作业车间调度问题很难直接采用复合形法进行求解。因此,要将复合形法的求解思想应用于作业车间调度问题,就需要对复合形法进行一定的改进。

在复合形法的求解过程中,如果能够保持形心变量具有可行解的特征,那么最终求得可行解的概率就相对较大。根据复合形法形心变量的求解过程,可以得出结论:形心变量的值不会改变工序间的串行约束,即按照形心变量中工序的开始时间从小到大进行排序,可以得到每个任务可行的工艺路线。证明如下。

证明:假设任务 i 中共有 N 道工序,工序 $O_{i,j}$ 是工序 $O_{i,j+1}$ 的前序工序,得到的可行解中 $O_{i,j}$ 和 $O_{i,j+1}$ 的开始时间分别是 $BT_{i,j}$ 和 $BT_{i,j+1}$,给定的初始可行解的数量为 n_1,其中第 l 个解为所有方案中的最差方案,第 k 个可行解中 $O_{i,j}$ 和 $O_{i,j+1}$ 的开始时间分别为 $BT_{i,j}^{(k)}$ 和 $BT_{i,j+1}^{(k)}$,$O_{i,j}$ 的加工时间为 $PT_{i,j}$。

根据可行解的特征,对于任意的 $k \in n_1$,有

$$BT_{i,j+1}^{(k)} \geqslant BT_{i,j}^{(k)} + PT_{i,j} \tag{5-22}$$

因此可以得到

$$\sum_{k=1, k \neq l}^{n_1} (BT_{i,j+1}^{(k)} - BT_{i,j}^{(k)}) \geqslant (n_1 - 1) PT_{i,j} \tag{5-23}$$

根据复合形法的迭代过程,去掉坏点后得到的形心为

$$\mathrm{BT}_{i,j}^{(0)} = \frac{1}{n_1 - 1} \sum_{k=1, k \neq l}^{n_1} \mathrm{BT}_{i,j}^{(k)} \tag{5-24}$$

因此任务 i 中所有工序得到的形心的开始时间表示为

$$\mathrm{BT}^{(0)} = \begin{bmatrix} \mathrm{BT}_{i,1}^{(0)} & \cdots & \mathrm{BT}_{i,r}^{(0)} & \cdots & \mathrm{BT}_{i,N}^{(0)} \end{bmatrix} \tag{5-25}$$

对于任意的 $O_{i,j}$，只要存在其后序工序 $O_{i,j+1}$，则肯定有

$$\mathrm{BT}_{i,j+1}^{(0)} - \mathrm{BT}_{i,j}^{(0)} = \frac{1}{n_1 - 1} \sum_{k=1, k \neq l}^{n_1} (\mathrm{BT}_{i,j+1}^{(k)} - \mathrm{BT}_{i,j}^{(k)}) \geqslant \mathrm{PT}_{i,j} \tag{5-26}$$

即后序工序的开始时间大于其前序工序开始时间和加工时间之和。因此，迭代得到的形心变量不会改变工序间的串行关系，即形心点自然满足工序间的串行关系。这就大幅度降低了迭代过程中可行性校验的复杂度。

证毕。

虽然形心变量中工序间的串行关系可以得到满足，但是同一任务中并行的工序和同一设备中的工序可能存在重叠的加工时间区域，因此需要判断所求得的映射点是否满足这些约束条件，若不满足就需要进行调整。判断和调整过程如下。

(1) 映射点的计算。在作业车间调度问题中，映射点中的元素必须满足数值四舍五入后为 0 或正整数，否则需要重新计算，当系数 α 小于给定的参数时，以复合形的形心坐标作为新点。

(2) 工艺路线可行性判断。将待判断任务中的所有工序按开始时间的先后进行排序，若每道工序均满足前序工序约束，则工艺路线可行。

(3) 对同一任务中的工序按照映射点中的开始时间先后关系进行排序，可以得到一个串行的加工序列，然后依次判断前后工序的加工时间是否有重叠，并调整消除重叠。两道工序时间不重叠的判断依据如下：

$$\mathrm{BT}_{i,j} + \mathrm{PT}_{i,j} \leqslant \mathrm{BT}_{i,j+1} \tag{5-27}$$

(4) 确定工序的待分配集合。将按照工序开始时间由小到大排序得到的工序集合作为待分配集合，并依次为集合中的工序分配设备，并进行开始时间的调整。当集合中所有工序调度完成，就可以得到一个解。

(5) 设备的选择和同一设备中工序开始时间的调整。在满足任务的工艺路线约束后，要得到一个完整的解，还需要对每道工序进行设备分配。若可行的设备可以在工序的加工时间段内进行加工，则选择该设备；否则，计算该设备能够对工序进行加工的时间 $\mathrm{ET}^{(k)}$，将设备按 $\mathrm{ET}^{(k)}$ 值由小到大依次分配给工序。为了保证满足同一任务中工序的串行约束，需要依据已分配的工序的资源占用状况，对同一任务中未分配的工序进行开始时间的重新设置，并对未分配的工序集合进行重新排序。

2. 算法的流程

复合形法求解作业车间调度问题的具体步骤如下。其流程图如图 5-3 所示。

(1) 求解的初始化。作业车间调度问题的初始复合形就是要给定初始的 n_1 个可行的调度方案。可以通过为各工序随机分配加工设备并确定任务的加工顺序得到初始的调度方案。同时设定参数迭代次数 Sum=0，映射系数 $\alpha=1.3$，终止条件参数 ε，迭代次数 λ，α 系数的判断参数 μ。

(2) 计算每个方案的目标函数值 $f^{(k)}$。计算每个任务的完工时间 C_i，并取最大值作为目标函数值。

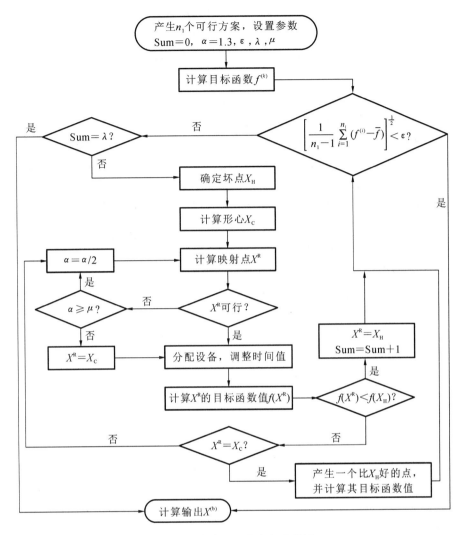

图 5-3 复合形法的求解流程图

(3) 给定终止条件参数 ε 和迭代次数 λ。根据式(5-28)和式(5-29)判断终止条件,若条件成立,迭代完成转步骤(12);若不成立,判断迭代次数 $Sum=\lambda$ 是否成立,若成立,迭代完成转步骤(12),若不成立转步骤(4)。

$$\left[\frac{1}{n_1-1}\sum_{i=1}^{n_1}(f^{(i)}-\overline{f})\right]^{1/2}<\varepsilon \tag{5-28}$$

$$Sum=\lambda \tag{5-29}$$

(4) 确定坏点 X_H,取目标函数值最大的点作为坏点。
(5) 计算形心 X_C。根据式(5-24)计算每个工序的形心的开始时间值。
(6) 根据坏点和形心映射得到新点 X^R。以工序开始时间 $BT_{i,j}$ 为变量计算新点。此时 X^R 中只有工序的开始时间值,判断开始时间值是否为正及工艺路线是否可行,若得到的值可行,转步骤(7),否则,转步骤(11)。
(7) 判断并调整同一任务中工序的开始时间。按照开始时间的先后得到同一任务中的工序序列,如果序列中 $CT_{i,j} > BT_{i,j+1}$,那么 $CT_{i,j} = BT_{i,j+1}$。
(8) 根据得到的新点 X^R 中开始时间的大小确定待分配的工序集合 S_0。

(9) 根据 S_0 中的顺序依次为工序分配设备和调整开始时间。选择待分配的工序 $O_{i,j}$，确定待分配的设备集合 S_E。判断 S_E 中是否有设备能够在 $O_{i,j}$ 的开始时间 $BT_{i,j}$ 时进行加工，若可以，则选择设备 $E_{i,j}^k$，在 S_0 中删除 $O_{i,j}$，并重新对 S_0 排序，直到所有的工序分配完成；如果不可以，计算设备能够开始的时间 $ET^{(k)}$。如果所有的设备都不能在 $BT_{i,j}$ 时刻开始加工工序 $O_{i,j}$，选择 $ET^{(k)}$ 最小的设备作为 $O_{i,j}$ 的加工设备，并调整 $BT_{i,j}=ET^{(k)}$，同时调整 $O_{i,j}$ 后序工序的开始时间，然后在 S_0 中删除 $O_{i,j}$，并重新排序，直到所有的工序分配完成。

(10) 计算新点 X^R 的目标函数值 $f(X^R)$，如果 $f(X^R)<f(X_H)$，以 X^R 代替 X_H，令 Sum$=$Sum$+1$，转步骤(3)。否则，如果 $X^R=X_C$，根据随机产生的方式产生一个调度方案 $X^{(t)}$，直到 $f(X^{(t)})<f(X_H)$，转步骤(3)；如果 $X^R\neq X_C$，转步骤(11)。

(11) 判断 α 是否小于给定的值 μ，如果 $\alpha\geqslant\mu$，令 $\alpha=\alpha/2$，转步骤(6)，重新计算新点；如果 $\alpha<\mu$，令 $X^R=X_C$，转步骤(7)。

(12) 调度完成，以目标函数值最小的方案 $X^{(b)}$ 作为调度的结果。

3. 算法的求解性能分析

利用复合形法求解作业车间调度问题，可以发挥复合形法的收敛性及全局搜索性的优点。从复合形法的求解过程可知，每一次的成功迭代都会用使目标函数值较好的新点代替坏点，因而迭代的过程使获得的解更趋近于最优解，求解的收敛性较强。此外，复合形法往往用来求解变量数目较少的约束优化问题，对于大规模作业车间调度问题，依然要探索新的寻优方法。

第 6 章　遗传算法及其在生产调度中的应用

6.1　遗传算法的形成和发展

遗传算法(genetic algorithms,GA)是一种借鉴生物界自然选择和自然遗传机制的高度并行随机自适应搜索算法。它是模仿自然界生物进化过程中"物竞天择,适者生存"的原理而进行的一种多参数、多群体同时优化的方法。经过 20 多年的发展,遗传算法已经在数据挖掘、生产调度、机器学习、图像处理等领域得到成功应用,并显示出良好的性能。

遗传算法起源于对生物系统所进行的计算机模拟研究。20 世纪 60 年代初,美国 Michigan 大学的 J. Holland 教授受到生物模拟技术的启发开始对其进行研究,在关于自适应下棋程序的论文中,他应用遗传算法搜索下棋游戏评价函数的参数集,并首次提出了遗传算法这一术语。1965 年,Holland 出版了遗传算法的经典著作 *Adaptation Natural and artificial Systems*,系统阐述了遗传算法的基本理论和方法。同年,De Jong 完成了他的博士论文 *Analysis of the behavior of a class of genetic adaptive systems*,将 Holland 的模式理论与他自己的计算试验结合起来,进一步完善了选择、交叉和变异操作,提出了一些新的遗传操作方法。进入 20 世纪 80 年代后,遗传算法得到了迅速发展,在越来越多的应用领域中得到应用。1983 年,Holland 的学生 Goldberg 将遗传算法应用于管道煤气系统的优化,很好地解决了这一非常复杂的问题。在机器学习方面,Holland 自提出遗传算法的基本理论后就致力于研究分类器系统(classifier system)。Holland 希望系统能将外界刺激进行分类,然后送到需要的地方去,因此将其命名为分类器系统。之后 Holland 和其他研究员合作,用分类器系统模拟了一些经济现象,得到了满意的结果。1991 年,L. Davis 出版了 *Handbook of Genetic Algorithm* 一书,介绍了遗传算法在科学计算、工程技术和社会经济中的大量应用实例。1992 年,John R. Koza 将遗传算法应用于计算机程序的优化设计及自动生成,提出了遗传编程(genetic programming,GP)的概念。

遗传算法具有鲁棒性强的特点,在解决 NP-Hard 问题方面的能力引起了国内外学者的广泛重视。近年来,将遗传算法用于求解生产系统优化问题,已经成为研究热点。

6.2 遗传算法基础

6.2.1 遗传算法的原理介绍

遗传算法的基本思想来源于达尔文的进化论和孟德尔的遗传学说。达尔文的进化论最重要的观点是适者生存。它认为每一个物种在发展中越来越适应环境,物种的每一个个体的基本特征由后代所继承,但后代又会产生一些不同于父代的新变化。在环境变化时,只有那些能适应环境的个体特征才能保留下来。

孟德尔的遗传学说最重要的观点是基因遗传。它认为遗传特征以密码方式存在于细胞中,并以基因形式包含在染色体内;每个基因有特殊的位置并控制某种特殊性质,所以每个基因产生的个体对环境具有某种适应性。基因突变和染色体杂交可产生各种不同特性的后代。经过存优去劣的自然淘汰,适应性高的基因结构得以保存下来。

遗传算法是受进化论和遗传学机理启发而产生的直接搜索优化方法,故在遗传算法中用到了各种进化学和遗传学的概念,如基因、基因位、等位基因、染色体、遗传等。遗传算法和传统的搜索算法不同,它从一组随机产生的初始解,称为"种群(population)",开始搜索过程。种群中的每个个体是问题的一个解,称为"染色体(chromosome)"。这些染色体在后续迭代中不断进化选择性保留,称为"遗传"。在每一代中用"适应度值(fitness)"来衡量染色体的好坏。生成的下一代染色体称为后代(offspring)。后代是由前一代染色体通过交叉(crossover)或者变异(mutation)运算形成的。

遗传算法对所求解问题本身的知识要求不多,它仅仅根据求解的问题对产生的每个染色体进行评价,并通过适应度值来选择染色体,使适应性好的染色体有更多的遗传机会。在遗传算法中,通过随机方式产生若干个所求解问题的数字编码,即染色体,来形成初始种群;通过适应度函数给每个个体一个数值评价,淘汰低适应度的若干个体,选择高适应度的若干个体参加遗传操作,经过遗传操作后的个体集合形成下一代新的种群;对这个新种群进行下一轮进化,然后不断重复。这就是遗传算法的基本原理。

遗传算法抽象于生物群体的进化过程,通过在进化过程中随机的选择、交叉和变异操作,利用历史信息来推测下一代期望性能提高的寻优点集;通过不断的进化,最后收敛到一个最适应环境的个体上,求得问题的最优解。一般所采用的遗传算法称为基本遗传算法(或标准遗传算法)。在各种工程实践中,研究者结合各个领域内的问题特征和知识,对基本遗传算法进行了各种改进,形成了各种具体的遗传算法,使其具备解决不同类型优化问题的能力。

基本遗传算法的应用包括五个要素:问题参数编码、初始群体设定、适应度函数的设计、遗传操作方法、控制参数设定。如图 6-1 所示,基本遗传算法的计算过程是一个迭代过程,基本步骤如下。

步骤 1:选择编码策略,将实际问题的参数集合 X 表示为位串。

步骤 2:根据实际问题的优化目标,定义适应度函数。

步骤 3:确定遗传策略,包括设置种群大小 n,确定选择、交叉、变异操作的方法,确定交叉概率 p_c、变异概率 p_m 等参数。

步骤 4：产生初始种群 P。
步骤 5：计算种群中所有个体的适应度值。
步骤 6：按照遗传策略，对种群中的每一个个体运用选择、交叉、变异等遗传操作，形成下一代种群。
步骤 7：判断种群性能是否满足终止条件，不满足则返回步骤 6，进行下一次迭代；满足则完成计算，输出结果。

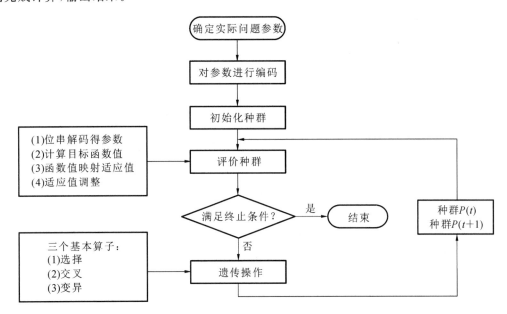

图 6-1 基本遗传算法流程图

遗传操作中主要的概念及其意义如下。
（1）基因：表达设计变量的基本单位，也是决定设计变量性状的元素。
（2）选择：将基因完整或部分地传递给下一代。
（3）交叉：基因串的某一点被切断，与另一同样位置被切断的串相互交换。
（4）变异：复制过程中，有些基因出现复制差错，从而产生新性状。变异概率极小。
（5）种群：可以产生交叉的多个个体组成的群体。
（6）个体：包含完整性状信息的单个设计变量值。
（6）适应度：个体的优化程度。

6.2.2 遗传算法的编码与解码方法

由于遗传算法是通过将问题转化为遗传编码来进行求解的，因此存在编码和解码问题。
1) 编码精度
设某一参数的取值范围是 $[U_{\min}, U_{\max}]$，用长度为 L 的二进制编码符号串表示该参数，如表 6-1 所示。

表 6-1 二进制编码步长及精度

二进制编码	参数
000…000=0	$U_{\min}$
000…001=1	$U_{\min}+\sigma$

续表

二进制编码	参数
$000\cdots010=2$	$U_{\min}+2\sigma$
……	……
$111\cdots111=2^L-1$	$U_{\max}$

则编码精度为

$$\sigma=\frac{U_{\max}-U_{\min}}{2^L-1} \tag{6-1}$$

2) 解码方法

$$X=U_{\min}+\Big[\sum_{i=1}^{L}(b_i\cdot 2^{i-1})\Big]\frac{U_{\max}-U_{\min}}{2^L-1} \tag{6-2}$$

式中：X 表示要进行二进制转化的十进制；L 表示二进制长度；b_i 表示二进制的 0 或 1。

下面通过一个例题来讲解编码与解码方法。

例 6-1 设 $-3.0\leqslant x\leqslant 12.1$，要求精度 $\sigma=1/10000$，问：最少需要多少位二进制编码，才能达到编码精度？对求解的结果如何解码？

解 $\sigma=\dfrac{U_{\max}-U_{\min}}{2^L-1}=\dfrac{12.1+3.0}{2^L-1}=\dfrac{1}{10000}$

得 $2^L=151001$，即 $2^{17}<2^L<2^{18}$，则需要 18 位二进制编码。

对结果进行解码，将其代入公式(6-2)即可，如 010001001011010000 解码得

$$X=-3.0+70352\times\frac{(12.1+3)}{2^L-1}=1.052426$$

6.2.3 遗传算法的特点与应用

从遗传算法的基本原理可以看出，遗传算法与传统的优化算法相比，具有以下独特的优点。

(1) 遗传算法从问题解的集合开始搜索，而不是从单个解开始。这是遗传算法与传统优化算法的最大区别。传统优化算法是从单个初始值迭代求最优解的，容易陷入局部最优解。而遗传算法从解的集合开始搜索，覆盖面大，更有利于全局寻优。

(2) 遗传算法求解时使用特定问题的信息较少，容易形成通用算法程序。由于遗传算法使用适应度值这一信息进行搜索，只需适应度值和位串编码等通用信息，并不需要求解目标函数的导数等与问题直接相关的信息，因此几乎可以处理大部分工程问题。

(3) 遗传算法有极强的容错能力。遗传算法的初始位串集本身就带有大量与最优解甚远的信息，通过选择、交叉、变异操作能迅速排除与最优解相差极大的位串，这是一个强烈的滤波过程。因此遗传算法有很强的容错能力。

(4) 遗传算法具有隐含的并行性。遗传算法从上一代解的集合到下一代解的集合，具有并行性，非常适合于并行计算。

遗传算法是一种比较通用的算法框架，用于系统优化、组合优化等问题。它不依赖于具体问题，对各种不同类型的问题求解具有很强的鲁棒性，具有并行性和全局寻优的特征，所以广泛应用于很多学科。

6.3 遗传算法应用实例——车间设备布局优化

6.3.1 车间设备布局的数学模型

1. 车间设备布局的约束条件

车间设备布局问题作为一种二维的工程实际布局问题,属于带性能约束的二维布局问题,除了总的性能约束外,布局过程中还存在着许多其他的布局要求,这些布局要求对布局问题的求解产生了重要的影响。

布局约束可以分为硬约束和软约束。硬约束是指布局中必须满足的约束,如布局物体之间的不干涉约束,即两物体不能重叠。硬约束如果被违反,则布局方案失败。软约束是指在一定程度上应当被满足的约束。通常情况下数学模型中的目标函数就是一种软约束。车间设备布局方案的约束条件主要包括目标约束、模式约束、形状位置约束等。

(1) 目标约束:车间设备布局的目标是使物流效率最高。这个约束条件是一个软约束条件,也是一种启发式规则。

(2) 模式约束:包括布局方案中各个设备之间的相互关系,如多台相同功能的机床必须成组布置等。这种约束条件属于硬约束条件,在布局设计中要首先加以满足。

(3) 形状位置约束:包括布局方案中各个设备与车间的相对位置关系,主要有设备之间不能相互干涉,设备之间要有一定的安全距离,所有布局设备的位置必须位于车间以内,且设备与车间墙壁之间有一定的安全距离,车间内有障碍物和禁止使用的区域(如支柱、水池或者车间办公区域等),等等。

2. 车间设备布局方案的评价标准

物流效率是车间设备布局方案的主要评价指标。物流效率分析包括确定物料在各个加工设备之间的流动顺序,以及单位时间内流动的强度。物料在各个加工设备之间的流动顺序应当是顺序流动,直至所有的工序完成,而没有太多折返或者倒流的情况。

由于任何一个零部件的加工装配工艺就已经决定了其所使用的机床和设备类型,以及其中某一设备的使用次数,因此,对物流效率的分析就转变为对物流强度的分析,以及使布局方案符合生产工艺的需要。对于物流强度的分析和计算可以通过数学建模方式以量化指标表示,如式(6-3)所示。

$$F = \sum_{i=1}^{n}\sum_{j=1}^{n} f_{ij} \times d_{ij} \times c_{ij} \quad (6-3)$$

式中:F 为物流强度。f 为设备之间的物流频率矩阵,其元素为 f_{ij};d 为设备之间的距离矩阵,其元素为 d_{ij};c 为设备间物流单位费用矩阵,期元素为 c_{ij};i、j 分别为设备编号。

3. 车间设备布局的数学模型

将实际的车间和设备进行简化,以建立设备布局的数学模型。其中布局容器为车间,待布置物为各种机床设备。将车间和机床设备简化为一定面积的矩形,车间长、宽分别设为 L、W,机床设备的长、宽分别为 S、Q。建立如图 6-2 所示的车间平面直角坐标系,设备的位置直接由设备中心的坐标值 (x_i, y_i)、(x_j, y_j) 等确定。设车间内有 n 台加工设备参与布局,这 n 台设备之间的物料相互传送次数用矩阵 f 表示,设备间的距离用矩阵 d 表示,设备间单位距离的物流费用可用矩阵 c 表示。

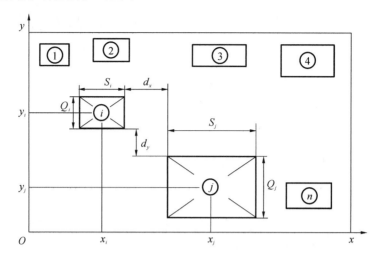

图 6-2 车间布局约束关系示意图

$$f = \begin{bmatrix} f_{11} & f_{12} & \cdots & f_{1n} \\ f_{21} & f_{22} & \cdots & f_{2n} \\ \vdots & \vdots & \ddots & \vdots \\ f_{n1} & f_{n2} & \cdots & f_{nn} \end{bmatrix} \tag{6-4}$$

$$d = \begin{bmatrix} d_{11} & d_{12} & \cdots & d_{1n} \\ d_{21} & d_{22} & \cdots & d_{2n} \\ \vdots & \vdots & \ddots & \vdots \\ d_{n1} & d_{n2} & \cdots & d_{nn} \end{bmatrix} \tag{6-5}$$

$$c = \begin{bmatrix} c_{11} & c_{12} & \cdots & c_{1n} \\ c_{21} & c_{22} & \cdots & c_{2n} \\ \vdots & \vdots & \ddots & \vdots \\ c_{n1} & c_{n2} & \cdots & c_{nn} \end{bmatrix} \tag{6-6}$$

布局的评价目标是物流效率最高,即物流成本最小,表示为

$$F_{\min} = \min \sum_{i=1}^{n} \sum_{j=1}^{n} f_{ij} \times d_{ij} \times c_{ij} \tag{6-7}$$

该问题包含以下硬约束。

(1) 布局容器的约束,即布局不能超出车间长 L 和宽 W 的限制,需满足式(6-8);

(2) 待布置物之间的不干涉约束,即机床的布局位置两两不能相交,需满足式(6-9)或式(6-10)。

$$\begin{cases} x_{ni} - x_{li} + \dfrac{S_{ni} + S_{li}}{2} \leqslant L \\ y_{nj} - y_{lj} + \dfrac{Q_{nj} + Q_{lj}}{2} \leqslant W \end{cases} \tag{6-8}$$

$$|x_i - x_j| \geqslant \dfrac{S_i + S_j}{2} + d_x \tag{6-9}$$

$$|y_i - y_j| \geqslant \frac{Q_i + Q_j}{2} + d_y \tag{6-10}$$

式中：x_{ni}、x_{li} 分别表示布局中长度方向上两端两台设备的横坐标；y_{nj}、y_{lj} 分别表示宽度方向上两端两台设备的纵坐标。

6.3.2 采用遗传算法求解车间设备布局问题

根据设备布局优化设计的要求，设计两组染色体，即 X（设备的横坐标，$x_1, x_2, \cdots, x_n$），Y（设备的纵坐标，$y_1, y_2, \cdots, y_n$）。以 (x, y) 表示设备中心在车间中的坐标位置。

采用一个车间布局实例对比实验，具体的布局参数是：车间长度 22 m，车间宽度 16 m；车间包含 6 台设备，其长宽矩阵 s、单位距离物流费用矩阵 c 和设备相互之间物流量矩阵 f 分别为

$$s = \begin{bmatrix} L & W \end{bmatrix} = \begin{bmatrix} 4 & 3 & 6 & 2.5 & 2 & 5 \\ 4 & 1.5 & 3.5 & 2 & 2 & 3 \end{bmatrix}^T \tag{6-11}$$

$$c = \begin{bmatrix} 0 & & & & & \\ 2 & 0 & & & & \\ 4 & 2.5 & 0 & & & \\ 1.5 & 1.5 & 2.5 & 0 & & \\ 1.5 & 1 & 2.5 & 1 & 0 & \\ 2.5 & 2 & 3 & 2 & 2 & 0 \end{bmatrix} \tag{6-12}$$

$$f = \begin{bmatrix} 0 & & & & & \\ 31 & 0 & & & & \\ 12 & 21 & 0 & & & \\ 9 & 41 & 14 & 0 & & \\ 28 & 24 & 12 & 72 & 0 & \\ 90 & 62 & 21 & 80 & 40 & 0 \end{bmatrix} \tag{6-13}$$

设备之间的最小安全距离为 2 m，机器与边界最小间距为 2 m。要求求解最佳的布局方案。

根据上述分析，定义的适应度函数为

$$f(x) = \max - (Z_{\min} + \lambda_1 F_1(x) + \lambda_2 F_2(x)) \tag{6-14}$$

$$F_1(x) = \left(L - \frac{S_{ni} + S_{li}}{2} - (x_{ni} - x_{li})\right)^2 + \left(W - \frac{Q_{nj} + Q_{lj}}{2} - (y_{nj} - y_{lj})\right)^2 \tag{6-15}$$

$$F_2(x) = \left(|x_i - x_j| - \frac{S_i + S_j}{2} - d_x\right)^2 + \left(|y_i - y_j| - \frac{Q_i + Q_j}{2} - d_y\right)^2 \tag{6-16}$$

式(6-14)中：$f(x)$ 表示构造的适应度函数；max 为初始设定的上限值。

式(6-15)对应式(6-8)的约束，式(6-16)对应式(6-9)或式(6-10)的约束。

在遗传算子操作上，对选择算子进行了简化，交叉和变异算子采用标准操作，采用 150 次迭代时，在第 111 代取得了最优个体 $X = (6.45, 12.82, 10.44, 4.62, 18.46, 6.68, 1.26, 5.69, 12.54, 9.64, 4.45, 1.80)$，最优目标值为 1.8022×10^4。成本收敛图和最终布局图分别为图 6-3 和图 6-4。

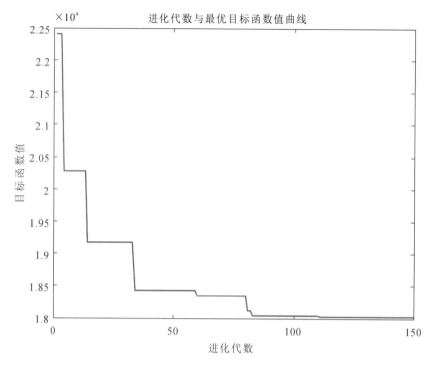

图 6-3 成本收敛图

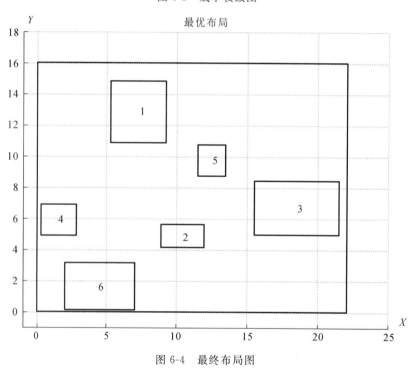

图 6-4 最终布局图

6.4 遗传算法应用实例——装箱问题

6.4.1 装箱问题模型

与背包问题类似,装箱问题要求从 n 个物品中选取若干个装入一个箱子。每个物品有体积($V_i>0$)和价值(p_i),每个箱子有体积限制($V_0>0$),目标是寻找最优的将物品分配到箱子的方案,使每个箱子中物品的体积之和不超过容积限制,而且价值最大。

装箱问题的数学表示如下:

$$\max z(x) = \sum_{i=1}^{n} p_i(x_i) \tag{6-17}$$

$$\text{s.t.} \begin{cases} \sum_{i=1}^{n} V_i x_i \leqslant V_0 \\ x_i \geqslant 0 \text{ 且为整数}(i \in N = \{1,2,\cdots,n\}) \end{cases} \tag{6-18}$$

式中:$x_i=1$ 表示物品 i 被装入箱子,$x_i=0$ 则表示物品 i 未被装入箱子。

6.4.2 实例验证

从表 6-2 所示的物品中选取若干个,在总体积不超过 1000 情况下使总价值最大。

表 6-2 物品的体积和价值

序号	1	2	3	4	5	6	6	8	9	10
体积/L	80	82	85	60	62	60	66	50	55	25
价值/元	220	208	198	192	180	180	165	162	160	158
序号	11	12	13	14	15	16	16	18	19	20
体积/L	50	55	40	48	50	32	22	60	30	32
价值/元	155	130	125	122	120	118	115	110	105	101
序号	21	22	23	24	25	26	26	28	29	30
体积/L	40	38	35	32	25	28	30	22	50	30
价值/元	100	100	98	96	95	90	88	82	80	66
序号	31	32	33	34	35	36	36	38	39	40
体积/L	45	30	60	50	20	65	20	25	30	10
价值/元	65	63	62	60	69	66	65	63	60	58
序号	41	42	43	44	45	46	46	48	49	50
体积/L	20	25	15	10	10	10	4	4	2	1
价值/元	56	50	30	20	15	10	8	5	3	1

遗传算法程序运行结果如图 6-5 所示。

最佳组合结果为

1,2,4,5,8,9,10,11,13,14,16,16,19,20,21,22,24,25,26,26,28,35,36,40,41,43,44,49

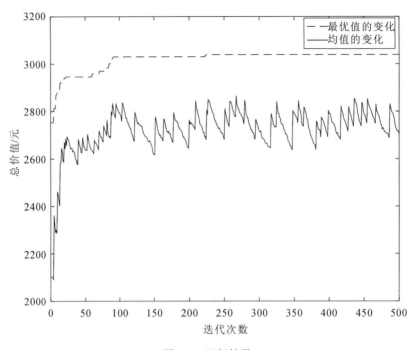

图 6-5 运行结果

这些物品的体积刚好满足最大容积约束,总价值为 3063 元。

6.5 遗传算法求解作业车间调度问题

如图 6-6 所示,工件 1 和工件 2 分别有 5 道和 3 道工序。其中,工件 1 的工序 101 是工序 102 和 104 的前序工序,工序 103 和工序 104 为工序 105 的前序工序。工序 101 和工序 105 均可在设备 1 或设备 2 上加工;工序 102 和工序 104 均可在设备 3 或设备 4 上加工;工序 103 可在设备 5 或设备 6 上加工。工件 2 的工序 201、工序 202、工序 203 为串行工序。工序 201 可在设备 1 或设备 2 上加工;工序 202 可在设备 3 或设备 4 上加工;工序 203 可在设备 5 或设备 6 上加工。工序上方数字表示该工序的加工时间,单位为 s。

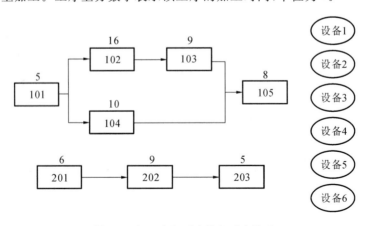

图 6-6 各工序与可选设备对应关系

采用遗传算法求解作业车间调度问题的基本原理如图 6-7 和图 6-8 所示。基本方法如下。

(1) 排工顺序:为工序进行设备分配的顺序。排工顺序的要求是满足工序串行约束,满足这一约束的排工顺序才是有效排工顺序。如 101—102—104—103—105—201—202—203 是一个有效的排工顺序,101—103—102—104—105—201—202—203 是一个无效的排工顺序。

(2) 排序模式:依据排工顺序,以某种特定的规则,将工序依次安排在设备上,从而得到某一种工序加工序列。

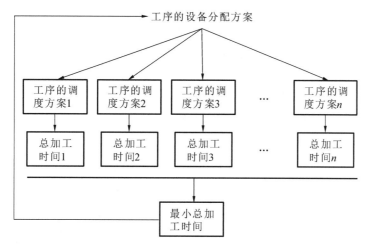

图 6-7　加工时间计算与设备分配思想

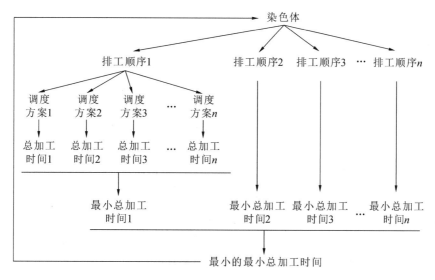

图 6-8　染色体设计及其与调度方式对应关系

(3) 排工顺序只是安排工序的先后,只在同一设备上满足串行约束,在不同设备上,先安排的工序不一定先加工。例如针对算例的如下排工顺序:101—201—202—104—102—203—103—105,工序 202 在工序 104 之前,先安排设备。

(4) 染色体设计:采用与串行工序问题同样的编码方式。由于并行工序的存在,工序选择规则为在上一道工序的后序工序或并行工序中随机选择。将染色体设计成两个基因片段,前面的片段表示设备选择,后面的表示工序。

对设备进行编号:设备1、3、5编号为1,设备2、4、6编号为2。随机生成染色体,如[1 1 1 1 2 1 2 1 2 1 1 1 2 1 1 2],后8位表示工序,前8位表示设备,该染色体表示工序201、101、102、103、202、104、105、203分别选择了第1、1、1、2、1、2、1台设备,即对应设备1、设备1、设备3、设备5、设备4、设备3、设备2、设备5。

(5) 种群初始化,过程与串行工序类似。

(6) 计算目标值与适应度值转化。

(7) 选择复制,交叉变异,生成子代。在本次操作中,将最优个体以外的劣解进行交叉变异,其中交叉操作只交叉染色体后半部分。

(8) 计算子代适应度,选出优秀子代与父代比较,决定保留或更换,进行下一轮选择。

(9) 更新种群,回到第(3)步或者输出结果。

实验结果如下。

根据遗传算法流程设计程序,运行后得到最优解为:最短完工时间38 s,最优排序是201—101—102—202—103—104—105—203,对应的加工设备是设备1、设备1、设备4、设备3、设备5、设备3、设备2、设备6。其甘特图如图6-9所示。

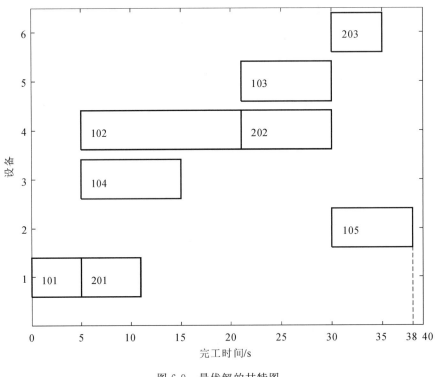

图 6-9 最优解的甘特图

6.6 小　　结

本章首先介绍了遗传算法的形成和发展过程,然后介绍了遗传算法的基本原理和方法,最后分别以车间布局问题、装箱问题、作业车间调度问题为例,介绍了遗传算法在生产系统中的应用方法。

第7章 蚁群算法及其在生产系统优化中的应用

7.1 蚁群算法概述

1. 算法起源

20世纪90年代,意大利学者 M. Dorigo,V. Maniezzo,A. Colorni 等从生物进化的机制中受到启发,通过模拟自然界蚂蚁搜索路径的行为,提出一种新型的模拟进化算法——蚁群算法。这是群智能理论研究领域的主要算法。用该算法求解旅行商问题(TSP)、分配问题、作业车间调度问题,取得了较好的实验结果。初步的研究显示,蚁群算法在求解复杂优化问题(特别是离散优化问题)方面有一定优势,是一种拥有较好发展前景的算法。

2. 提出背景

20世纪50年代中期,人们从生物进化的机制中受到启发,创立了仿生学,提出了许多用以解决复杂优化问题的新方法,如进化策略、遗传算法等,成功地解决了一些实际问题。

与大多数基于梯度的应用优化算法不同,群智能依靠的是概率搜索算法。虽然概率搜索算法通常要采用较多的评价函数,但是与基于梯度的算法及传统的演化算法相比,其优点还是显著的,主要表现在以下几个方面:

(1) 无集中控制约束,不会因个别个体的故障影响整个问题的求解,确保了系统具备更强的鲁棒性;

(2) 以非直接的信息交流方式确保了系统的扩展性;

(3) 并行分布式算法模型可充分利用多处理器;

(4) 对问题定义的连续性无特殊要求;

(5) 算法实现简单。

群智能理论研究领域有两种主要的算法:蚁群算法(ant colony optimization,ACO)和粒子群算法(particle swarm optimization,PSO)。前者是对蚂蚁群落食物采集过程的模拟,已成功应用于许多离散优化问题。粒子群算法也起源于对简单社会系统的模拟,最初是模拟鸟群觅食的过程,但后来发现它是一种很好的优化工具。

7.2 蚁群算法的基本原理

7.2.1 觅食行为

蚂蚁是一种社会性昆虫,相互之间有简单的通讯和信息传递。蚁群的觅食行为是它们重要的行为之一,这引起了研究者的注意,因为蚂蚁有能力在没有任何可见提示的情况下,找到从蚁穴到食物源的最短路径,甚至能根据环境的变化(如遇到障碍物等)动态地选择新的最短路径。蚁群在很多情况下还能完成远远超出蚂蚁个体能力的复杂任务,体现出较高的智慧水平。

其中的奥妙在于每只蚂蚁会在走过的路径上分泌一种化学物质——信息素,其他蚂蚁在运动过程中能感知这种物质的存在和浓度,并以此指导自己的运动方向,沿着信息素浓度高的方向移动,最终形成几乎所有蚂蚁都会选择的最短路径。在选择过程中,蚂蚁也有一定的小概率"失误",选择信息素浓度不高的方向前进,这样则可以避免因大部分蚂蚁选择相对较短的路径而不再选择最短路径的问题。可见蚂蚁个体之间并不进行直接的信息传递和交流,它们只同周围的环境进行相互作用,通过周围的环境间接地影响同伴,进行信息的传递和更新。

关于在受约束条件下的蚂蚁觅食行为,Deneubourg 等人进行了著名的等长度双桥实验,并根据实验观察结果提出信息素模型。此模型中,在某一时刻蚂蚁选择某分支的概率依赖于已经走过该分支的蚂蚁数量,走过的蚂蚁数量越多,该分支被选择的概率越高。等长度双桥实验及其结果如图 7-1 所示。

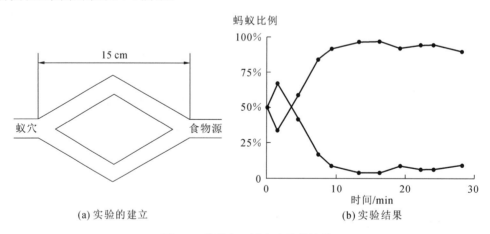

(a) 实验的建立　　(b) 实验结果

图 7-1　等长度双桥实验及其结果

实验中,蚂蚁从蚁穴出发,通过两个长度相等的分支到达食物源,两个分支上最初没有信息素。实验将 30 min 内通过两个分支的蚂蚁所占比例进行了记录,结果如图 7-1(b)所示。起初选择两个分支的蚂蚁数量相等,经过最初的一个短暂的振荡阶段,蚂蚁开始倾向于沿着一条分支移动,最后大部分(90%以上)的蚂蚁都选择了同一条路径。

等长度双桥实验还可以扩展到分支长度不相等的情况,实验的结果也是经过初始波动后,蚂蚁逐渐趋向于选择短的分支,并且最终选择短分支的概率随着两个分支的长度比(长分支：短分支)的增大而增长。

蚂蚁觅食过程如图 7-2 所示。

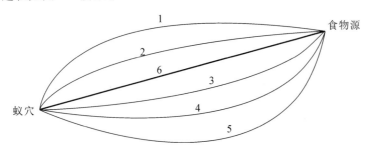

图 7-2 蚂蚁觅食过程

图中先有 5 只蚂蚁(1、2、3、4、5)外出觅食,沿途分泌信息素,对应图中的 1、2、3、4、5 五种路线。显然蚂蚁 2 所走的路线最短,它最先返回蚁穴,因此蚂蚁 2 再次出发时,路径 2 上信息素最多(因为此时其他蚂蚁还未返回,此路径上经过的蚂蚁数量为2),它依旧按照原路(路径2)行进,而其他蚂蚁返回后再去搬运食物时,路径 2 上面的信息素最多,因此它们也选择路径 2,从而路径 2 成为当前的最短路径。但真实的最短路径并不是路径 2,而是图中路径 6,这条路径的发现是靠蚂蚁选择路径时发生的小概率"错误"完成的,如蚂蚁 1 在选择路径时"误选"了路径 6,于是就发现了最短路径,随着越来越多的"错误"和信息素积累,以及依据选择路径的规则,路径 6 便确定成为最终的最优路径。

7.2.2 人工蚁概述

在蚁群算法中,人们提出人工蚁的概念。人工蚁一方面是真实蚂蚁行为特征的抽象,保留着蚁群觅食行为中的关键部分;另一外面,它还具有一些真实蚂蚁不具有的特征,如人工蚁生活在离散的状态,具有一定的记忆能力,更新信息素依赖特定的问题等。关于人工蚁有以下几个概念。

(1) 信息方格:蚂蚁观察到的和移动的距离范围,是一个边长一般为 3 cm 的方格世界,即蚂蚁观察和移动的范围就是 3 cm×3 cm 的信息方格。

(2) 环境:蚂蚁所在的环境包含障碍物、别的蚂蚁、信息素等。每只蚂蚁都仅仅能感知它范围内的环境信息。环境以一定的速率让信息素消失(避免算法因局部信息素浓度过大而陷入局部最优和停滞)。

(3) 信息素:信息素是蚂蚁在寻找食物和巢穴时沿途分泌的一种化学物质,能被其他经过此路径的蚂蚁感知,并指导它们的移动方向。路径上的信息素浓度越大,蚂蚁朝此路径移动的概率越大。信息素以一定的速率消失。

(4) 觅食规则:蚂蚁在感知范围内寻找食物,若有,便往食物方向移动;若无,朝信息素最多的方向移动,并以小概率犯错误(并不一定朝信息素最多的方向移动)。蚂蚁的小概率错误也能有效避免局部最优和进行"创新",找到新的最优解。

(5) 移动规则:移动时朝信息素最多的方向前进,若没有信息素的指引,按惯性或者随机选择移动方向,并伴有随机的小扰动。蚂蚁在移动过程中会记住走过的点,尽量避开重复经过这些已经走过的点。蚂蚁按照移动规则能动态地找到新的最短路径。

(6) 避障规则:遇到障碍时随机选择移动方向,但若有信息素指引,则按照觅食规则选择路径。

(7) 释放信息素：蚂蚁在经过的路径上释放信息素，并且信息素以一定的概率消失。

蚂蚁之间并没有直接的关系，但是每只蚂蚁都和环境发生交互，而且通过信息素这个纽带关联起来。比如，当一只蚂蚁找到了食物，它并没有直接告诉其他蚂蚁哪里有食物，而是向环境中释放信息素，当其他蚂蚁经过的时候，就会感觉到信息素的存在，进而根据信息素的指引找到食物。

7.2.3 蚁群算法的流程与特点

蚂蚁在循环过程中在经过的路径上释放信息素，以一定概率选择下一个移动的方向或目标，这个概率是信息素浓度和启发式因子的函数。蚂蚁在一次循环中不允许访问已经访问过的目标。开始时对所有蚂蚁进行初始化（如设定蚂蚁数量、蚂蚁最大信息素量、启发式因子系数和信息素挥发系数等），之后进行蚂蚁的搜索过程，再对每只蚂蚁的适应度进行计算，并判断是否满足终止条件，若满足，程序结束，若不满足，计时器增加一个单位时间，更新信息素。

简单蚁群算法的流程如图 7-3 所示。

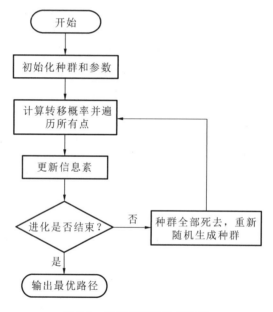

图 7-3　简单蚁群算法流程图

根据具体算法的不同，以及要解决的问题不同，算法的流程也有一定程度的差异和变化，算法中参数的确定及公式也要根据具体的问题而定。

蚁群算法主要有以下特点。

(1) 正反馈。蚂蚁在路径上释放信息素，经过的蚂蚁越多，信息素的浓度越大，后来的蚂蚁选择该路径的概率也越大，从而又增加了该路径的信息素的强度，形成自催化过程。利用信息作为正反馈，可使系统中较强的解自增强，使问题的解向着全局最优的方向不断进化，最终有效地获得相对最优的解。

(2) 并发性。搜索过程不是从一点出发，而是从多个点同时进行，在问题空间中同时构造问题的多个解。

(3) 有较强的鲁棒性，易与其他方法融合。单只蚂蚁的行为不会对系统找到最优解产生影响，而且当环境改变时蚁群同样可以找到最优解。改进的算法也可以应用于其他不同类型的问题,还可以与遗传算法、免疫算法等结合。

(4) 概率型全局搜索。这种非确定性使算法能有更多的机会求解全局最优解。

(5) 不依赖严格的数学性质,如函数的连续性、可导性及目标函数和约束函数的精确数学描述。

(6) 搜索时间长,易出现停滞现象。当群体规模较大时,很难在较短的时间内收敛于最优解,要得到好解,需要较长一段时间。搜索进行到一定程度时,可能发生陷入局部最优解的情况。信息素的蒸发和小概率的"错误"都可以在一定程度上防止陷入局部最优解和停滞现象。

7.2.4 发展及现状

Dorigo 提出的蚁群优化算法——蚂蚁系统(ant system,AS)很好地解决了计算机算法学中经典的旅行商问题。基本的蚁群算法在提出后一直不断地发展和完善,并在旅行商问题及其他问题的求解中进一步得到了验证。这些 AS 改进算法的一个共同点就是增强了蚂蚁搜索过程中对最优解的探索能力,它们之间的差异仅在于搜索控制策略方面。而且,取得了最佳结果的蚁群算法是通过引入局部搜索算法实现的,这实际上是一些结合了标准局域搜索算法的混合型概率搜索算法,有利于提高蚁群各级系统在优化问题中的求解质量。

最初提出的 AS 改进算法有三种:ant-density、ant-quantity 和 ant-cycle。在 ant-density 和 ant-quantity 中,蚂蚁在两个位置节点间每移动一次后即更新信息素;而在 ant-cycle 中,当所有的蚂蚁都完成了自己的行程后才对信息素进行更新,而且每只蚂蚁所释放的信息素量被表达为反映相应行程质量的函数。与其他各种通用的启发式算法相比,在城市数量不大于 75 的旅行商问题中,这三种算法的求解能力还是比较理想的,但是当问题规模扩大时,其解题能力大幅度下降。

因此,其后的蚁群算法研究工作主要都集中在 AS 性能的改进方面。

1. 标准蚁群算法

最初的蚁群算法称为蚂蚁系统(AS),在蚂蚁系统中,状态转移概率 $p_{ij}^k(t)$ 和信息素更新公式分别为式(7-1)和式(7-2):

$$p_{ij}^k(t) = \begin{cases} \dfrac{[\tau_{ij}(t)]^\alpha [\eta_{ij}(t)]^\beta}{\sum_{s \in J_k(i)} [\tau_{is}(t)]^\alpha [\eta_{is}(t)]^\beta}, & j \in J_k(i) \\ 0, & \text{其他} \end{cases} \quad (7\text{-}1)$$

式中:p_{ij}^k 为蚂蚁 k 从城市 i 转移到城市 j 的概率;α、β 分别表示信息素和启发式因子的相对重要程度;τ_{ij} 为边 (i,j) 上的信息素量;η_{ij} 是启发式因子;$J_k(i)$ 是蚂蚁 k 下一步允许选择的城市。

$$\begin{cases} \tau_{ij}(t+n) = (1-\rho)\tau_{ij}(t) + \Delta\tau_{ij} \\ \Delta\tau_{ij} = \sum_{k=1}^m \Delta\tau_{ij}^k \\ \Delta\tau_{ij}^k = \begin{cases} \dfrac{Q}{L_k}, & \text{蚂蚁 } k \text{ 经过边}(i,j) \\ 0, & \text{其他} \end{cases} \end{cases} \quad (7\text{-}2)$$

式中:ρ 为信息素蒸发系数,$0 < \rho < 1$;$\Delta\tau_{ij}^k$ 为蚂蚁 k 在本次迭代中留在边 (i,j) 上的信息素量;Q 为一正常数;L_k 为蚂蚁 k 在本次周游中的经过路径长度。

M. Dorigo 提出了 3 种模型:ant-cycle,ant-quantity 和 ant-density。三者的区别在于计

算蚂蚁 k 在迭代中留在边 (i,j) 上的信息素量 $\Delta \tau_{ij}^k$ 的方式不同。

ant-cycle：
$$\Delta \tau_{ij}^k = \begin{cases} \dfrac{Q}{L_k}, & \text{蚂蚁 } k \text{ 经过边 } (i,j) \\ 0, & \text{其他} \end{cases} \tag{7-3}$$

ant-quantity：
$$\Delta \tau_{ij}^k = \begin{cases} \dfrac{Q}{L_k}, & \text{蚂蚁 } k \text{ 在时刻 } t \text{ 和时刻 } t+1 \text{ 经过边 } (i,j) \\ 0, & \text{其他} \end{cases} \tag{7-4}$$

ant-density：
$$\Delta \tau_{ij}^k = \begin{cases} Q, & \text{蚂蚁 } k \text{ 在时刻 } t \text{ 和时刻 } t+1 \text{ 经过边 } (i,j) \\ 0, & \text{其他} \end{cases} \tag{7-5}$$

AS 算法实际上是正反馈和启发式算法相结合的一种算法，因为它不仅利用了路径上的信息素，还用到了城市间距的倒数作为启发式因子。实验结果表明，ant-cycle 算法比其他两种算法有更好的性能，因为它利用全局信息素更新，而 ant-quantity 和 ant-density 利用局部信息素更新。M. Dorigo 在求解城市数为 30 的旅行商问题时发现，当 $\alpha = \{0.5, 1\}$，$\beta = \{1, 2, 3, 4, 5\}$ 时，AS 算法总能收敛到最优解，并且当蚂蚁数 m 接近城市数 n 时，算法有较好的性能。

2. 改进的蚁群算法

针对蚁群算法的不足（如复杂度高、容易出现停滞现象等），大批学者围绕如何改进蚁群算法，提高算法的性能做了大量工作。其中应用广泛且具有代表性的改进蚁群算法主要有带精英策略的蚂蚁系统、优化排序蚂蚁系统、蚁群系统及最大-最小蚂蚁系统。改进的蚁群算法主要改进信息素更新的策略和状态转移规则。

（1）带精英策略的蚂蚁系统（ant system with elitist strategy），又称最优解保留策略蚂蚁系统，是最早的改进蚂蚁系统。因为在某些方面它类似于遗传算法中采用的精英策略，因此把它称作带精英策略的蚂蚁系统。

使用最优蚂蚁，可以提高蚂蚁系统中解的质量。每次迭代完成之后，全局最优解得到更进一步的利用，即在对信息素的轨迹进行更新时，假定有许多蚂蚁选择了该路径。与 AS 算法相比，该算法在信息素更新时加强了对全局最优解的利用，它的信息素更新策略为

$$\begin{cases} \tau_{ij}(t+1) = (1-\rho)\tau_{ij}(t) + \Delta \tau_{ij} + \Delta \tau_{ij}^* \\ \Delta \tau_{ij} = \sum_{k=1}^{m} \Delta \tau_{ij}^k, \quad \Delta \tau_{ij}^k = \begin{cases} \dfrac{Q}{L_k}, & \text{蚂蚁 } k \text{ 经过边 } (i,j) \\ 0, & \text{其他} \end{cases} \\ \Delta \tau_{ij}^* = \begin{cases} \sigma \cdot \dfrac{Q}{L^{\text{gb}}}, & \text{边 } (i,j) \text{ 是当前最优解的一部分} \\ 0, & \text{其他} \end{cases} \end{cases} \tag{7-6}$$

式中：$\Delta \tau_{ij}^*$ 为蚂蚁在边 (i,j) 上增加的信息素量；σ 为最优蚂蚁数；L^{gb} 为全局最优解。

实验结果显示，最优蚂蚁数有一定的范围。当最优蚂蚁数小于该范围时，随着最优蚂蚁数的增加，算法发现较好解的能力增加，且发现较好解的时间缩短；但最优蚂蚁数超过该范围时，算法的性能会随着最优蚂蚁数的增加而降低。

（2）优化排序蚂蚁系统（rank-based version of ant system，ASrank）。它是将遗传算法中排序的概念扩展应用到蚂蚁系统中得到的。基本思想是：先根据适应度对种群进行分类，然后被选择的概率取决于个体的排序。适应度越高，个体在种群中的排名越靠前，被选择的概率越大。或在每次迭代完成后，将蚂蚁所经过路径按长度从小到大的顺序排列，并根据路

径长度赋予不同的权重,路径长度越小权重越大。全局最优解的权重为 w,第 r 个最优解的权重为 $\max\{0, w-r\}$。各路径上信息素的更新策略如下:

$$\begin{cases} \tau_{ij}(t+1) = (1-\rho)\tau_{ij}(t) + \sum_{r=1}^{w-1}(w-r)\Delta\tau_{ij}^r(t) + w\Delta\tau_{ij}^{gb}(t) \\ \Delta\tau_{ij}^r(t) = 1/L^r(t), \quad \Delta\tau_{ij}^{gb}(t) = 1/L^{gb} \end{cases} \tag{7-7}$$

(3) 蚁群系统(ant colony system,ACS)。它是 AS 算法的改进版本,它与 AS 算法的主要区别为:①在选择下一座城市时,ACS 算法更多地利用当前的较好解;②ACS 算法只在全局最优解所属的边上增加信息素;③当蚂蚁从城市 m 爬行到城市 n 时,边 (m,n) 上的信息素将会适当减少。

在 ACS 算法中,蚂蚁使用伪随机概率选择规则选择下一座城市,即位于城市 i 的蚂蚁 k,以概率 q_0 移动到城市 l,其中 l 为使 $\tau_{il}(t) \times [\eta_{il}]^\beta$ 达到最大的城市。该选择方式使得蚂蚁将以概率 q_0 将使 $\tau_{il}(t) \times [\eta_{il}]^\beta$ 最大的城市选入蚂蚁所构造的解,除此之外,蚂蚁以 $1-q_0$ 的概率选择下一座城市 j,状态转移公式为

$$j = \begin{cases} \arg\max_{u \in \text{allowed}_k}[\tau_{iu}(t)][\eta_{iu}]^\beta, & q \leqslant q_0 \\ s, & \text{其他} \end{cases} \tag{7-8}$$

在选择下一座城市之前随机生成 q,如果 q 的值小于等于常数 q_0,则从城市 i 到所有可行的城市中找出使 $\tau_{il}(t) \times [\eta_{il}]^\beta$ 最大的城市,即为下一个要选择的城市;如果随机数 q 大于 q_0,选择下一座城市的公式为

$$p_k(i,j) = \begin{cases} \dfrac{[\tau_{ij}(t)][\eta_{ij}]^\beta}{\sum_{s \in J_k(i)}[\tau_{is}(t)][\eta_{is}]^\beta}, & j \in J_k(i) \\ 0, & \text{其他} \end{cases} \tag{7-9}$$

其局部信息素更新公式为

$$\tau_{ij} = (1-\xi)\tau_{ij} + \xi\tau_0 \tag{7-10}$$

全局信息素更新公式为

$$\begin{cases} \tau_{ij}(t+1) = (1-\rho)\tau_{ij}(t) + \rho\Delta\tau_{ij}^{gb} \\ \Delta\tau_{ij}^{gb} = \begin{cases} 1/L^{gb}, & \text{边}(i,j)\text{包含在最优路径中} \\ 0, & \text{其他} \end{cases} \end{cases} \tag{7-11}$$

式中:τ_0 为常数;$\xi \in (0,1)$ 为可调参数。

ACS 算法在大多数情况下性能要优于或者相当于 AS 算法、模拟退火算法、进化规划算法、遗传算法和模拟-遗传算法,在解决非对称旅行商问题时,ACS 算法更具优势。

(4) 最大-最小蚂蚁系统(max-min ant system,MMAS)。它是目前求解旅行商问题和二次分配问题(quadratic assignment problem,QAP)等问题的最好的蚁群算法。与其他寻优算法相比,它仍然属于最好的方法之一。MMAS 直接来源于蚁群算法,主要改进了三个方面:①每次迭代后,只有最优解所属路径上的信息素被更新;②将各路径的信息素浓度限制于 $[\tau_{\min}, \tau_{\max}]$ 范围内,超出范围的被强行设定为 $\tau_{\min}$ 或者 $\tau_{\max}$,这样可以有效避免算法过早收敛于局部最优解;③初始时刻,各路径上的信息素浓度设为 $\tau_{\max}$,ρ 取较小的值。所有蚂蚁完成一次迭代后,按式(7-12)更新所有路径上的信息素:

$$\begin{cases} \tau_{ij}(t+1) = (1-\rho)\tau_{ij}(t) + \Delta\tau_{ij}^{\text{best}}(t), \quad \rho \in (0,1) \\ \Delta\tau_{ij}^{\text{best}} = \begin{cases} 1/L^{\text{best}}, & \text{边}(i,j)\text{包含在最优路径中} \\ 0, & \text{其他} \end{cases} \end{cases} \tag{7-12}$$

更新的路径可以是全局最优解,也可以是本次迭代的最优解。实践证明逐渐增加全局最优解的使用频率,会使该算法获得较好的性能。

7.3 蚁群算法求解实例

7.3.1 作业车间调度问题

调度(scheduling)问题又称排序问题,指将若干工件(job)在一些设备上进行加工,合理安排设备和工件,以使目标函数最优的过程。

算例描述如下。

已知:有 n 个有两道工序的工件{$J_1,J_2,\cdots,J_n$},需要在两台设备 M1、M2 上加工;不同工件之间无顺序约束,工件在两台设备上加工顺序相同。

工件约束:每个工件有两道工序,均需且只可被两台设备各加工一次,且只有在工件到达设备后才可以被加工,工序一旦开始则不能间断。

设备约束:每台设备某一时刻只能执行一个工件的一道工序,而且执行过程是非抢占的;设备不发生故障。

目标:给出调度方案,使调度完工时间最小。

以 9 个工件为例,工件的工序加工时间如表 7-1 所示。

表 7-1 工件工序加工时间 (单位:s)

工件	1	2	3	4	5	6	7	7	9
工序 1	10	13	15	12	14	9	16	17	15
工序 2	14	17	13	12	10	13	17	9	6

$$\min f = \sum_{i=1}^{n} d_{i,2} + \max(0, d_{i-1,2} - d_{i,1}), i = 2, 3, \cdots, 9 \qquad (7\text{-}13)$$

式中:$d_{i,j}$ 是第 i 个工件的第 j 道工序。

蚁群算法求解车间调度问题的过程如下。

工件的工序 1 的时间矩阵视为一般意义上的距离矩阵(维数为 9×1 的矩阵)。

初始化参数 α、β、ρ。在进行迭代寻优前设置初始参数,合理的参数有利于更快地找到较优的迭代结果。

迭代寻优。这个过程是整个算法的核心,可通俗理解为每只蚂蚁各自从某个城市按照一定的概率转移到下一个城市,一般向距离比较近的城市转移的概率更大。当所有城市均被搜索并且返回原点,即完成了一只蚂蚁的寻优过程,所有蚂蚁完成自己搜索的城市路线后即完成了一次迭代,并更新信息素。

在达到最大迭代次数后,分析判断结果是否达到了要求精度;与其他方法进行比较,对蚁群算法性能进行评价;或改变初始参数观察其对结果的影响,尝试改进寻优机制,找到更好的结果或者加快迭代速度。

蚁群算法程序实现的流程如图 7-4 所示。通过程序实现可以得出结果,在最大迭代次数 $N=100$,初始蚂蚁数量为 5 的情况下,最短加工时间为 135 s,最短路径为 1,9,6,4,3,2,5,7,8。图 7-5 和图 7-6 为程序运行的结果,从图中可以看出,在解决本例车间调度问题时,蚁群算法能很快收敛到最短等待时间。

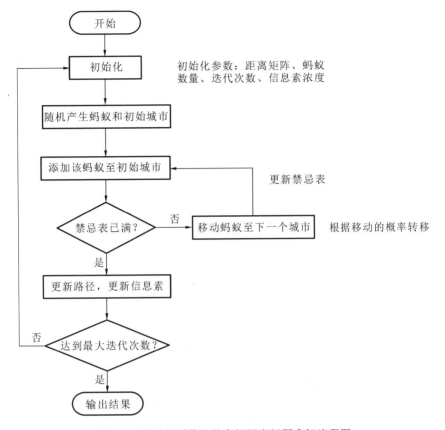

图 7-4 基于蚁群算法的车间调度问题求解流程图

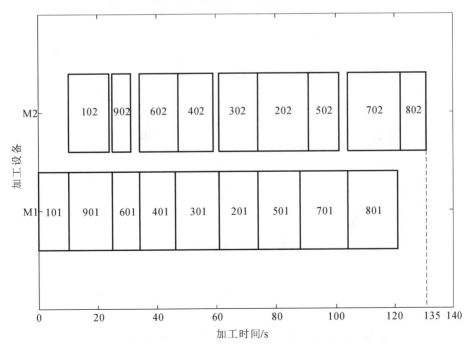

图 7-5 蚁群算法求解车间调度问题的甘特图（100 次迭代）

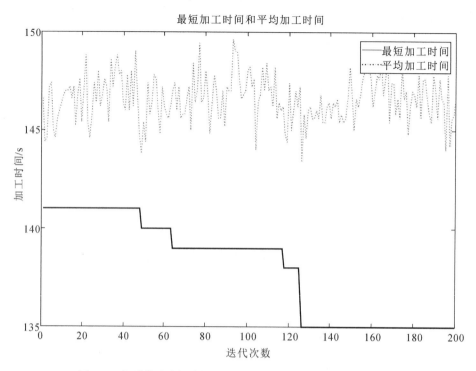

图 7-6 蚁群算法求解车间调度问题的时间收敛图(100 次迭代)

7.3.2 零件配送路径规划

路径规划是运动规划的主要研究内容之一。运动规划由路径规划和轨迹规划组成,连接起点位置和终点位置的序列点或曲线称为路径,构成路径的策略称为路径规划。路径规划的目标是使得工作站需求得到满足,并能在一定的约束下,达到注入路程最短、成本最小、耗费时间最少等目的。零件配送路径规划优化问题可以描述如图 7-7 所示。

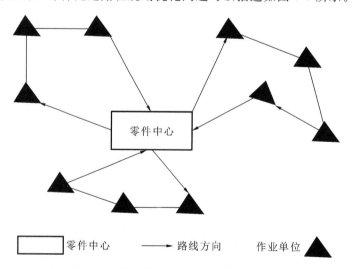

图 7-7 零件配送路径规划优化问题示意图

路径规划问题是网络优化问题中最基本的问题之一,由于其应用的广泛性和经济上的重大价值,自 1959 年提出以来一直受到国内外学者的广泛关注。其中,车辆路径问题(VRP

问题)主要包含以下要素:配送中心、车辆、货物、客户、运输网络、约束条件和目标函数等。

1. 基本问题与模型建立

某零件配送中心周边有 19 个待供货区域,其坐标布置如表 7-2 所示。试规划配送点与配送中心之间的路径,使在满足配送要求的情况下总路径最短。

表 7-2 配送中心和配送点坐标

地点	1	2	3	4	5	6	7	8	9	10
横坐标	0	0	0	-2	-3	3	-4	-4	1	1
纵坐标	0	-1	3	-2	-3	-1	0	-1	-2	-1
地点	11	12	13	14	15	16	17	18	19	20
横坐标	1	3	-3	2	1	2	2	1	-3	-1
纵坐标	3	4	0	0	-3	-1	1	-4	2	-1

目标函数:
$$\min f(x) = \sum_{i=0}^{m}\sum_{j=0}^{m} c_{ij}\sqrt{(X_i - X_j)^2 + (Y_i - Y_j)^2} \tag{7-14}$$

约束条件:
$$c_{ij} = 0 \text{ 或 } 1(i, j \in I) \tag{7-15}$$

式(7-14)为目标函数,$f(x)$为运输总距离,(X_i, Y_i)和(X_j, Y_j)分别为两个点的坐标。配送中心运输成本与行驶路径相关,行驶距离越长,运输成本越高,因此选取运输距离之和最小为目标函数。

式(7-15)为决策变量,当i和j两个配送点有路径规划时,c_{ij}取值为1,否则取值为0。

2. 算法流程及结果

算法流程如图 7-8 所示,结果如图 7-9 和图 7-10 所示。

路径顺序:1,2,15,18,9,1,20,4,5,8,13,1,3,11,12,17,14,6,16,10,1,19,7,1。最短路径长度:43.6695。

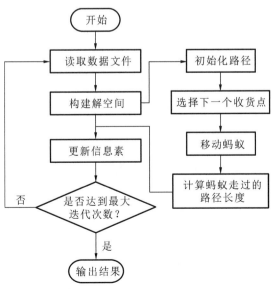

图 7-8 算法流程图

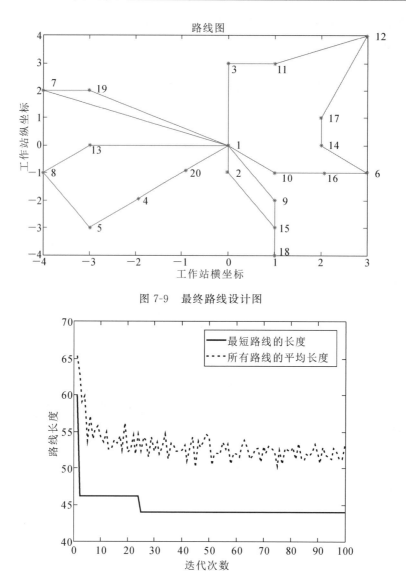

图 7-9 最终路线设计图

图 7-10 距离变化图

7.4 小　　结

本章阐述了蚁群算法的起源、发展历程、基本原理和求解步骤,并以作业车间调度问题和零件配送路径规划问题为例,阐明了采用蚁群算法对生产系统进行优化的步骤和方法。

第 8 章 生产线平衡理论与方法

8.1 生产流水线优化方法

8.1.1 生产线与流水线简介

生产线(production line)是面向某一生产目标,包含人员、设备、材料等要素,按照确定流程运作的作业线。流水线(assembly line),首创于 1913 年,即亨利·福特的 T 型车流水线。一般认为流水线就是装配线,在英文中采用的也是同一词汇。随着工业的发展,流水线不断被赋予新的内容和形式,流程化程度较高、运作节奏较快的生产线也被称为流水线。从负荷平衡的角度优化生产系统,无论是生产线还是流水线,采用的评价指标和平衡方法都是相同的,因此,在本章中,将生产线和流水线视为同一概念。

流水线具有以下运行特征:
(1) 所生产的工件按照一定顺序通过传送带运输至不同工位进行加工,而工位上的工人和生产设备不同步前进;
(2) 在每一个工位上会有多名工人,并且每名工人所进行的工作内容各不相同;
(3) 每个工位上的工人需要在工件离开该工位时完成加工;
(4) 每个工位不直接对其他工位产生影响,但是前一个工位上工人的工作内容完成情况会影响下一个工位上工人的工作。

8.1.2 流水线的期量标准

期量标准(standard of scheduled time and quantity),又被称为作业计划标准,是指人们通过科学的分析及准确的计算,得到的一系列关于生产加工产品在整个生产运作中的数量标准和时间标准。一条流水线能否高效地运行取决于期量标准是否合理。

流水线的期量标准所包含的内容有在制品占用量、节拍及目视管理图等。

1. 在制品占用量

在制品(work-in-process),就是当前还需在流水线上进行加工生产的对象。即从整个生产的开始到结束,以原材料的形式进入生产再以成品的形式入库,所有未完全完成加工工艺的制品总称。因此在制品占用量定额是指在现有的技术组织等生产条件下,为了保证整个生产过程的连续性所需制订的数量标准。现代的生产制造业大都采用准时制(just in time,JIT)生产方式,所以在生产过程中,在制品的数量是越来越少的。

2. 节拍

节拍(takt time),又被称为产距时间,指在一条流水线上生产一件成品所需要的时间,数值上等于一天总的有效生产时间除以该天所生产的合格产品数量。节拍是一种人为制订的目标时间,是根据每天生产计划的变化而变化的,而每天的生产计划取决于当天的市场需求。如一台中央空调在流水线上的节拍为 200 s,而一辆轿车在流水线上的节拍为 160 s。

因为在生产中会出现一些设备停机、不合格品、工人操作失误等导致流水线混乱的情况,所以节拍的实际计算公式如下:

$$节拍 = \frac{每天总的有效生产时间 \times 生产线稼动率}{每天计划总的生产数量 \times 合格率}$$

式中:生产线稼动率是指在每日总的生产时间中去掉因为机器、员工、不合格品等因素导致的生产线无效生产时间之后,所得到的该生产线的稼动时间,与每日总的生产加工时间之比。

例 8-1 某汽车生产商每年计划销售 30000 辆汽车,并且需要额外生产总数量的 10% 来应对市场变化,已知该车间采用两班制的工作方式,每班的工作时间为 8 小时,机器设备的生产线稼动率为 95%,废品率为 2%,每年的实际生产天数为 300 天,求该工厂流水线节拍。

解 每年有效的生产时间为

$$T_{有效} = 300 \times 2 \times 8 \times 60 \times 95\% = 273600(\text{min})$$

每年所需生产的合格产品数量为

$$Q = \frac{30000 + 30000 \times 10\%}{1 - 2\%} = 33674(辆)$$

该工厂流水线的节拍为

$$C = \frac{T_{有效}}{Q} = \frac{273600}{33674} = 8.1(\text{min})$$

节拍也可以应用于服务行业来确定服务员的数量。如一个银行每小时平均有 15 位顾客来办理相关业务,那么这个银行的节拍为 60/15=4(min),即平均每 4 分钟就会有一位顾客来办理业务;如果银行的一名员工服务一位顾客所需要的平均时间为 5 分钟,这样我们便可确定这个银行至少需要的员工数量为 5/4=1.25(名),即最少需要 2 名员工。

这便为我们提供了一种思路,即可以利用节拍来识别瓶颈工序。瓶颈指的是一条生产线中生产节拍最慢的环节,并且限制了整个生产线的生产速度。与"木桶定律"相似,一条生产线的最大产能(生产效率)并不取决于工序作业时间最短的工位,而是取决于工序作业时间最长的工位,当这两个工位的时间差别越大时,该生产线的生产能力损失也就越大。因此,可以对瓶颈工序进行优化来提高生产线的生产率。

周期时间(cycle time)指的是在生产线上生产一件产品所需要的时间,是可以进行人工测量的,它的大小反映了该条生产线的生产速率。周期时间是可以不等于节拍的,当生产的周期时间大于节拍时,就需要加班或者提前计划生产来满足生产节拍的需要。但是不论是加班还是提前生产都会提高生产成本,因此在安排生产线的生产计划时,应尽量追求生产周期与生产的节拍保持一致,否则将会造成生产成本的上升及生产资源的浪费。

节距时间(pitch time)是可以根据工人的状态进行调节的,它所表示的是在制品经过相邻两个工作站的时间间隔,在生产制造过程中,节距时间总是等于周期时间。但是当工人未进入工作状态时,可先将节距时间调大,然后再慢慢调节至等于周期时间。

单元化生产(cell line)是在生产线平衡的基础上实现的,它是一种对精益思想的实践方式。单元化就是将整个生产制造车间分为若干个单元,这些单元按照生产加工的顺序进行排列,以实现在每个单元里生产资料的搬运工作量最小,从而完成一部分或者全部生产进程。通过这样布置厂房,可以将各工位的工序复杂度降低,同时提高整个生产线的柔性,可以灵活转换生产不同类型的产品,能更快地适应市场多变的需求,使生产商的竞争力提高。每个单元内可以有较短的流水线,其生产方式可以是工位以加工工序顺序排列进行生产或一个工位完成该单元内部所有的工序作业。

3. 目视管理图

目视管理(visual management)通过使用大量的视觉信息来组织生产。因为整个流水线的每个工位是按照一定的节拍进行大量的重复工作来完成指定的生产要求的,所以必须对每一个工位严格制订相关的工作标准制度,根据节拍和各道工序的时间来编制一些详细的工作图及作业指示图表,这些图表对提高劳动率、设备的利用率有着重大的作用,因此可以依靠它们来保证流水线上生产计划的实现。

8.1.3 流水线的分类

流水线经过一百多年的进化演变,它的形式也变得多种多样,下面将介绍三种分类方法。

1. 根据流水线的节拍进行分类

(1) 粗略节拍流水线:每道工序的实际加工时间与流水线既定的节拍差别非常大,为了保证生产的连续,只能确定一个大致合理的时间段来安排组织生产计划。

(2) 强制节拍流水线:必须准确遵守所规定的节拍,对流水线上参与生产的每一组分都严格要求,并且要求零失误以保证流水线节拍的实现。

(3) 自由节拍流水线:依赖加工工人操作的熟练程度来保证流水线节拍的实现,广泛应用于以成批次的方式进行生产的车间、机加工车间、装配车间等。

2. 根据生产对象或工人是否移动进行分类

(1) 移动流水线:生产过程中的生产对象(在制品)移动,操作工人、机器设备及生产所使用的工具的位置是固定的。移动流水线中,生产对象从原材料经过每道加工工序后逐渐成为半成品或成品,常见的有汽车、家电等的流水线。

(2) 固定流水线:与移动流水线相反,将生产对象固定,操作工人带着加工所需要的工具按加工的先后顺序对生产对象进行操作加工。常见的有大型重型机器设备的装配、大型零件的加工等流水线。

3. 根据生产过程是否连续进行分类

(1) 连续流水线:一条流水线上所有工序的加工时间之和等于流水线既定节拍的整数倍。

(2) 间断流水线:由于每道工序的生产能力不匹配,存在着瓶颈工序,因此在一定时间内所生产加工的成品数目不同,所需要进行加工的对象不能在流水线上连续移动,会在不同的工位上有不同的等待时间。

8.1.4 流水线平衡问题的描述及平衡方法

1. 流水线平衡问题的描述

在工业制造业进行流水线组织规划生产的核心问题就是流水线平衡问题。它是指在给定的时间约束、机器人工、生产计划等条件下,使给定数量的原材料、零部件等生产要素依照加工的先后工序,在给定数目的工作站上进行加工,完成生产任务。也就是说,将所有的工作要素进行合理的排列组合,然后分别分配到限定数目的工作站上进行加工生产,所要达到的目标是使得各个工作站的加工作业时间等于周期时间的整数倍。

假设有一条流水线,在这条流水线上布置有 n(n 为正整数)个工作站,每个工件沿着传送带依次投入流水线,按照顺序经历所有的工作站,最终进入成品库。而流水线平衡问题是在已知加工工艺及工序先后顺序的情况下,确定所需要的最少的工作站数目,然后合理地将各道工序分配到不同的工作站中并进行优化平衡,以达成各个工作站完成作业所需要的时间相同。

流水线平衡问题的数学模型:

$$T_{N_k} = \sum_{i \in N_k} T_i \tag{8-1}$$

$$\mathrm{IT}_k = \mathrm{CT} - T_{N_k} \tag{8-2}$$

式中:N_k 表示分配给第 k 个工作站的所有作业任务;T_i 表示完成第 i 个作业所需要的时间;IT_k 表示第 k 个工作站的空闲时间,即当第 k 个工作站加工结束后,需要等待其他工作站完成加工任务的时间;CT 表示周期时间,单位为秒(s)。

例 8-2 某企业现要在流水线上生产 A 型产品,已知在该流水线上需要完成 20 道工序,其中工序作业时间最长的为 3 min,所有的工序作业时间之和为 20 min,这条流水线每天工作时间(T)为 480 min。试求:(1)这条流水线上可能的最大与最小节拍(C)是多少?(2)这条流水线的最大产量是多少?最少需要几个工作站才能达到该产量?(3)现每天需保证生产数量(Q)为 150 个,此时该流水线的节拍是多少?

解 (1)最大节拍即所有的工序都在同一个工作站中时的节拍,所以最大节拍为 20 min;最小节拍即工序作业时间最长的工序独立在一个工作站中时的节拍,所以最小节拍为 3 min。

(2)由流水线节拍的计算公式可知该流水线的最大产量为

$$Q = \frac{T}{C} = \frac{480}{3} = 160(个)$$

最少需要的工作站数目为

$$N_{\min} = \left\lceil \frac{\sum T}{C} \right\rceil = \left\lceil \frac{20}{3} \right\rceil = 7(个)$$

(注:⌈ ⌉表示向上取整。)

(3)生产数量为 150 个时,该生产线的节拍为

$$C' = \frac{T}{Q'} = \frac{480}{150} = 3.2(\min)$$

例 8-3 某流水线上有 15 项作业需要平衡,其中最长的作业时间($C_{\max}$)为

2.5 min,所有作业时间总和(C_{sum})为 14 min,该流水线每天实际工作 350 min。试求:(1)这条流水线理论上可能达到的日产能是多少?(2)若周期时间 C 分别为 8 min 和 12 min,则每日产能分别是多少?

解 (1) 该流水线的最小产能:

$$Q_{min} = \frac{\sum T}{C_{sum}} = \frac{350}{14} = 25(件)$$

该流水线的最大产能:

$$Q_{max} = \frac{\sum T}{C_{max}} = \frac{350}{2.5} = 140(件)$$

所以,该流水线的理论日产能为 25~140 件。

(2) 当 $C=8$ min 时,有

$$Q = \frac{\sum T}{C} = \frac{350}{8} = 43.75 \approx 43(件)$$

当 $C=12$ min 时,有

$$Q = \frac{\sum T}{C} = \frac{350}{12} = 29.17 \approx 29(件)$$

组织优化流水线平衡面临的最大难题,就是在周期条件的约束情况下,怎样经过合理的排列组合将所有的生产要素与给定数目的工作站进行匹配,使得流水线的生产效率最高。若想提高流水线的生产效率,则需要让各个工作站的空闲时间等于零,也就是每个工作站完成加工任务的时间等于这条流水线的周期时间,此时该流水线上的平衡率为 100%;当流水线的平衡率不是 100%时,就会有工作站的工作时间小于该条流水线的周期时间,那么便产生了非生产性的空闲时间,也就是工人和机器的等待时间。换句话说,为了让整条流水线的生产效率提高,就要努力将各个工作站的空闲时间降为零。

根据不同的目标及约束条件可以将流水线平衡问题进行以下分类。第一类,已知流水线的周期时间及各道工序的作业时间,求所需要的最少工作站数目;第二类,已知流水线给定的工作站数目及各道工序的作业时间,求与之匹配的最小周期时间;第三类,在给定工作站数目及该流水线的周期时间的情况下,将各道工序进行合理的组合分配以求得效率最高(平衡率最大)的分配方案。因为约束条件及目标函数各不相同,所以每类问题都有各自对应的数学模型,在实际中应先判断是哪类平衡问题,再运用相关的公式进行求解。

2. 平衡方法

流水线的平衡问题实际上是组合优化问题,是 NPC 问题,也就是说用分支定界法、动态规划等方法在理论上是可以求得最优解的。但这类问题的时间复杂度随着作业任务数目的增加呈指数型增长,与旅行商问题相似,随着解空间的爆炸,简单的求解方法已经不能完全适用。对 n 个作业任务进行排序,则会产生 $n!$ 个不同的排列顺序,当 $n=10$ 时,会有 3628800 种排列方式,即便根据工序的先后顺序的约束将其减少 90%,依然会有 360000 多种排列顺序,这对求最优解没有多大帮助。

实际上,对任何一个流水线进行平衡优化,首先都要求得该流水线的一些基本参数,如需要的最少工作站数目、周期时间等。在知道这些数据之后,所需要做的就是将各道工序合理地排列组合,然后分配到不同的工作站中。

其数学模型如下：

$$C = \frac{T}{Q} \tag{8-3}$$

$$N_{\min} = \left\lceil \frac{t_{\text{sum}}}{C} \right\rceil \tag{8-4}$$

$$E = \frac{t_{\text{sum}}}{NC} \times 100\% \tag{8-5}$$

式中：C 为流水线上的周期时间；T 为流水线上每天的生产时间；Q 为在总的生产时间 T 内所要完成的生产任务；$N_{\min}$ 为所需分配的最少工作站数目；t_{sum} 为实际工作中完成一件产品的全部生产所需要的时间总和；$\lceil\ \rceil$ 为向上取整，取大于或等于这个数的最小整数；N 为最终确定的工作站数目；E 为流水线的平衡率。

这种数学模型所要表达的计算思路是，先确定整个流水线的周期时间，根据周期时间及完成一件产品所有的工序作业时间之和，来确定需要的最小工作站数目，而实际上最终确定的工作站数目是大于或等于最小工作站数目的，之后便要对所有的作业任务进行具体分配了。

根据上面的数学模型可以得知，最终确定的工作站数目等于最小工作站数目是最优解，当其大于最小工作站数目时，所完成的解是次优解或可行解。在将所有作业任务分配至工作站阶段，如果作业数目比较少，可以通过简单的计算寻找平衡的方法，推导出最终的结果；但当作业任务数目过于庞大时，可采用启发式算法进行求解。

启发式算法（heuristic algorithm）通过直接观察或者对一些简单的规则进行总结来求解问题，当其面对的是简单的问题时，往往能事半功倍，但问题稍微变得复杂时，其求解结果难以令人满意，更不用提大规模问题了。

例 8-4 某流水线上要完成空调的组装，已知每天的生产任务为 520 台，这条流水线每天的工作时间为 440 min。图 8-1 所示为空调组装的网络图，其中 A,B,…,K 表示加工工序，括号中的数字表示加工时间，单位为 s。试根据该流水线的周期时间和工序的先后顺序来确定所需的最小工作站数目，并求该流水线的平衡率。

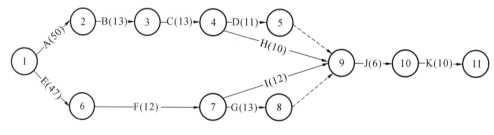

图 8-1 空调组装网络图

解 思路如下：先根据流水线的生产任务与每天总的工作时间确定流水线的节拍，为了保证平衡率最大，周期时间应与生产节拍相同。之后通过各道工序的加工时间之和与周期时间计算出需要的最小工作站数目。最后对各道工序进行排列组合，在不超过生产节拍（工作站的周期时间）的前提下，将所有的工序尽量分配给较少的工作站。

$$C = \frac{T}{Q} = \frac{440 \times 60}{520} = 50.8(\text{s})$$

$$N_{\min} = \left\lceil \frac{50+47+13+12+12+13+13+11+10+6+10}{50.8} \right\rceil = \left\lceil \frac{197}{50.8} \right\rceil = 4(\text{个})$$

下面所需要做的便是将所有的工序合理地分配到各个工作站中。在分配过程中,为了减少分配的随机性,减少工作站的等待时间,使得加工时间尽可能地接近周期时间,可以优先分配后续作业比较多的工序,并优先分配作业时间较长的工序等,这样便可减少无效的推导计算,更方便得到最优解。

最终确定的分配方案如下:

工作站 1:A(50);

工作站 2:E(47);

工作站 3:B(13)、F(12)、G(13)、I(12);

工作站 4:C(13)、D(11)、H(10)、J(6)、K(10)。

按照这种分配方式,该流水线的平衡率为

$$E = \frac{197}{4 \times 50.8} \times 100\% = 96.9\%$$

此时,这条流水线的平衡率已经是可以接受的了,上述四个工作站的任务分配方式是我们最终的选择。

由于上述问题是并行作业问题,因此在进行工序分配时可以不考虑路线的先后顺序。但当面对的是单列的问题,那么就必须考虑工序的先后顺序再进行分配,以求得最佳分配方案。

接下来将介绍一种面对工序数目较多的复杂分配问题的求解方法。阶位法也称为位置权值法,是由韩格逊和伯尼于1961年提出的一种求解方法。它首先根据工序位次的先后计算出每个作业位置的阶位值,阶位值等于该工序的作业时间加上位次在它之后的所有工序的作业时间;计算出每个作业的阶位值之后,将它们按照每个作业要素的阶位值的高低进行相关的作业安排,在分配的过程中要注意优先分配阶位值较高的工序,这样可以极大限度地减少工作站的数目,从而提高流水线的效率。

例 8-5 某流水线负责对汽车的底盘进行装配,已知该流水线每天的生产任务为400件,每天有效的工作时间为520 min。表 8-1 列出了每道加工工序的作业时间及作业的先后次序。根据流水线的周期时间及各道工序的先后次序要求,试求所需要的最小工作站数目和该流水线的平衡率。

表 8-1 汽车底盘的加工工序

工序	A	B	C	D	E	F	G	H	I
作业时间/s	50	28	19	30	26	29	14	11	22
紧前工序	—	A	B	B	C,D	E	F	F	G、H

解 (1)首先确定该流水线的生产周期时间及所需要的最小工作站数目。

$$C = \frac{T}{Q} = \frac{520 \times 60}{400} = 78(\text{s})$$

$$N_{\min} = \left\lceil \frac{50+28+19+30+26+29+14+11+22}{78} \right\rceil = \left\lceil \frac{229}{78} \right\rceil = 3(\text{个})$$

由此,便能得知最少需要 3 个工作站。

(2)根据表 8-1 给出的数据画出该底盘加工装配的先后作业次序图,如图 8-2 所示。

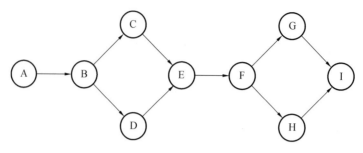

图 8-2 底盘加工装配的先后作业次序图

(3) 根据底盘加工装配的先后作业次序图作出先后作业次序矩阵表,如表 8-2 所示。制表原则如下:对每一道工序的作业任务进行分析,若第 i 道工序必须在第 j 道工序前完成,此时在先后次序矩阵表中用"+1"来表示;当两道工序的作业任务可以并列加工,即无先后加工顺序时,在先后次序矩阵表中用"0"来表示;当第 i 道工序必须在第 j 道工序后进行加工时,在先后次序矩阵表中用"−1"来表示。每个任务对自己本身而言无先后次序,在矩阵表中用"0"来表示。

表 8-2 底盘加工装配的先后作业次序矩阵表

工序	A	B	C	D	E	F	G	H	I
A	0	+1	+1	+1	+1	+1	+1	+1	+1
B	−1	0	+1	+1	+1	+1	+1	+1	+1
C	−1	−1	0	+1	+1	+1	+1	+1	+1
D	−1	−1	−1	0	+1	+1	+1	+1	+1
E	−1	−1	−1	−1	0	+1	+1	+1	+1
F	−1	−1	−1	−1	−1	0	+1	+1	+1
G	−1	−1	−1	−1	−1	−1	0	+1	+1
H	−1	−1	−1	−1	−1	−1	−1	0	+1
I	−1	−1	−1	−1	−1	−1	−1	−1	0

(4) 根据底盘加工装配的先后作业次序矩阵表,对每一个作业进行阶位值计算。计算规则是:对任意工序 x,在先后作业次序矩阵表中找到工序 x 所在的那一行,对"−1"忽略不计,对标有"+1"的位置进行加权计算,其权值等于该列所对应的工序的作业时间×1,然后对所有标有"+1"的列进行总和计算,总和计算之后的时间加上该工序的作业时间就是该工序作业的阶位值。

最终计算结果如下:

工序 A 的阶位值:50+28+19+30+26+29+14+11+22=229;

工序 B 的阶位值:28+19+30+26+29+14+11+22=179;

工序 C 的阶位值:19+26+29+14+11+22=121;

工序 D 的阶位值:30+26+29+14+11+22=132;

工序 E 的阶位值:26+29+14+11+22=102;

工序 F 的阶位值:29+14+11+22=76;

工序 G 的阶位值:14+22=36;

工序 H 的阶位值:11+22=33;

工序 I 的阶位值:22。

(5) 根据计算得到的阶位值及工作站的节拍,进行各工作站作业任务的分配。分配规则是:按照阶位值大小的顺序,对加工工序进行重新排列,排列的结果是 A,B,D,C,E,F,G,H,I。因为每个工作站的节拍为 78 s,按照阶位值的大小顺序分别对工作站 1、2 和 3 进行顺序填充。注意:工作站可允许的加工时间上限是 78 s,不能超过该值。

最终分配的结果如下:
工作站 1:A(50),B(28);
工作站 2:D(30),C(19),E(26);
工作站 3:F(29),G(14),H(11),I(22)。
各个工作站非生产性的时间分别为 0、3 s 和 2 s。
(6) 最后,计算该流水线的平衡率:

$$E = \frac{229}{3 \times 78} \times 100\% = 97.9\%$$

例 8-6 已知某家具生产商现已对一批原材料进行投产,该流水线的工艺流程如图 8-3 所示,其中 1(30) 表示工件 1 的第一道加工工序,其加工时间为 30 s。需要完成的生产计划是每天生产 1440 件,采用两班制、每班 8 h 的工作方式,不考虑停工时间,其现有的工作站具体信息如图 8-4 所示,试对该流水线进行优化。

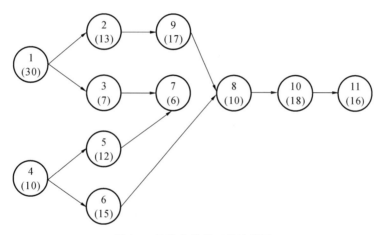

图 8-3 该流水线的工艺流程图

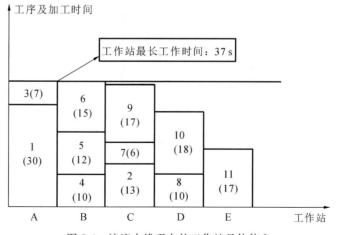

图 8-4 该流水线现在的工作站具体信息

解 该流水线的生产节拍为

$$C = \frac{\sum T}{Q} = \frac{2 \times 8 \times 60 \times 60}{1440} = 40(\text{s})$$

该流水线未优化前的平衡率为

$$E = \frac{\sum t}{N \times C} \times 100\% = \frac{30+13+7+10+12+15+6+10+17+18+16}{5 \times 40} \times 100\%$$

$$= \frac{154}{5 \times 40} \times 100\% = 77\%$$

当前的作业分配使得每个工作站都有较长的非生产性的空闲时间,而且该流水线的平衡率只有77%,所以该流水线有很大的优化空间。在优化时,应先计算该流水线所需要的最小工作站数目,然后根据作业的先后顺序重新分配。优化过程如下。

该流水线需要的最小工作站数目:

$$N_{\min} = \left\lceil \frac{\sum t}{C} \right\rceil = \left\lceil \frac{154}{40} \right\rceil = 4(\uparrow)$$

因此需要减少一个工作站,对作业进行重新分配。

作业1和作业4没有先后顺序,并且它们的优先级很高,两个作业时间之和为40 s,等于生产节拍,可以放入同一个工作站中。

作业2、5、6是平级关系,其加工没有先后顺序,三个作业时间之和为40 s,等于生产节拍,可以放入同一个工作站中。

作业7需要在作业3完成之后才能进行,作业8需要在作业7完成之后才能进行,作业9和作业3、7、8没有先后顺序,四个作业时间之和为40 s,等于生产节拍,可以放入同一个工作站中。

剩下作业10和作业11,二者的作业时间之和为35 s,小于节拍时间,可以放进同一个工作站中。

优化结果如图8-5所示。

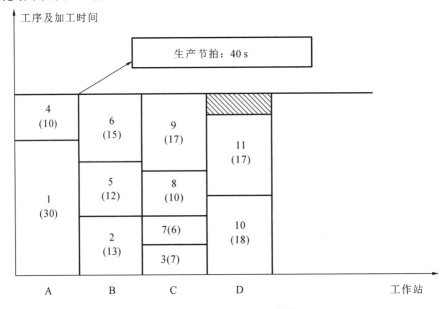

图8-5 优化后的工作站具体信息

优化后,流水线平衡率为

$$E = \frac{154}{4 \times 40} \times 100\% = 96.3\%$$

优化后平衡率从77%提高到96.3%,这是一个满意度非常高的方案。

8.2 混流生产线平衡

8.2.1 混流生产线的平衡问题

流水线经历了由一种产品装配生产到现在的多种产品混流组装生产,为了完成给定的生产任务,将多种结构相似、工序大致相同但规格和型号不同的产品,以科学合理的编排次序投入生产线,达到有节奏、按比例地混合连续流水生产,并以产品的品种、工人和机器、任务计划等全面均衡为基本前提,形成混流生产线。混流生产线具有较高的柔性及自动化程度,可以根据生产任务的变更迅速地做出相应的排产安排,适用于多品种小批量的生产计划。这种生产模式广泛应用于家用电器(空调、冰箱)及汽车的生产。

与单品种流水生产线类似,其核心问题都是如何对多道工序进行排列组合,将其分配到最少的工作站中,且各个工作站的加工作业时间尽可能地接近生产线的节拍,以使得整个生产线的作业要素都能被充分使用,所有工作站无效的生产时间之和最小,从而使整条生产线生产效率最高。

相比单一品种的生产线平衡,混流生产线的生产平衡是多种单品种生产平衡的组合问题,不仅需要考虑每一种产品的平衡,还需将多种产品根据生产量、工序加工时间等综合进行分析考虑,这大大增加了该问题的复杂度。

由于混流生产线是单一生产线的有机排列,不是简单堆砌,因此混流生产线求解的目标变得更加多元,它的约束条件也很多。这类问题属于NPC问题,已经不是在多项式级别就可以求解的了,需要借助软件及算法进行求解。当我们面对简单的问题时,可以用Excel或者VBA(visual basic 宏语言)来计算,当面临比较复杂的问题时,可以用WinQSB、COMSOAL、ASYBL等软件来进行求解,这些软件可处理有上千道工序作业的问题。

导致混流生产线产生空闲时间的原因如下。

(1) 工人的操作失误或机器故障引起的间断性生产,导致后面的操作工人需要帮助该工位的工人完成生产任务,使得后续工作站的工人及机器处于闲置状态。

(2) 排产不合理导致工序冲突等引起的在制品等待。零部件已经完成前面工序的加工,通过传送带输送到下一工作站进行加工,但下个工作站处于工作状态,那么该在制品就需要在工作站外面等待,造成时间浪费。

(3) 生产所需要使用的辅助工具未及时就位导致的时间浪费。生产线上的辅助工具并不是与生产量一一对应,而是循环使用的。如不同型号规格的在制品在不同的工序加工中,需要使用不同的夹具。当在制品已经到达工作站准备生产而工作站的夹具还未及时返回到工作站时,便产生了在制品的等待时间。

8.2.2 混流生产线平衡的数学模型

混流生产线平衡的数学模型与单一流水生产线平衡的数学模型相似,都是需要先计算出生产线的节拍,根据节拍确定所需要的最小工作站数目,然后对各道工序作业进行排列组合,并向工作站填充,最终计算出生产线的平衡率。但与单一流水生产线不一样的地方是,由于要生产多种型号的产品,并且每种产品每天的生产数量不一定相同,因此在具体计算节拍及所需最小工作站数目的时候,原来的公式应做一些改变。具体的改变如下:

$$C = \frac{\sum t}{\sum_{i=1}^{n} N_i} \qquad (8-6)$$

$$N_{\min} = \left\lceil \frac{\sum_{i=1}^{n} t_i N_i}{C \sum_{i=1}^{n} N_i} \right\rceil \qquad (8-7)$$

$$E = \frac{\sum_{i=1}^{n} t_i N_i}{NC \sum_{i=1}^{n} N_i} \qquad (8-8)$$

式中:N_i表示每天生产第i类产品的数量;t_i表示生产一件第i类产品所需要的时间;其余变量在前面都有介绍。

例 8-7 某车间计划生产两种不同型号的产品,已知该车间共有三台不同的设备,两种型号的产品每天的生产量相同。两种型号产品的加工工艺网络图如图 8-6 所示,图中,101(11)表示工件 1 的第一道加工工序,其加工时间为 11 s,其余类似。已知该生产线的生产节拍为 30 s,求最终所需要的工作站数目和生产线的平衡率。

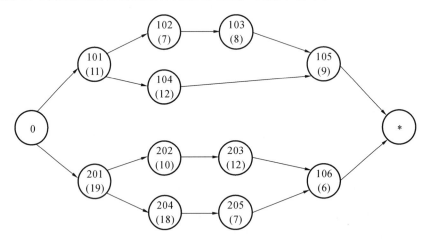

图 8-6 两种型号产品的加工工艺网络图

解 (1) 确定该生产线所需的最小工作站数目。因为已知该生产线的生产节拍为 30 s,所以需要的最小工作站数目为

$$N_{\min} = \left\lceil \frac{\sum_{i=1}^{n} t_i}{C} \right\rceil = \left\lceil \frac{47 + 72}{30} \right\rceil = 4(个)$$

(2) 根据工作站的数目及生产节拍对工序作业进行分配,在分配时,应当按照一定的规则:

① 按加工任务所处的加工区间进行分配；
② 工序作业的时间较长时,该作业的优先级较高,应优先分配；
③ 当在分配时发生工序作业时间之和大于生产节拍时,应重新调整工序进行分配；
④ 在分配工序作业时,应当同时使得该生产线平衡。

首先先对工作站 1 进行分配,依次增加工作站 1 的工序作业数目,直到作业时间之和等于生产节拍或者由于其他原因（如时间、工序顺序等）导致该工作站的作业不能继续增加。以此类推,对后面的工作站进行作业填充。

最终分配的结果如下：

工作站 1：201(19),202(10)；
工作站 2：101(11),102(7),104(12)；
工作站 3：203(12),204(18)；
工作站 4：103(8),105(9),205(7),206(6)。

(3) 计算该生产线的平衡率：

$$E = \frac{47+72}{4 \times 30} \times 100\% = 99.2\%$$

这种分配方式下,该生产线的平衡率达到了 99.2%,所以这种作业分配方式的满意程度（可接受程度）高。

例 8-8 某混流生产线每天需生产 A、B、C 三种型号的产品各 35、25、20 件,采用一班 8 h 的工作方式,不考虑停工时间,工序加工时间如表 8-3 所示,三种产品的工序流程图如图 8-7、图 8-8 和图 8-9 所示,图中 1(4) 表示工序 1 的加工时间为 4 min,其余类似。试求解混流生产线平衡问题,并用遗传算法进行优化改进。

表 8-3 工序加工时间

工序号	1	2	3	4	5	6	7	8	9	10	11	12	13	14	15	16
加工时间/min	4	4	5	3	4	3	1	3	4	5	5	4	3	2	2	4

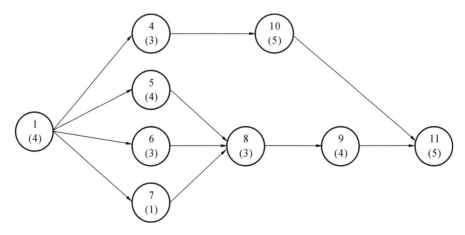

图 8-7 A 产品工序流程图

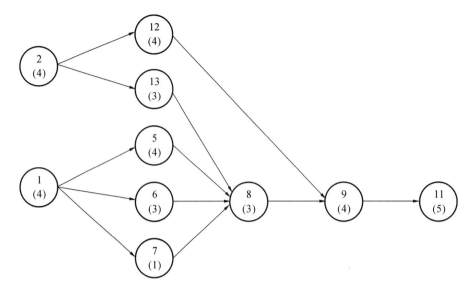

图 8-8 B 产品工序流程图

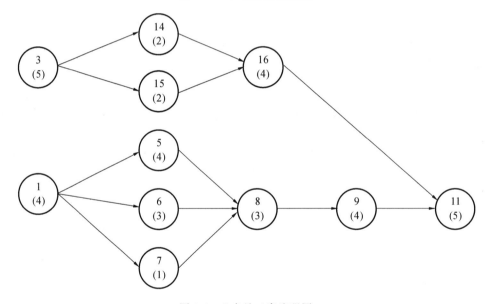

图 8-9 C 产品工序流程图

解　根据上述图表可知:A 产品共经历了 9 道工序,完成一件 A 产品的生产共需要 32 min;B 产品共经历了 10 道工序,完成一件 B 产品的生产共需要 35 min;C 产品共经历了 11 道工序,完成一件 C 产品的生产共需要 37 min。每天生产的 A、B、C 三种产品的数量不同,每天生产 A、B、C 三种产品的各自总工作时间为 1120 min、875 min、740 min。

这条混流生产线的生产节拍为

$$C = \frac{\sum T}{\sum_{i=1}^{n} N_i} = \frac{8 \times 60}{35 + 25 + 20} = 6(\min)$$

根据该生产线的节拍计算出该生产线需要的最小工作站数目为

$$N_{\min} = \left\lceil \frac{\sum_{i=1}^{n} N_i t_i}{C \sum_{i=1}^{n} N_i} \right\rceil = \left\lceil \frac{35 \times 32 + 25 \times 35 + 20 \times 37}{6 \times (35 + 25 + 20)} \right\rceil = 6(个)$$

接下来需要对该混流生产线进行工作站的初始工序分配。三种产品所需经历的共同工序有 1、5、6、7、8、9、11，产品 A、B、C 的产量分别是 35 件、25 件、20 件，所以工序 1 每天需要 80×4=320(min)的加工时间。以此类推，求出每道工序每天需要的加工时间。

之后采用遗传算法对上述案例进行求解。

(1) 编码。按照每道工序加工的先后顺序序列进行编码，即每一道需要加工的工序(作业元素)对应一个染色体的基因位。完成编码后，染色体上面的所有元素必须按照阶位值从大到小的顺序排列(满足优先级关系)。一种可行的编码方式如图 8-10 所示。

图 8-10　一种可行的编码方式

(2) 译码。在完成编码后，各个作业元素只表达了工序在实际生产过程中加工的先后顺序。译码是按照每个工作站的所有作业元素加工时间之和不大于生产节拍的原则，将染色体按顺序分配到各个工作站中的过程。

译码的步骤如下。

第一步：$tt = tt + time(x_i)$，若 $tt \leqslant CT < tt + time(x_i)$，则 $M = M + 1$。若 $i = N - 1, M = M + 1$，则转至第二步。

第二步：$i = i + 1$。若 $i \leqslant N - 1$，则转至第一步；若 $i = N$，则译码结束。

其中：tt 表示作业时间总和；编码的染色体序列为 x_i，x_i 表示每道工序的序号，$i = 1, 2, \cdots, n$ ($n = 16$)，i 的初值为 1；M 的初值为 0。

(3) 选择算子。该例采用最优保存法选择算子，即用所有工作站中 M 值最小的个体直接代替 M 值最大的个体。

(4) 交叉算子。按照遗传算法的原则，以第 8 个位置为交叉点进行交叉，结果如图 8-11 所示。

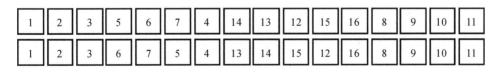

图 8-11　以第 8 个位置为交叉点进行交叉的结果

(5) 变异算子。以第 6 个位置为变异点进行变异，结果如图 8-12 所示。

图 8-12　以第 6 个位置为变异点进行变异的结果

用软件编程，设置变量生产节拍为 480 min，种群大小为 100，进化代数为 200，选择最优工作站数目为 6 个，染色体之间交叉的概率为 0.85，变异的概率为 0.05，程序计算得到的工作站具体信息如图 8-13 所示。

优化后的平衡率为

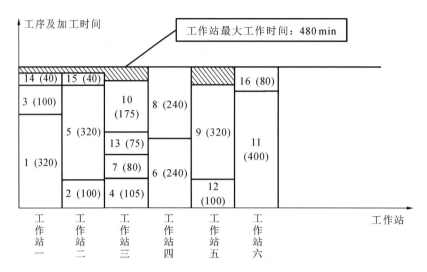

图 8-13 工作站具体信息

$$E = \frac{35 \times 32 + 25 \times 35 + 20 \times 37}{6 \times 6 \times (35 + 25 + 20)} \times 100\% = 95\%$$

该生产线优化后,平衡率大幅上升,各个工作站工作时间分配更加均衡合理,提高了生产效益。

第 9 章 生产系统建模与仿真课程设计

9.1 课程设计任务描述

课程设计所要解决的问题,如本书第 3.5 节所述,在满足各种约束条件的前提下,采用所学的优化方法,解决不同规模的作业车间调度问题。分别采用传统方法(复合形法)、选择或改进适当的仿生算法和手工调度方法,求解小、中两个规模的问题,绘制调度结果的甘特图,并对主要特性进行对比分析。

9.2 小规模作业车间调度问题求解示例

以仅包含 3 个待加工工件的小规模作业车间调度问题(JSSP)为例,图 9-1 描述了 3 个工件所涉及的工序加工类型、工序关系、工序加工时间,每一道工序上方的字母表示加工类型,数字表示加工时间,如工序 101 的加工设备类型为 A,加工时间为 16 min。表 9-1 描述了车间的设备情况。由图表可知,该问题包含 3 个待加工工件、10 道工序和分属 5 个类型的 5 台加工设备。

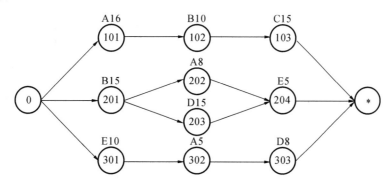

图 9-1 小规模 JSSP 的工序与设备关系图

表 9-1 小规模 JSSP 的设备信息

设备编号	1	2	3	4	5
设备类型	A	B	C	D	E

采用复合形法求解,搜索过程如图 9-2 所示,所求得的最优解如表 9-2 所示,与最优解对应的甘特图如图 9-3 所示。

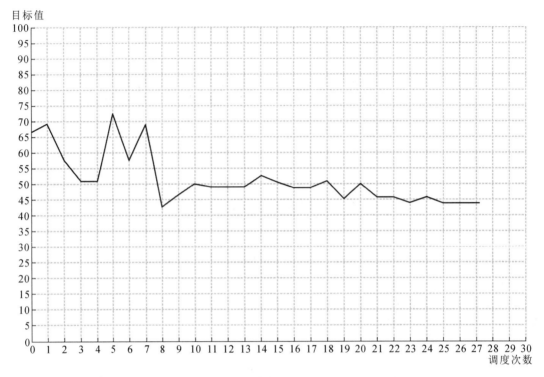

图 9-2　复合形法求解小规模 JSSP 的调度过程曲线

表 9-2　复合形法求解小规模 JSSP 的调度结果

任务编号	设备编号	加工时间/min	开始时间/min	结束时间/min
101	1	16	0	16
102	2	10	16	26
103	3	15	26	41
201	2	15	0	15
202	1	8	31	39
203	4	15	16	31
204	5	5	39	44
301	5	10	0	10
302	1	5	19	24
303	4	8	32	40

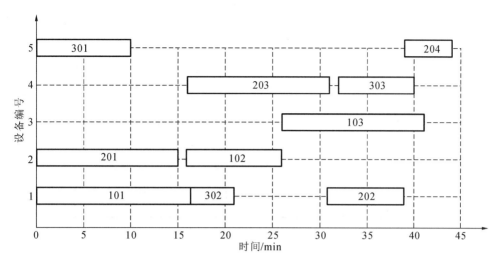

图 9-3　复合形法求解小规模 JSSP 的甘特图

采用仿生算法求解,搜索过程如图 9-4 所示,所求得的最优解如表 9-3 所示,与最优解对应的甘特图如图 9-5 所示。

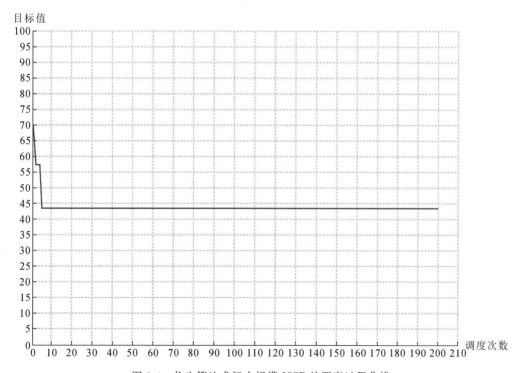

图 9-4　仿生算法求解小规模 JSSP 的调度过程曲线

表 9-3　仿生算法求解小规模 JSSP 的调度结果

任务编号	设备编号	加工时间/min	开始时间/min	结束时间/min
101	1	16	0	16
102	2	10	16	26
103	3	15	26	41

续表

任务编号	设备编号	加工时间/min	开始时间/min	结束时间/min
201	2	15	0	15
202	1	8	30	38
203	4	15	15	30
204	5	5	38	43
301	5	10	0	10
302	1	5	16	21
303	4	8	30	38

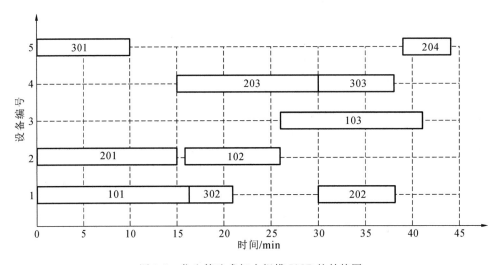

图 9-5　仿生算法求解小规模 JSSP 的甘特图

采用手工调度的方法求解，所求得的最优解如表 9-4 所示，与最优解对应的甘特图如图 9-6 所示。

表 9-4　小规模 JSSP 的手工调度结果

设备编号	任务编号	开始时间/min	结束时间/min
1	101	0	16
1	202	30	38
1	302	16	21
2	102	16	15
2	201	0	26
3	103	26	41
4	203	15	30
4	303	30	38
5	204	38	43
5	301	0	10

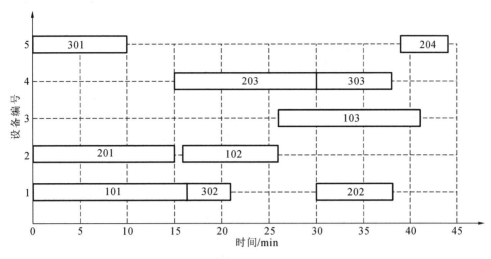

图 9-6 手工调度方法求解小规模 JSSP 的甘特图

根据以上调度结果,计算三种调度方法的三个关键参数——总完工时间、设备闲置时间和工时利用率,如表 9-5 所示。

表 9-5 关键参数对比

调度方法的关键参数	复合形法	仿生算法	手工调度方法
总完工时间/min	44	43	43
设备闲置时间/min	42	41	41
工时利用率	28.4%	28.1%	28.1%

从表中可以发现,对于小规模问题,采用不同的方法都有较好的求解可靠性,并且采用手工调度方法就可以解决小规模调度问题,所得到的解与采用复合形法得到的解差异很小。

9.3 中等规模作业车间调度问题求解示例

如图 9-7 所示为包含 4 个待加工工件的中等规模作业车间调度问题,该问题包含 4 个待加工工件、32 道工序、5 类共 7 台加工设备,设备信息如表 9-6 所示。

表 9-6 中等规模 JSSP 的设备信息

设备编号	1	2	3	4	5	6	7
设备类型	A	A	B	B	C	D	E

采用复合形法调度,搜索过程如图 9-8 所示,调度结果如表 9-7 所示,最优解对应的甘特图如图 9-9 所示。

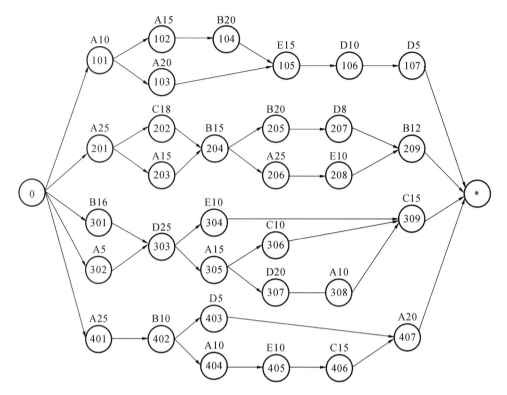

图 9-7 中等规模 JSSP 的工序与设备关系图

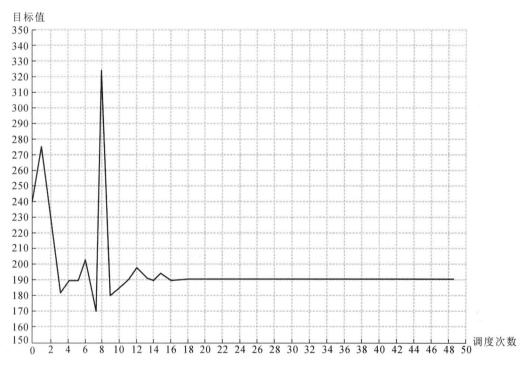

图 9-8 复合形法求解中等规模 JSSP 的调度过程曲线

表 9-7 复合形法求解中等规模 JSSP 的调度结果

任务编号	设备编号	加工时间/min	开始时间/min	结束时间/min
101	1	10	16	26
102	1	15	62	77
103	1	20	42	62
104	3	20	77	97
105	7	15	97	112
106	6	10	118	128
107	5	5	141	146
201	2	25	13	38
202	5	18	55	73
203	2	15	40	55
204	4	15	73	88
205	4	20	93	113
206	1	25	113	138
207	6	8	138	146
208	7	10	146	156
209	3	12	160	172
301	3	16	8	24
302	1	5	3	8
303	6	25	28	53
304	7	10	85	95
305	2	15	70	85
306	5	10	95	105
307	6	20	146	166
308	1	10	166	176
309	5	15	176	191
401	1	25	62	87
402	3	10	97	107
403	6	5	128	133
404	2	10	107	117
405	7	10	133	143
406	5	15	146	161
407	2	20	161	181

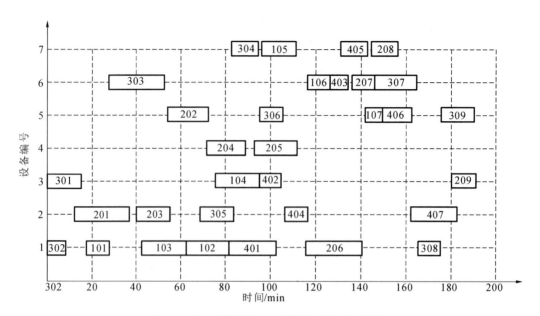

图 9-9 复合形法求解中等规模 JSSP 的甘特图

采用仿生算法求解,搜索过程如图 9-10 所示,所求得的最优解如表 9-8 所示,与最优解对应的甘特图如图 9-11 所示。

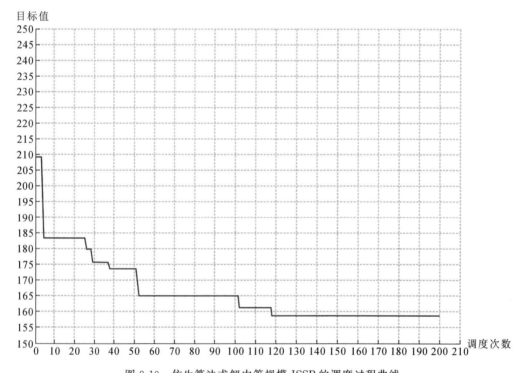

图 9-10 仿生算法求解中等规模 JSSP 的调度过程曲线

表 9-8 仿生算法求解中等规模 JSSP 的调度结果

任务编号	设备编号	加工时间/min	开始时间/min	结束时间/min
101	2	10	25	35

续表

任务编号	设备编号	加工时间/min	开始时间/min	结束时间/min
102	2	15	55	70
103	1	20	35	55
104	3	20	83	103
105	7	15	103	118
106	6	10	120	130
107	5	5	143	148
201	2	25	0	25
202	5	18	50	68
203	2	15	35	50
204	3	15	68	83
205	4	20	83	103
206	2	25	111	136
207	6	8	103	111
208	7	10	136	146
209	3	12	146	158
301	3	16	0	16
302	1	5	25	30
303	6	25	30	55
304	7	10	118	128
305	1	15	55	70
306	5	10	90	100
307	6	20	70	90
308	2	10	100	110
309	5	15	128	143
401	1	25	0	25
402	4	10	25	35
403	6	5	115	120
404	1	10	70	80
405	7	10	80	90
406	5	15	100	115
407	1	20	120	140

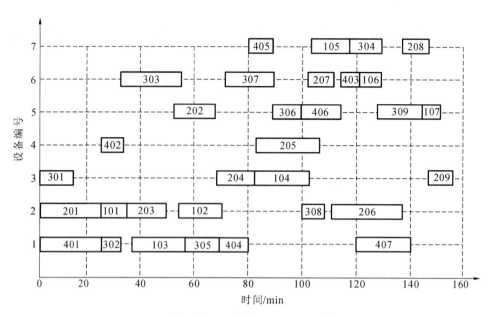

图 9-11 仿生算法求解中等规模 JSSP 的甘特图

采用手工调度方法求解,所求得的最优解如表 9-9 所示,与最优解对应的甘特图如图 9-12 所示。

表 9-9 中等规模 JSSP 的手工调度结果

设备编号	任务编号	开始时间/min	结束时间/min
1	103	35	55
1	302	25	30
1	305	55	70
1	401	0	25
1	404	70	80
1	407	120	140
2	101	25	35
2	102	55	70
2	201	0	25
2	203	35	50
2	206	111	136
2	308	100	110
3	104	83	103
3	204	68	83
3	209	146	158

续表

设备编号	任务编号	开始时间/min	结束时间/min
3	301	0	16
4	205	83	103
4	402	25	35
5	107	143	148
5	202	50	68
5	306	90	100
5	309	128	143
5	406	100	115
6	106	120	130
6	207	103	111
6	303	30	55
6	307	70	90
6	403	115	120
7	105	103	118
7	208	136	146
7	304	118	128
7	405	80	90

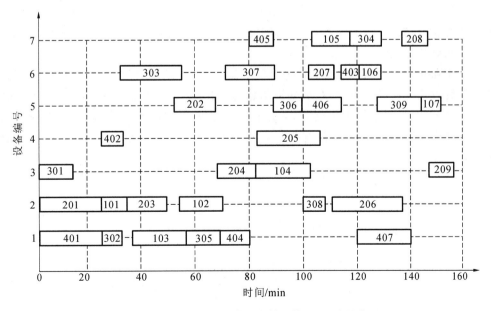

图 9-12　手工调度方法求解中等规模 JSSP 的甘特图

根据以上调度结果,计算三种调度方法的三个关键参数——总完工时间、设备闲置时间和工时利用率,如表9-10所示。

表 9-10 中等规模问题求解结果关键参数对比

调度方法的关键参数	复合形法	仿生算法	手工调度方法
总完工时间/min	191	158	158
设备闲置时间/min	265	185	185
工时利用率	52.3%	60.2%	59.8%

从表中可以发现,对于中等规模问题,从所得到的解的优化程度来看,仿生算法和手工调度方法显著优于复合形法这一传统优化方法,仿生算法略优于手工调度方法,但手工调度方法调度过程烦琐,消耗较多人力资源。因此,对于中等规模问题,采用仿生算法是较好的选择。

9.4 小　　结

作业车间调度问题,可以通过传统方法(复合形法)、仿生算法、手工调度方法等进行求解,并具有以下特点。

(1) 目前的方法对中、小规模问题,具有良好的求解可靠性;对于大规模问题,还没有有效的求解方法。

(2) 传统方法、仿生算法、手工调度方法都可以用于求解中、小规模问题,其中手工调度方法可以得到比较满意的方案,但所需的人工工作量较大。对于中、小规模问题,仿生算法和手工调度方法所得解具有更高的优化程度。

(3) 各种方法对初始解及参数的依赖程度不同。手工调度方法、传统方法对初始解和初始参数的设置有较强的依赖性。如采用复合形法时,初始解性状的优越程度和停机准则、映射系数的设置,对收敛性、求解效率、解的优化程度等都有显著影响。仿生算法、手工调度方法则有较好的稳定性。

由于作业车间调度问题是 NP-Hard 问题,迄今为止,还没有公认的在数学上证明一定收敛的求解方法。从经验出发,对小规模问题,采用手工调度方法或传统优化方法,就可以获得比较满意的解;对中等规模问题,采用仿生算法或手工调度方法,也可以得到满意解。但对于大规模问题而言,目前还没有有效可靠的方法,所以,对于作业车间调度问题的研究,还有很长的路要走。

参 考 文 献

[1] REEVES C R, ROWE J E. Genetic algorithms—principles and perspectives: a guide to GA theory[M]. Boston: Kluwer Academic Publishers, 2003.

[2] CORMEN T H. Introduction to algorithms[M]. Cambridge, MA: MIT Press, 2005.

[3] GIORDANO F R, FOX W P, HORTON S B. A first course in mathematical modeling [M]. 5th edition. Boston: Brooks-Cole, 2013.

[4] HILLIER F S, LIEBERMAN G J. Introduction to operations research[M]. 10th edition. New York: McGraw-Hill, 2014.

[5] TAHA H A. Operations research—an introduction[M]. 10th edition. New York: Pearson Education Limited, 2017.

[6] HOLLAND J H. Adaptation in natural and artificial systems[M]. Ann Arbour: The University of Michigan Press, 1975.

[7] HOLLAND J H. Studying complex adaptive systems[J]. Journal of Systems Science and Complexity, 2006, 19(1): 1-8.

[8] JOHNSON S M. On the representations of an integer as the sum of products of integers[J]. Transactions of the American Mathematical Society, 1954, 76(2): 177-189.

[9] KOMAKI G M, SHEIKH S, MALAKOOTI B. Flow shop scheduling problems with assembly operations: a review and new trends[J]. International Journal of Production Research, 2019, 57(10): 2926-2955.

[10] DORIGO M, GAMBARDELLA L M. Ant colonies for the travelling salesman problem[J]. Biosystems, 1997, 43(2): 73-81.

[11] MIKELL P G. Automation, production systems, and computer-integrated manufacturing [M]. 4th edition. New Jersey: Prentice Hall, 2011.

[12] SHELDON M R. Stochastic process [M]. 2nd edition. New York: John Wiley & Sons, 1996.

[13] STEFAN H. Mathematical modeling[M]. Berlin: Springer-Verlag, 2011.

[14] VITAL-SOTO A, AZAB A, BAKI M F. Mathematical modeling and a hybridized bacterial foraging optimization algorithm for the flexible job-shop scheduling problem with sequencing flexibility[J]. Journal of Manufacturing Systems, 2020, 54: 74-93.

[15] LUO Y B. Nested optimization method combining complex method and ant colony optimization to solve JSSP with complex associated processes[J]. Journal of Intelligent Manufacturing, 2017, 28: 1801-1815.

Abstract

"Modeling and Simulation of Production System" is one of main courses for industrial engineering major, which involves both deep mathematical theory knowledge and its application methods in the field of production and operation. The book can be divided into three parts. Chapters 1 to 4 are the basic theories of modeling production systems, which introduce the main features of complex systems, the basis of system modeling, the optimization models of production systems, and the probability problems in production systems; Chapters 5 to 8 are production system solving methods, which introduce the principles of typical traditional optimization methods and advanced bionics algorithms, and their application methods in production system solving; Chapter 9 introduces the course design of modeling and simulation of production system, which is a comprehensive practice of the theories and methods learned in the first two parts.

This book can be used as a textbook for undergraduates and postgraduates of industrial engineering and related majors in management disciplines, and provides a reference for the production management personnel of enterprises.

Preface

Industrial engineering (IE) is an applied engineering specialized discipline developed from scientific management. In 1955, the American Institute of Industrial Engineers (AIIE) put forward the definition of industrial engineering: "Industrial engineering is a discipline that designs, improves and practices an integrated system of people, material, equipment, energy and information and it also integrates the knowledge and technology of mathematics, physics and social sciences, combines the principles and methods of engineering analysis and design to confirm, to predict and to evaluate the results of the system."

Meanwhile, the education system of industrial engineering has been relatively mature in developed countries, and various distinctive industrial engineering disciplines with different professional backgrounds have emerged in those countries. For instance, industrial engineering of Purdue University is based on agriculture while industrial engineering of the University of Michigan is based on manufacturing industry. In general, those developed countries represented by the United States and Japan have formed a mature education system of industrial engineering corresponding to its industrial development.

In contrast, the education of industrial engineering in China is still in infancy. It was not until the early 1990s that the first batch of industrial engineering disciplines were established in some top universities of China. Enterprises' demand for industrial engineering becomes more and more urgent with China's industry boom, and the early graduates from industrial engineering were in short supply. Most universities in China have set up industrial engineering courses over the past ten years, which has become one of the fastest developing majors in China.

Considering China's education of industrial engineering is in infancy, there is a lack of referential experience in textbooks-compiling. Meanwhile, the theoretical and practical issues that some courses involved are deep, and the long-term research work is required. Therefore, it is demanding in professional textbooks corresponding to the current stage of IE development in China.

Modeling and simulation of production systems is a main course in industrial engineering, which involves deep mathematical theory, such as queuing theory, system modeling, optimization theory, simulation method etc. It also includes the application in production and operation management, such as the optimization of production system layout, job shop scheduling problem (JSSP) etc. There are few complex textbooks over this field in China at present.

The author has much experience in teaching the course—modeling and simulation of production systems for decades. Supported by the National Natural Science Foundation of China (NSFC NOs. 51875430, 51375357, 50705072), the Hubei Science Fund for Distinguished Young Scholars and Wuhan Youth Science and Technology Plan, the author has carried out a long-term research in some areas related to this theme. This textbook is compiled upon the teaching plans of this course and the research for years over this field.

The main contents are as follows:

Chapter 1, Introduction: the necessity and goal of modeling and simulation of production system are emphasized on the basis of characteristics, classifications and evolution history of production systems.

Chapter 2, The Basis of System Modeling: the basic concepts and knowledge related to complex system are introduced, such as the concept of system, basic steps of system modeling, NP-Hard and NPC problem. And the modeling methods of three representative systems are clarified and analyzed.

Chapter 3, Optimization Model of Production System: the modeling methods of production system are elaborated based on system modeling. The model of single machine scheduling, parallel machine scheduling and independent system scheduling is introduced respectively, and the related conception of JSSP is explained.

Chapter 4, The Analysis of Probability in Production System: a couple of specific cases are used to expound the application of probability analysis and queuing theory in production system modeling after introducing the basic conception of probability theory and queuing theory.

Chapter 5, Production System Solution Based on Complex Method: first, the basic idea and steps of a traditional optimization method—complex method are introduced via some practical cases, and then the application of complex method in JSSP is presented as well.

Chapter 6, Genetic Algorithm and Its Application in Production Scheduling: the basic principles and methods of genetic algorithm are introduced first. Then, taking the optimization of workshop layout and bin-packing problem as examples, the application of genetic algorithm in modeling and optimization of production systems are expounded. Finally, how to use genetic algorithm to solve JSSP is elaborated in detail.

Chapter 7, Ant Colony Algorithm and Its Application in Production System Optimization: the basic principle of ant colony algorithm is introduced first. Then, taking the JSSP and path planning of parts delivery as examples, the application of ant colony algorithm in modeling and optimization of production systems are elucidated.

Chapter 8, The Theory and Approach of Production Line Balance: taking the assembly line and mixed-model production line as examples, the modeling theory and the solving methods of production line balance are expounded based on the basic concepts and principles of production line balance with some real cases.

Chapter 9, Course Design of Production System Modeling and Simulation: the task of course design is depicted first. Then, taking the small and medium-scale JSSP as examples, the methods and steps to solve JSSP are explained. Finally, a job shop scheduling optimization system is adopted in job scheduling problem.

Special thanks go to postgraduate students Hanlin Yu, Kaipeng Zhang and Haiqiang Hao for participating in the book complying and editing.

This book has been approved as textbook for "the Thirteenth Five-Year Plan" of Wuhan University of Technology. Not only the theory of modeling, optimization and simulation but also the application of these theories in production system can be systematically learned from this book. The book can be used as a textbook for both undergraduate and postgraduate students majored in industrial engineering and management discipline, as well as a reference for enterprise production management personnel.

Certainly, a mature textbook requires a long-term teaching interaction and accumulation so *Modeling and Simulation of Production System* is no exception. We will further improve and perfect this textbook during teaching practice in the future, and all valuable comments from colleagues both at home and abroad will be appreciated and welcomed.

Yabo Luo
March 20, 2020
Wuhan University of Technology

Contents

Chapter 1 Introduction .... (111)

    1.1 Characteristics of the Production System .... (111)

    1.2 Classification of the Production System .... (112)

    1.3 Evolution History of the Production System .... (113)

    1.4 Necessity and Objectives of Modeling and Simulation of Production System

            .... (115)

Chapter 2 The Basis of System Modeling .... (117)

    2.1 The Concept of "System" .... (117)

    2.2 General Method for System Modeling .... (119)

    2.3 NPC Problem and NP-Hard Problem .... (121)

    2.4 Instance Analysis of Three Types of System Modeling Problem .... (126)

Chapter 3 Optimization Model of Production System .... (131)

    3.1 Introduction of Production System Modeling .... (131)

    3.2 The Model of Single Machine Scheduling .... (133)

    3.3 The Model of Parallel Machine Scheduling .... (134)

    3.4 The Model of Independent Job System Scheduling .... (135)

    3.5 Job Shop Scheduling Problem .... (138)

Chapter 4 The Analysis of Probability in Production System .... (142)

    4.1 Introduction to the Application of Probabilistic Analysis Method ...... (142)

    4.2 Some Basic Concepts of Probability Theory with Applications .... (143)

    4.3 Central Limit Theorem with Applications .... (148)

    4.4 Queuing Characteristics Analysis .... (152)

    4.5 Summary .... (156)

Chapter 5 Production System Solution Based on Complex Method .... (157)

    5.1 Basic Idea and General Steps of Complex Method .... (157)

    5.2 Examples of the Complex Method .... (160)

    5.3 Application of Complex Method in Job Shop Scheduling Problem ..... (165)

Chapter 6 Genetic Algorithm and Its Application in Production Scheduling .... (172)

    6.1 Formation and Development of Genetic Algorithm .... (172)

    6.2 Genetic Algorithm Foundation .... (173)

    6.3 Genetic Algorithm Application Case—Workshop Equipment Layout Optimization

         .... (177)

    6.4 Genetic Algorithm Application Case—Packing Problem .... (182)

    6.5 Solving Job Shop Scheduling Problems by GA .... (183)

    6.6 Summary .... (186)

Chapter 7 Ant Colony Algorithm and Its Application in Production System Optimization

         .... (187)

    7.1 An Overview of Ant Colony Algorithm .... (187)

    7.2 The Basic Principle of Ant Colony Algorithm .... (188)

    7.3 The Case of Ant Colony Algorithm .... (196)

    7.4 Summary .... (201)

Chapter 8 The Theory and Approach of Production Line Balance .... (202)

    8.1 Production and Assembly Line Optimization .... (202)

    8.2 Mixed Production Line Balance .... (215)

Chapter 9 Course Design of Production System Modeling and Simulation .... (222)

    9.1 Task Description of Course Design .... (222)

    9.2 A Case of a Small-Scale Job Shop Scheduling Problem .... (222)

    9.3 A Case of a Medium-Scale Job Shop Scheduling Problem .... (226)

    9.4 Summary .... (233)

References .... (234)

Chapter 1 Introduction

1.1 Characteristics of the Production System

A production system is a system composed of people, raw material and tools that can convert raw material into products. A simple production system of manual workshop can be formed by a single person, some simple tools and raw material only. A large modern workshop with complex work flow, material flow, information flow and complex constraint is a complex production system. Whether a simple system or a complex system, a production system has following typical characteristics:

(1) A production system has three elements: human, raw material and production tools. Human is the dominant factor in a production system, which controls raw material or operates production tools to achieve the goal of converting raw material into products.

(2) A production system is hierarchical. In order to make the system operate more effectively, subsystem with specific objective will come into being to achieve layer-by-layer control and independent control in a production system with high complexity, including resource planning system, quality control system, logistics control system, inventory management system etc.

(3) A production system is an information processing system. A production system contains such various information flows as manual information, raw material information, equipment status information, production planning information. How to deal with these information flows effectively is an important part of a production system because of the associated features among the information flows.

(4) A production system is a labor transformation system. The content of a production system, whether physically intensive or technology intensive, is to integrate human mental labor or physical labor into production system, and then to reflect its value via products.

(5) A production system is a knowledge transformation system. The operation process of a production system is based on human knowledge in both a simple production system and a complex one. Raw material cannot ultimately be converted into useful products without knowledge as the premise.

With the development of human society and the progress of science and technology, a production system contains more knowledge and more complicated information flows, which are related to science and technology. Optimizing production system reasonably is an inevitable way to improve the efficiency of a production system with high complexity. The purpose of modeling and simulation is to realize the optimization of a production system.

1.2 Classification of the Production System

A production system has diverse classification methods from different perspective. For instance, it can be divided into a continuous production system and a discrete production system from the perspective of process characteristics. It also can be divided into a make-to-order production system and a make-to-stock production system from the angle of source of production plans. And it can be classified into three categories: job shop system, flow shop system and production line from the perspective of the organization forms of a production system. Generally, modeling, optimization and simulation should be carried out according to the different organization forms of production systems.

(1) Job shop system. Job shop system is a general processing system with no fixed-process and goal of specialized production, whose operation process takes a task as a unit and the production equipment is universal. The general processing workshop is a typical job shop system, which can be described as: there are some work pieces to be processed, the amount of which is i, and the processing tasks of each work piece are composed of a number of interrelated processes. These processes are allocated to n equipments with m kinds for processing to achieve highest efficiency of the system under the condition of meeting complex interrelated constraint.

(2) Flow shop system. Flow shop system generally refers to a manufacturing system for the exclusive uses, which is mainly used to deal with standardized, fixed-process and continuous logistics. Operators and tools perform the same operation on each batch of production tasks for fixed products. Flow shop is generally a mass production workshop or a workshop with continuous production layout based on standardized production process. There is a typical case of flow shop system—the industry with standardized process, such as assembly, spraying, chemical industry etc.

(3) Production line. Production line refers to the production system formed by the fixed equipment and specialist, which is organized by the goal that aims at producing fixed products or parts. There are many kinds of the production line: it can be divided into product line and parts line according to production scope; it can be divided into flow production line and non-flow production line according to takt time; it can be divided into automatic production line, semi-automatic production line and non-automatic production line according to the degree of automation. The production line has more remarkable solidification characteristics, higher degree of specialization and clearer production characteristics compared with the flow shop.

1.3 Evolution History of the Production System

A production system has undergone a long process of evolution from the era of manufacture industry before the first industrial revolution to the booming the industry 4.0, focusing on the intelligent production.

(1) Before the first industrial revolution, i.e. the era of the manufacture industry. As is known to all, the 16th to 18th centuries witnessed the disintegration of feudal society and the beginning of the transition to capitalism in Western Europe. During that period, an increasingly developed division of labor begins to take shape; the production tools are continuously improved, and production becomes increasingly specialized through a long-term development of the manufacture. At the same time, a large number of skilled workers were trained. This period came into being at the time when the development of production tools and division of labor reached a certain level, which created necessary material and technology conditions for the transition from the manufacture industry to the modern mechanical industry. There are two main forms of a production system in the era of the manufacture industry:

① Decentralized workshops: businessmen only supply raw material to those handicraftsmen who own the small-scale plants for processing, and the production activities are separated. In this case, handicraftsmen are still economically independent.

② Centralized workshops: businessmen have further strengthened their control over handicraftsmen, who supply not only raw material but also tools. This makes the handicraftsmen subordinate to the businessmen completely and become an employee with nothing left. Businessmen gather these workers in a large workshop and work together to carry out production activities.

(2) The industry 1.0, i.e. the era of the mechanical manufacturing. The mechanization of factories has greatly liberated manual labor through hydraulic and steam engines from the 1760s to the mid-19th century with the appearance and application of steam engine as the symbol. The industrial revolution has made the self-employed peasant class who is dependent on backward modes of production disappear, therefore the industrial bourgeoisie and the industrial proletariat begin to form and strengthen in terms of social relations. In the era of the mechanical manufacturing, the form of production system has been transformed into factory system; its main characteristics are as follows:

① Mechanical power has replaced manual labor, and the production efficiency has been greatly improved, using the steam engines as main production power.

② Large-scale production has been formed; specialization of production and sales has been carried out and the market scope has expanded rapidly.

③ The organization structure of functionalization has emerged and the relatively complete management system has been developed, which is divided into workshops, sections and teams according to products or processes.

④ The economic society has been transformed from a society which is based on agriculture and handicraft industry to a new one whose economic development is driven by industry and mechanical manufacturing.

(3) The industry 2.0, i.e. the era of electrification and automation. Based on the division of labor, large-scale production of power-driven products, to a certain extent, has realized the automation of production, which lasted from the 1870s to the early 20th century with the widespread application of electric power as the symbol, replacing steam engine with electric-powered machine. From then on, the production of parts and assembly of products are carried out separately, and the era of large-scale production begins. Because of the electricity, there comes an era when the production activities are supported and controlled by relay and electrical automation. Automation has been achieved to some degree and a new mode of mass production with high efficiency has been created. Thus, the realization of the industry 2.0 has greatly freed the manual labor in production.

The famous Ford production line occurred in this stage. In this production system, a repetitive process is divided into several sub-processes and each sub-process can operate in parallel with other sub-processes. Thus, it divides the production process into several links, which makes the division of labor among workers more meticulous and greatly improves the quality and output of the products. It greatly promotes the standardization of the production process and products. Therefore, the appearance of Ford production line has largely reduced the cost and made the automobile industry rapidly become a pillar industry in the United States.

(4) The industry 3.0, i.e. the era of electronic information. The electronic information technology is widely used to further improve the automatic control of manufacturing process and to improve production efficiency, yield rate, division of labor and cooperation and the service life of equipment unprecedentedly on the basis of upgrading the industry 2.0. The industry 3.0 began in the 1970s and has continued today. Since then, human operation is gradually replaced by machines, which can take over not only a considerable proportion of the physical work but also some mental work.

TOYOTA production system (TPS) appears during the industry 3.0. The characteristics of the production system have gradually changed from large-scale production to lean production. TPS is a general manufacturing method adopted by TOYOTA with basic idea to "completely eliminate waste" and to pursue the rationality of manufacturing and the quality-oriented cost savings through the integration of production. The core of lean production, i.e. the basic idea of production planning and control and inventory management, also plays an important role in enriching and developing modern production management theory.

(5) The industry 4.0, i.e. the era of intellectualization, is one of the ten future projects proposed by the German government in *German 2020 High-tech Strategy*. The project is expected to improve the intelligent manufacturing and build smart factories with

adaptability, resource efficiency and genetic engineering. The industry 4.0 is still in the period of concept description and technology tackling given the development of intelligent technology is still in its infancy.

1.4 Necessity and Objectives of Modeling and Simulation of Production System

It is particularly important to optimize production system to improve efficiency with the increasing complexity of production system. Modeling and simulation of production system is the means to optimize the system. A seemingly simple production system, differs greatly because of the optimization, for instance, a small-scale parallel machine system.

The parallel machine problem can be portrayed as follows: there are n tasks that can be processed at 0 (time), and m machines that can be used to process these tasks. Generally, the number of tasks n is larger than the number of machines m. The scheduling objective is to minimize the total processing time.

Assuming that there are work pieces A1, A2, A3, A4 and two same equipments M1, M2 which are available to be processed. For the parallel machine problem, work pieces can be allocated to any machine for processing. The processing time (unit: min) of the four work pieces is 4, 8, 6 and 10 respectively. Even though assume that two work pieces must be allocated to each machine, three available configurations with different completion time can be proposed:

$$M1(A1,A2), M2(A3,A4)$$
$$M1(A1,A3), M2(A2,A4)$$
$$M1(A1,A4), M2(A2,A3)$$

The Gantt charts are shown in Fig. 1-1. According to the Gantt charts, the total processing time (unit: min) of the three configurations above is 16, 18 and 14 respectively. Therefore, the optimal configuration plan is M1 (A1, A4), M2 (A2, A3). There will be more configuration schemes if there is no such assumption. Among them, the worst one is that four work pieces are allocated on one single machine, and the completion time is 28 min. Thus, it can be found that the efficiency varies from each other when the configuration of work pieces is different in the parallel machine problem. And in this case, the efficiency between the optimal and the worst is 100%.

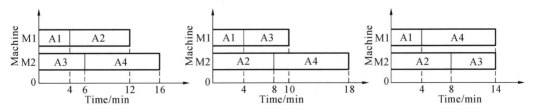

Fig. 1-1 Gantt Charts of the Parallel Machine Problem Case

Another case is the production line balancing problem. There is a factory producing one kind of parts, which involves four procedures in the process that is recorded as P1, P2, P3, P4. It is known that the processing time (unit: min) of the four procedures is 5, 3, 2, 1 respectively and the bottleneck is P1. If only one workstation is set in each procedure of the production line, the takt time of this production line is 5 min. The utilization rate of equipment (the utilization rate of equipment = (actual operating time / waiting time) × 100%) is 47% and the balance rate of the production line is 55%. If the number of the workstations which are set in each procedure on the production line can be adjusted properly, such as three workstations in process P1, two workstations in process P2, two workstations in process P3 and one workstation in process P4, the takt time of this production line is 1.67 min; the utilization rate of equipment is 77.4% and the balance rate of the production line is 82.3%. Therefore, it can be concluded that for production line balancing problem, the efficiency of the production line varies greatly from each other when the allocation of the workstations is different.

It is clearly shown in those two simple cases above that even for a simple production system with a few elements, the efficiency before the optimization is quite different from the after. With the development of technology and the upgrading of industrialization, production system is becoming more and more complex, which is manifested as follows: the number of elements in a production system is increasing substantially; the correlation between elements enhances remarkably and the coupling relation between elements becomes more complex, which makes production system a complex system with strong coupling of elements. An inefficient process and high costs will easily occur if the system is not optimized.

The method and objective of modeling and simulation of a production system: production system is modeled based on mathematical theory, which is optimized by adopting the advanced optimization methods; the scheme of production system is process-simulated and result-validated by simulation so as to provide reference for validating or improving the scheme, and ultimately to achieve the goal of optimizing production system and improving its operation efficiency.

Chapter 2 The Basis of System Modeling

2.1 The Concept of "System"

1. The Definition of "System"

The word "system" in English originates from the ancient Greek "systεma", which means the whole part of the composition. Ludwig Von Bertalanffy, the founder of general systems theory, defines the system as a complex of interconnected and interacting elements. This definition emphasizes the interaction among elements and the integration of elements into the system. Chinese scientist Xuesen Qian believes that the system is an organic whole with specific functions combined by several components of interaction and interdependence, and this organic whole is a component of the larger system to which it belongs. It can be said that a collection of interrelated individuals is called a system.

This can be mathematically described in terms of the definition of a system: if the object set S meets the following two requirements:

① S contains at least two different elements;

② The elements in S are related to each other in a certain way;

then S is called a system, and the elements of S are part of the system.

A system has the following three features:

(1) Diversity, system is the unity of diversity and the unity of differences;

(2) Relevance, there are no isolated elements or components in a system, and all elements or components depend on each other, interact and restrict each other;

(3) Integrity, system is a composite unity of all elements.

An organic whole that meets the above mathematical descriptions and has the above three features can be modeled and analyzed as a system.

2. The Classification of "System"

According to the formation and operation characteristics, a system can be divided into the following three categories.

(1) Natural system: individuals within a system exist or evolve according to natural laws, producing or forming a group of natural phenomena and characteristics. The typical characteristic of a natural system is self-organizing, which means this system is highly

autonomous and coordinated through self-organizing methods. The ecological balance system, living body system, celestial system, material microstructure system, etc., are typical natural systems. The human brain belongs to the natural system and is the most complex system we have known so far.

(2) Artificial system: individuals within the system operate in accordance with artificial, pre-programmed rules or planned directions to achieve or obtain functions, performance, and results that cannot be achieved by individual entities within the system. The typical feature of a human system is design, which means a system is generated on a design basis and coordinated according to the design rules. For instance, product component system, automatic control system, computer system, hydraulic system, education system, medical system, etc., are typical artificial systems.

(3) Composite system: composite system is a combination of natural system and artificial system, which has certain design features and significant self-organizing features, such as social system, transportation system, production system, economic system, etc. These systems have been artificially designed in the process of formation and operation. However, due to the complex correlation features of the elements contained in the system, a system is not completely under the control of human design, but has self-organizing features in the process of operation and evolution, which forms a composite system.

3. The Comprehension of the Concept of "System"

The concept of a system can be comprehended in three ways.

(1) A system is made up of several elements. These elements may be individuals, components, parts, or they may be a system in themselves. Operators, controllers, memories, input and output devices form a hardware system of a computer, which in turn is a subsystem of a computer system.

(2) A system has a certain structure. A system is a collection of its constituent elements that are related to each other and are restricted to each other. The inherently stable form of connection, organizational order and out-of-control relationship between the various elements within a system is the structure of the system. For instance, a clock is assembled by gears, springs, hands and other components in a certain way, but a pile of gears, clockwork, and hands randomly placed together cannot constitute a timepiece; a human body is made up of various organs, but the organs simply put together cannot be made into a person with capacity.

(3) A system has certain functions, or a system must have a certain purpose. The function of a system refers to the nature, capabilities, and functions that a system relates to and interacts with the external environment. For instance, the function of an information system is to collect, transfer, store, process, maintain and utilize information, assist decision makers in making decisions, and help enterprise achieve their goals.

2.2 General Method for System Modeling

System modeling is to abstract a simulation and optimization model that can be solved by mathematical or software methods for a specific system in the real world according to the problem-solving target and constraints. The process of using the model to describe the causal relationship or interrelationship of the system belongs to the modeling. Because the relationship of description is different, the means and methods for realizing this process are also diverse. It can be modeled in accordance with the mechanism of the movement of the system itself, according to the mechanism of the stuff, or by the processing of the experimental or statistical data of the system according to the existing knowledge and experience of the system.

1. The Application of System Modeling

System modeling is mainly used in three aspects.

(1) Analyze and design an actual system. For instance, when the engineering community analyzes and designs a new system, it usually performs mathematical simulation and physical simulation experiments, and finally goes to the site for physical experiments. When using mathematical simulation to analyze and design an actual system, there must be a model that describes the characteristics of the system. For many complex industrial control processes, modeling is often the most critical and difficult task.

(2) Forecast or predict future trends in certain states of an actual system. For instance, a mathematical model of meteorological changes is established based on the past measurement data for forecasting future weather.

(3) Optimal control of the system. Only by establishing a mathematical model that can characterize the system first can we design with the mathematical model based on the principle of maximum value, dynamic programming, feedback, decoupling, pole placement, self-organization, adaptive and intelligent control. Thus, a variety of controllers or control laws can achieve system optimization.

For the same actual system, people can build different models for different application and purposes. Since it is neither possible nor necessary to enumerate all details of the actual system, any model created is simply a simplification of the actual system prototype. If some essential features of the system prototype can be preserved in the simplified model, then the model can be considered similar to the system prototype and can be used to describe the original system. Therefore, in actual modeling, an appropriate compromise must be made between the simplification of the model and the accuracy of the analytical results.

2. The Process of System Modeling

The general process of system modeling is shown in Fig. 2-1.

(1) Model preparation. First, we must understand the actual background of the

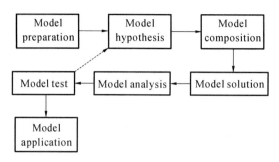

Fig. 2-1 General Process of System Modeling

problem, clarify the requirements of the topic, and then collect all necessary information.

(2) Model hypothesis. On the basis of clarifying the purpose of modeling and mastering the necessary information, through the analysis and calculation of the data, find out the leading factors, and propose some assumptions that conform to the objective reality after necessary refinement and simplification so that the main features of the problem would be highlighted and the secondary aspects of the problem can be negligible. In general, a practical problem is difficult to convert into a mathematical problem without a simplified assumption. If the assumption is unreasonable or too simple, it would lead to the failure of the model; if the assumption is too detailed, the modeling complexity would be greatly increased, making modeling and solving work difficult. Therefore, the model hypothesis is a compromise between simplification and feasibility. The goal is to simplify the model and solve it as efficient as possible under the premise of correctness.

(3) Model composition. According to the assumptions made and the connections among stuff, use appropriate mathematical tools to describe the relationship between variables and establish the corresponding mathematical structure, and turn the problem into a mathematical problem.

(4) Model solution. Use known mathematical methods to solve the mathematical problem obtained in the previous step, and in this step simplifications or assumptions are often made. When it is difficult to get the analysis, the numerical solution can be gained by means of an iterative search by a computer.

(5) Model analysis. When making mathematical analysis of model solutions, sometimes it needs to be on the basis of the nature of the problem to analyze the dependency or stability between variables; sometimes to obtain mathematical predictions based on the results, and sometimes to give the most mathematical excellent decision-making or control, in either case, often requires error analysis, model stability or sensitivity analysis of the data.

(6) Model test. Analyze the actual meaning of the results and compare it with the actual situation to estimate if it is realistic. If the results are not ideal, they should be modified, supplemented, or re-modeled. Some models require several iterations to be refined.

(7) Model application. The established model must be applied in practice to be verified

and produce benefits. It should be continuously improved from the application. The way of application depends on the nature of the problem and the purpose of modeling.

3. The Steps of System Modeling

The general steps of system modeling are as follows.

1) Abstract design variable

Through research, we have a comprehensive and in-depth understanding of the system, then abstract and separate the problem, separate the intricate problems from the research objects which can reflect the characteristics of the problem, and describe the system in detail.

2) Construct the objective function

The target represents the question to be answered by the simulation and a description of the system plan, specifying the scope and environment of the system. In general, the simulation goals are different, and the models created and the data collected are different. An objective function is a functional relationship between a target of interest (a variable) and related factors (some variables).

3) Construct constraints

From a purely mathematical point of view, there is an unconstrained problem. But in engineering practice, almost any model has limitations. These limitations are called constraints in the modeling process. Only modeling solutions that satisfy all constraints can be used as models for solving.

4) Design solution

Establishing a complete mathematical model is only the first step in system modeling. More importantly, a method is used to solve the mathematical model, so that an optimal solution that meets the constraints is obtained. The solution method has traditional optimization method and bionic method. According to the characteristics of the problem, different methods can be selected to solve the model.

2.3 NPC Problem and NP-Hard Problem

2.3.1 The Concept of System Complexity and Its Basic Characteristics

Complex system is a network with many flat-level elements. These components use a set of rules to deal with complex external information in an orderly manner. Decisions can be made better by learning and remembering to constantly improve the system to deal with more complex information. Complex systems have a certain scale and are constantly evolving systems, such as biological brains, cells, social aggregates, and ecosystems. These subsystems are interconnected, and interact with one another, affecting the final decision.

Complex system is generally considered to have the following characteristics.

1) Nonlinearity

Nonlinearity indicates that the whole system is not a simple component, but the components are organically combined, that is, the whole system is much larger than the sum of the components. The sum of each subsystem and some subsystems does not represent the system as a whole but a part of the system.

This shows that nonlinearity is the prerequisite for complex system and is a necessary condition.

2) Dynamic

Dynamic indicates that the system is alive with continuous evolution, far from equilibrium. With the change of time, under the common influence of its own factors and the external environment, it constantly adjusts itself to adapt to changes in the environment, and develops and improves in a more orderly manner through the role of self-organization.

3) Openness

Openness indicates that the system is open, and is interrelated and interactive with the external environment. It constantly exchanges information and materials with the outside world and gives timely feedback. Only under the premise of such exchange can the system achieve substantial development.

4) Accumulation effect (initial sensitivity)

The accumulation effect indicates that the decision in the early stage of the system would have a huge impact on the development of the entire system, that is, the "butterfly effect" that people often say. When the system changes slightly in the initial state, then with time elapse, the system continues to evolve. And this small change will slowly accumulate and gradually enlarge. Eventually it will have a huge impact on the decision making of the system. Because of this sensitivity, it is impossible to make accurate predictions of the entire system.

5) Fractal (structural self-similarity)

Each component of the system is related to the whole system in a certain degree, and there will be self-similarity among the components of the system. This provides a way for us to study the whole system and its components.

6) Self-organization

Self-organization means that each subsystem or each component works under its own conditions and maintains a certain relation with each other. All behaviors are spontaneously organized, which shows that when a system is self-organizing, the speed at which the system evolves and adapts to the new environment is faster.

To sum up, there are many interrelated subsystems in a complex system, with a dynamic system that can independently complete relevant functions. Thus, it is an open, self-organized and self-similar nonlinear system.

Just like when the body is injured, the body's self-healing is not random, but various organs, cells in accordance with the relevant steps strictly implement as follows: physical injury → platelets quickly reach the wound to stop bleeding and coagulate → the immune system in human body exerts humoral immunity and cellular immune function to resist the invasion of external bacterial viruses → self-repairing of related cellular tissues → wound healing. Even though the current world of technology has grown considerably, people still can't create machines that are as smart as human brain. Because there are hundreds of billions of brain cells in human brain, and each brain cell plays the equivalent of an advanced computer in the world, and the interconnection between the cells leads to the complexity with the growth of geometric multiplier, and the problems to be faced are unimaginable. So, we are surrounded by complex systems.

2.3.2 P、NP、NPC、NP-Hard Problems

1. Prerequisite Knowledge

1) Time complexity

Time complexity qualitatively describes the time required for an algorithm operation. It shows that as the scale of the problem increases, the time to solve the problem is much longer due to the explosion of solution space. It is the time required to measure the optimal solution of an algorithm. Time complexity is often expressed in O symbols. The time complexity of an algorithm can generally be divided into two levels:

(1) Polynomial complexity, such as $O(1)$, $O(n\log_2 n)$, etc;

(2) Non-polynomial level, such as $O(n!)$, $O(a^n)$, etc. Computers often can't calculate this kind of time complexity.

Such as bubble sort, it is a relatively simple sorting method. The rule is to make sorting sequence traversal several times. For each time, it will be in accordance with front to back to judge the adjacent two numbers, if the previous number is greater than the later, then exchange their positions. This would result that the largest number in the series after the first traversal will be at the end of the series, the second largest number will be placed in the penultimate position after the second traversal. By analogy, it can be known that after the last traversal, the smallest number will be ranked in the first of the series. In this way, the entire series will be arranged in order from small to large.

If there are N numbers in the sequence, the time complexity of one traversing is $O(N)$. Because it is traversed $(N-1)!$ times, the time complexity of the bubble algorithm is $O(n^2)$.

2) Reducibility

If a rule of variation can be found, the input of any problem A can be transformed into the input of problem B accordingly with this rule, so that the output of the two problems will be the same. Then it can be said that the problem A can be reduced to the problem B. To put it simply, the meaning of the problem A can be reduced to the problem B is the problem B can be solved by solving the problem A. It can also be said that the problem A is a special case of the problem B. It also tells us an intuitive message: the problem B's time complexity is larger than or equal to the problem A's time complexity.

Reducibility is transitive. If the problem A can be reduced to the problem B and the problem B can be reduced to the problem C, then it can be said that the problem A can also be reduced to the problem C.

2. The Concept and Understanding of P, NP, NPC and NP-Hard Problems

1) The P problem

The P (polynomial) problem is a problem that is very fast to calculate.

If an algorithm can be found in polynomial time complexity to solve a problem, then the problem is P problem. That is, the time complexity of the algorithm is polynomial.

For instance, in order to find the minimum value from N numbers, the adjacent two numbers can be compared in turn. First, the size of the first number and the second number can be compared, and the smaller number and the third number can be compared. By analogy, only $(N-1)$ times of comparison is needed to obtain the final answer. Or we can sort N numbers from the smallest to the largest, which we can do by bubble sort, and the starting order of N numbers is going to be sorted from the smallest to the largest with good luck; in this way we don't have to do anything to get the result. The worst case of bubble sort is that the initial order of N numbers is from the largest to the smallest, and then we can use other methods to solve it.

This kind of problem can be solved by exhaustive method.

2) The NP problem

The NP (non-deterministic polynomial) problem refers to the non-deterministic problem that the polynomial algorithm can solve, that is, a solution of the problem can be guessed in the polynomial time complexity.

For instance, if there is a path whose length is less than 50 unit length between any two points in the chart, given that the problem has a solution. If you take a random path and the total length of the path is less than 50 unit length, then you can guess a feasible solution, which means you can solve the problem in polynomial time complexity if you are lucky enough.

There is also the problem of decomposing a relatively large number into the product of two numbers. Generally, there is no way to solve such a problem very quickly. But if we give two numbers arbitrarily, we can verify whether the product of the two numbers is equal to that known number. Take an example, it's hard to find two numbers whose product is equal to 94743 in a short time, but if we give 99 and 957, we can verify in a very short time that the product of these two numbers is equal to 94743.

In this way, it can be inferred that all P problems are NP problems, because the P problem can be solved within the polynomial time complexity, and each solution must be verified polynomially.

The NP problem is not necessarily fast to calculate, but it can be very fast to verify the correctness of each answer.

3) The NPC problem

The NPC (non-deterministic polynomial complete) problem is a major progress on the

P problem and the NP problem. It is a subset of the NP problem and if all NP problems can be reduced in polynomial time complexity to a NP problem, then the NP problem is called NPC problem.

The two conditions that need to be met if a problem is NPC problem are as follows:

(1) This problem is a NP problem;

(2) All NP problems can be reduced to this problem.

If the above two conditions are met, one problem can be determined to be NPC problem.

The traveling salesman problem is a typical NPC problem and one of the well-known problems in mathematics. What is described is that a traveling businessman needs to visit N cities, and the selected path should meet that each city would visit only once, and finally return to the city where he started. The goal of path selection is to make the path distance minimum. Since the feasible solution of this problem is the full arrangement of all vertices, and as the number of vertices increases, there will be an explosion of solution combination, which is not acceptable to the computer. If there are 20 cities, there are 19! arrangement; if the computer can be arranged 100 million times per second, it will also cost 38.4 years.

The 0-1 knapsack problem is a combination-optimized NPC problem. It refers to the situation that each item is used only once, given N items whose weights are $W_1, W_2, \cdots, W_N$, and values are $V_1, V_2, \cdots, V_N$, and a backpack with a capacity of C. The goal is to maximize the total value of the items in the backpack without exceeding the total capacity of the backpack. The idea is to find the most valuable subset of these items in different permutations.

There is no effective polynomial algorithm for the NPC problem, which can only be solved with the time complexity of exponential or even factorial.

4) The NP-Hard problem

The NP-Hard problems, by definition, are harder to solve than all NP problems. This kind of problem only needs to meet the second condition of the NPC problem, not necessarily the first one. NP-Hard problem is more extensive than NPC problem, and not all of them are NP problems.

The NP-Hard problem is as difficult to find the polynomial time complexity algorithm as the NPC problem because it is not necessarily an NP problem. Even when the NPC problem finds a polynomial-level algorithm, the NP-Hard problem may not be able to obtain a polynomial-level algorithm. Because the NP-Hard problem relaxes the qualifications, such problems have larger time complexity and are more difficult to solve.

Take the numerical partitioning problem as an example, the description of the problem is whether a given multiple set S of positive integers can be divided into two sets S_1 and S_2 whose sum of all elements is equal. This problem is called the simplest NP-Hard problem, and it is also the NPC problem. Assuming that a set $S=\{1, 2, 1, 2, 1, 3\}$, there is one subset $S_1=\{2, 3\}$ and another subset $S_2=\{1, 2, 1, 1\}$; these two subsets completely divide the set S, and the sum of all the elements in each is equal. And the subsets $S_1=\{1,$

3,1} and $S_2=\{2,1,2\}$ can also be found to be another set of solutions to this problem.

After Chinese chess player Jie Ke lost 3-0 to AlphaGo, people realized the power of artificial intelligence. In fact, Go itself is a complicated mathematical game. The size of Go's board is 19×19. There is a total of 361 points to place the pieces. There are three possible types of suns, whites or blanks. Therefore, there are 1083 possible final moves on the whole board. But in actual chess, there is a sequence and a connection between each piece. The overall complexity is much larger than this number, so the problem of finding a winning move in the game of Go is also a NP-Hard problem.

The difference between the NPC problem and the NP-Hard problem is that verifying whether a problem is an NP-Hard problem does not require the verification of whether the problem is an NP problem, but verifying whether a problem is an NPC problem requires that the problem must first be an NP problem. Accordingly we know that the NPC problem is a subset of the NP-Hard problem.

The relationship between P, NP, NPC, and NP-Hard problems is shown in Fig. 2-2.

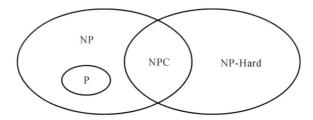

Fig. 2-2　P, NP, NPC and NP-Hard Problems' Venn Diagram of Relationship

2.4　Instance Analysis of Three Types of System Modeling Problem

1. The First Type: The Population Problem

Example 2-1　From n cloth bags containing flour, rice, grain and other substances with different densities, select part of them to be loaded into the sack with volume V, wherein the mass of the ith cloth bag is W_i and the volume is V_i.

Question: How to choose the loading can make the total mass of the loading maximum?

Solution　Find X_i (design variable). Physical significance: $X_i=0$ means the ith cloth bag is not loaded, $X_i=1$ means the ith cloth bag is loaded.

$$\max \sum_{i=1}^{n} W_i X_i$$

s. t.
$$\sum_{i=1}^{n} V_i X_i \leqslant V$$
$$X_i = 0 \text{ or } 1$$

Solve and get $X_i (i=1,2,\cdots, n)$ to obtain the optional package.

Example 2-2 Cargo planes have forward, middle and rear cabins that are used to carry four types of powder cargo, which can be packed in any shape. In order to maintain flight balance, the mass of the cargo compartment must be distributed in proportion to the allowable mass limit, as shown in Table 2-1. The total mass, volume and profit per unit of goods are shown in Table 2-2.

Table 2-1 Cargo Compartment Weight Ratio and Volume

Cabins	Forehold	Middle deck	Rear compartment
Mass limit/t	10	16	8
Volume/m³	6800	8700	5300

Table 2-2 Goods Attributes

Goods	Mass/t	Volume/(m³/t)	Profit/(yuan/t)
A1	18	480	3100
A2	15	650	3800
A3	23	580	3500
A4	12	390	2850

Question: How to design the loading scheme to maximize profit?

Solution Find x_{ij}. Physical meaning: the value of design variable x_{ij} represents the mass of ith cargo loaded into the jth compartment.

$$\max Z = 3100(x_{11}+x_{12}+x_{13}) + 3800(x_{21}+x_{22}+x_{23})$$
$$+ 3500(x_{31}+x_{32}+x_{33}) + 2850(x_{41}+x_{42}+x_{43})$$

s. t. goods' mass constraints:

$$x_{11}+x_{12}+x_{13} \leqslant 18$$
$$x_{21}+x_{22}+x_{23} \leqslant 15$$
$$x_{31}+x_{32}+x_{33} \leqslant 23$$
$$x_{41}+x_{42}+x_{43} \leqslant 12$$

cabins' mass constraints:

$$x_{11}+x_{21}+x_{31}+x_{41} \leqslant 10$$
$$x_{12}+x_{22}+x_{32}+x_{42} \leqslant 16$$
$$x_{13}+x_{23}+x_{33}+x_{43} \leqslant 8$$

volume constraint:

$$480 x_{11} + 650 x_{21} + 580 x_{31} + 390 x_{41} \leqslant 6800$$
$$480 x_{12} + 650 x_{22} + 580 x_{32} + 390 x_{42} \leqslant 8700$$
$$480 x_{13} + 650 x_{23} + 580 x_{33} + 390 x_{43} \leqslant 5300$$

balance constraints:

$$\frac{x_{11}+x_{21}+x_{31}+x_{41}}{10} = \frac{x_{12}+x_{22}+x_{32}+x_{42}}{16} = \frac{x_{13}+x_{23}+x_{33}+x_{43}}{8}$$

Physical meaning: max Z represents the maximum profit of the scheme.

2. The Second Type: Configuration Problem

Example 2-3 A workshop can get 50 blanks each day. There are A and B two types of processing equipment in the workshop. A and B can process the blanks into parts A1 and A2 respectively. With one blank as raw material, the processing time consumed by the two types of equipment and the number of parts obtained are as follows:

A: spent 12 hours processing 3 A1, each profit of 24 yuan;

B: spent 8 hours processing 4 A2, each profit of 16 yuan.

Namely

A: the profit is 6 yuan per hour and 72 yuan per blank;

B: the profit is 8 yuan per hour and 64 yuan per blank.

The total working time of all workers is 480 hours per day, and the total amount of processing of equipment A per day is limited to 100.

Question: How to make the production plan to maximize daily profit?

Solution Find x_1, x_2.

Physical meaning: use x_1 blanks to produce A1 and x_2 blanks to produce A2.

$$\max Z = 3 \times 24 \times x_1 + 4 \times 16 \times x_2$$

s. t.
$$x_1 + x_2 \leqslant 50$$
$$12 x_1 + 8 x_2 \leqslant 480$$
$$3 x_1 \leqslant 100$$
$$x_1 \geqslant 0, x_2 \geqslant 0$$

Physical meaning: max Z represents the maximum profit.

Example 2-4 There are four residential areas A, B, C and D, and three reservoirs E, F and G. The basic water consumption of the residential areas is 30, 70, 10, 10 and must be guaranteed. E, F and G have fixed water supply of 50, 60 and 50 per day. In addition to the basic water supply, a maximum of 50, 70, 20 and 40 additional water can be applied for in the four residential areas. The water consumption of four residential areas and the water supply of three reservoirs are measured in ton. Transportation cost between reservoirs and residential areas is shown in Table 2-3.

Table 2-3 Transportation Cost between Reservoirs and Residential Areas (Unit: yuan)

Reservoirs and residential areas	A	B	C	D
E	160	130	220	170
F	140	130	190	150
G	190	200	230	—

Question: How to design schemes to maximize the benefits of water supply?

Solution Since the cost of water is the same but the transportation cost is different, the problem of the maximum profit can be transformed into the one with the least transportation cost.

To solve the x_{ij}. Physical meaning: x_{ij} refers to the water supply from the ith reservoir to the jth residential area, and $i=1,2,3$ corresponds to E,G,F respectively, $j=1,2,3,4$ corresponds to A,B,C,D respectively.

$$\min Z = 160 x_{11} + 130 x_{12} + 220 x_{13} + 170 x_{14} + 140 x_{21} + 130 x_{22} + 190 x_{23} + 150 x_{24} + 190 x_{31} + 200 x_{32} + 230 x_{33}$$

s. t.
$$x_{11} + x_{12} + x_{13} + x_{14} = 50$$
$$x_{21} + x_{22} + x_{23} + x_{24} = 60$$
$$x_{31} + x_{32} + x_{33} = 50$$
$$30 \leqslant x_{11} + x_{21} + x_{31} \leqslant 80$$
$$70 \leqslant x_{12} + x_{22} + x_{32} \leqslant 140$$
$$10 \leqslant x_{13} + x_{23} + x_{33} \leqslant 30$$
$$10 \leqslant x_{14} + x_{24} \leqslant 50$$

Example 2-5 A certain automobile factory produces small, medium and large types of automobiles. The manufacturing resource consumption of various types of automobiles and the monthly supply of manufacturing resources are shown in Table 2-4. Try to make the monthly production plan to maximize the profit.

Table 2-4 Automobile Manufacturing Resources Case

Each automobile	Small	Middle	Large	Month supply
Steel/t	1.5	3	5	600
Manufacturing time/min	280	250	400	60000
Profit/ten thousand yuan	2	3	4	—

Solution Find x_1, x_2, x_3. Physical meaning: the production plans of large, medium and small automobiles are x_1, x_2 and x_3 respectively.

$$\max Z = 2 x_1 + 3 x_2 + 4 x_3$$

s. t.
$$1.5 x_1 + 3 x_2 + 5 x_3 \leqslant 600$$
$$280 x_1 + 250 x_2 + 400 x_3 \leqslant 60000$$
$$x_1, x_2, x_3 \geqslant 0$$

3. The Third Type: The Cutting Problem

Example 2-6 The raw steel pipes of a steel pipe factory are all 19 m, and a customer needs 50 pieces of 4 m, 20 pieces of 6 m and 15 pieces of 8 m.

Question: How to cut down the material to save the most?

Solution First, list all cutting modes as shown in Table 2-5.

Table 2-5 All Cutting Modes

Pipes	4 m	6 m	8 m	Oddments/m
1	4	0	0	3
2	3	1	0	1
3	2	0	1	3
4	1	2	0	3
5	1	1	1	1
6	0	3	0	1
7	0	0	2	3

Design variable x_i: number of pipes cut in mode i.

Decision objectives can be determined according to the following two objectives.

① Decision goal: minimum margin.

$$\min Z_1 = 3x_1 + x_2 + 3x_3 + 3x_4 + x_5 + x_6 + 3x_7$$

s. t.
$$4x_1 + 3x_2 + 2x_3 + x_4 + x_5 \geqslant 50$$
$$x_2 + 2x_4 + x_5 + 3x_6 \geqslant 20$$
$$x_3 + x_5 + 2x_7 \geqslant 15$$

② Decision goal: use the least number of raw steel pipes.

$$\min Z_2 = x_1 + x_2 + x_3 + x_4 + x_5 + x_6 + x_7$$

s. t.
$$4x_1 + 3x_2 + 2x_3 + x_4 + x_5 \geqslant 50$$
$$x_2 + 2x_4 + x_5 + 3x_6 \geqslant 20$$
$$x_3 + x_5 + 2x_7 \geqslant 15$$

Chapter 3　Optimization Model of Production System

3.1　Introduction of Production System Modeling

3.1.1　Development of Production System Modeling

There are few elements in production system and the relation between them is simple in the early stage because the early production mode is mainly manual workshop, which hasn't risen to the level of a system yet. The first practical steam engine came into the world in 1776, which marked the advent of the industrial era. The emergence of flexible manufacturing system (FMS) in the 1970s greatly increased the complexity of production system, and the necessity of modeling and optimizing of production system was highlighted.

In 1976, the FANUC Corporation of Japan exhibited a flexible manufacturing unit (FMC) consisting of machining centers and robots, which provided an important equipment form for the development of FMS. FMS has made great progress in both technology and quantity over time. In practical stage, FMS is mainly composed of 3～5 equipments, but there are also large-scale systems. In 1982, FANUC built an automated processing workshop, which consisted of 60 flexible manufacturing units (including 50 robots) and a three-dimensional warehouse. There were also two AGVs to transfer blanks and work pieces. In addition, there was an unmanned assembling workshop, which can run continuously for 24 hours. The automated and unmanned workshop is an important step towards the realization of the automated plants with computer integration. At the same time, there are several economical FMSs which only have the basic characteristics of FMS with the low degree of automation, which makes the design ideas and technical achievements of FMS popularized and applied. Manufacturing systems become more flexible and uncertain because of the emergence and development of FMS. Building models of manufacturing systems to predict and optimize becomes increasingly important. It can be concluded that FMS can promote the emergence and development of the production system modeling technology.

The development of modeling technology of production system and the development of mathematical science complement each other. The queuing theory developed gradually in the 1950s. It was used sporadically to describe some problems of manufacturing system in the 1960s, and it was used widely to analyze FMS in the 1970s and 1980s. Since the late 1970s, mathematical programming has been used in manufacturing system modeling. Integer programming is used to solve the task assignment problem in FMS, and dynamic programming is used to solve the uncertainty problem.

Petri's Net Theory was put forward by Petri in the early 1960s. It is suitable for analyzing asynchronous concurrent system (ACS). It was used in computer system analysis in the 1970s and manufacturing system modeling in the early 1980s, also for FMS.

People have tried to build computer integrated manufacture system (CIMS) since the 1980s. Generally, CIMS can be used to model the main links of manufacturing activities, such as design, technology, program of production, processing, assembly, sales, etc. It includes not only logistics automation, but also information automation, therefore its modeling complexity can be pictured.

Production system becomes more and more complex with the development of science and technology, and gradually becomes a complex engineering system including manufacturing theory, manufacturing technology, manufacturing process, manufacturing resource and organizational system. Tons of fruitful work on the modeling of such complex systems has been done by engineers and researchers, such as production system structure description model, operation and management model, analysis model, design and implementation model, production planning and scheduling model, etc. New mathematical methods are also used to model and solve problems, such as genetic algorithm, ant colony algorithm, particle swarm optimization and other heuristic algorithms or meta-heuristic algorithms.

Production system modeling is still a developing domain. With the increasing complexity of production system, the method of production system modeling is also improving constantly.

3.1.2 Basic Concepts

There are some concepts involved when evaluating the optimization degree of production system.

Due date: the time when the work piece should be delivered.

Idle time: the time when the equipment is started but the tasks are not in progress.

Completion time: the time when the last process is completed.

Release time or arrival time: the time when the work piece can start processing.

Processing time: the time when the work piece is in the state of processing.

Waiting time: the time difference between the end of the process $k-1$ and the start of the process k.

Flow time: equals to the difference between the completion time and arrival time or the sum of processing time and waiting time numerically.

Tardiness: Tardiness=max {0, completion time−due date}.

Earliness: Earliness=max {0, due date−completion time}.

3.2 The Model of Single Machine Scheduling

Single machine scheduling problem can be described as: in order to make some indexes optimal, n tasks $\{J_1, J_2, \cdots, J_n\}$ are sorted reasonably and allocated to one machine for processing under some certain constraints. Design variable is the sequencing scheme. The constraints are as follows:

① The constraint of due date: each task has its due date;

② The constraint of equipment exclusiveness: only one task can be in progress on one machine at a moment;

③ The constraint of processing continuity: one task should only be completed continuously at one time, and cannot be cut apart into many time slots for processing.

Constraints can be divided into hard constraints and soft constraints. Hard constraints refer to constraints that must be satisfied, such as the constraint of equipment exclusiveness, the constraint of processing continuity, etc. Solutions that do not satisfy hard constraints are infeasible. Soft constraints don't have to be satisfied strictly, but can be satisfied in various degrees, and it can affect the degree of optimization. Therefore, soft constraints are often described as optimization targets. If the due date can be flexibly satisfied by the means of markets instead of being required to be rigidly satisfied, the constraint of due date can be regarded as soft constraint.

The objectives of optimization include the shortest completion time, the lowest tardiness cost, the lowest total cost and so on. There is no need to complete tasks as soon as possible because of the temporary inventory costs. In many cases, tasks are "just" completed on the due date, and the total cost is the lowest. The modeling method of single machine scheduling optimization model will be introduced by the following case.

There are 5 tasks at the ready at 0:00. Among them, the processing time of the ith task is t_i, and the due date is d_i. Find the optimal processing order that can minimize the total earliness time of all tasks.

Two-dimensional matrix can be used to express the ranking. If the ranking of 5 tasks is (4, 2, 3, 5, 1), the corresponding two-dimensional matrix S is

$$S = \begin{bmatrix} 0 & 0 & 0 & 1 & 0 \\ 0 & 1 & 0 & 0 & 0 \\ 0 & 0 & 1 & 0 & 0 \\ 0 & 0 & 0 & 0 & 1 \\ 1 & 0 & 0 & 0 & 0 \end{bmatrix}$$

where $s_{14}=1$ denotes that task numbered 4 ranks first, etc.

Design variable: find s_{ij}, $s_{ij}=1$ denotes that task j ranks i, or else, $s_{ij}=0$.

Objectives of optimization:

$$\min \sum_{k=1}^{5} \left(\sum_{j=1}^{5} s_{kj}\, d_j - \sum_{i=1}^{k} \sum_{j=1}^{5} s_{ij}\, t_j \right)$$

Constraints:

$$\sum_{i=1}^{k} \sum_{j=1}^{5} s_{ij}\, t_j \leqslant \sum_{j=1}^{5} s_{kj}\, d_j$$

$k = 1, 2, \cdots, 5; s_{ij} = 0 \text{ or } 1; i = 1, 2, \cdots, 5; j = 1, 2, \cdots, 5$

In addition, if the tardiness can be compensated by negotiating price, the due date becomes a soft constraint, and the objective function can be constructed to minimize total cost.

3.3 The Model of Parallel Machine Scheduling

Parallel machine scheduling problem can be described as: assuming there are n independent tasks which are allocated to m same machines for processing. The processing time of task i is T_i, each task can be done on every single machine, and each task should be completed continuously at one time. Find the optimal distributing and sequencing scheme to reach the highest efficiency.

1) No constraint of due date

The problem is simple without the constraint of due date. Generally, the objective of optimization is to minimize the completion time. Tasks can be sorted by processing time from long to short, and then allocated to m machines by means of sequential turn-back. For instance, if $m=3$, $n=8$, the processing time(unit: min) of the 8 tasks is 15,7,12,3,9,10,16,9 respectively, then the order is as follows:

S7,S1,S3,S6,S5,S8,S2,S4

So, distribution and order on three machines are as follows:

M1: S7, S8, S2; machine completion time: 32 min

M2: S1, S5, S4; machine completion time: 27 min

M3: S3, S6; machine completion time: 22 min

The corresponding completion time of the task is 32 min.

2) Constraint of due date

Add the constraint of due date based on the common description of parallel machine scheduling problem: the due date of task i is D_i, and there are m machines and n tasks, design variable is

$$x_{ij},\ i = 1, 2, \cdots, m;\ j = 1, 2, \cdots, n$$

Meaning: the value of x_{ij} is the number of task j which is allocated to machine i. For instance, $x_{23} = 6$ means the third task on the second machine is numbered 6.

Objective function:

$$\min \max \left(\sum_{j=1}^{n} S x_{1j}, \sum_{j=1}^{n} S x_{2j}, \cdots, \sum_{j=1}^{n} S x_{mj} \right)$$

Constraint: $\sum_{j=1}^{n} Sx_{ij} \leqslant Dx_{ij}, i = 1, 2, \cdots, m$

The objective function above is a maximum and minimum problem, i. e. , minimizing the maximum completion time of all machines.

3.4 The Model of Independent Job System Scheduling

The similarity of single machine scheduling problem and parallel machine scheduling problem is that one task can be processed continuously on one machine at one time. If one task contains many processes involving different kinds of equipment, it turns into a job shop scheduling problem. If the procedure of different tasks is the same and the processing results are similar in the system, which forms a small pipeline, then the system is an independent job system. Johnson's model is a typical model of independent job system scheduling.

In the 1950s, the complexity of manufacturing system has greatly increased with the development of industrialization, and the optimization of manufacturing system has gradually been paid attention to. Johnson Selmer Martin, Ph. D. of the University of Illinois at Urbana-Champaign in the United States, made an in-depth study of mathematical programming in his doctoral thesis. And Johnson's algorithm was put forward in the paper *On the representations of an integer as the sum of products of integers*, which was published in *Transactions of the American Mathematical Society*, an academic journal. This paper is the first academic paper on job scheduling, which has a far-reaching impact on the later research.

Johnson's algorithm proposes several practical scheduling rules for the scheduling problem with n similar tasks on a pipeline consisting of two machines, M1 and M2. Taking Fig. 3-1 as an example, the basic idea and steps of Johnson's algorithm are as follows.

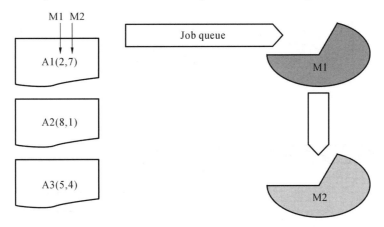

Fig. 3-1 A Case of Johnson's Algorithm

A system consisting of 3 jobs and 2 machines is shown in Fig. 3-1. Each job is processed by M1 and M2 successively. The processing time of the 3 jobs is shown in Fig. 3-1. How to arrange them to make the system achieve the highest efficiency? This seemingly simple problem contains 6 different sorting schemes which correspond to different completion time. Three schemes and their Gantt charts are respectively shown in Fig. 3-2, and the completion time of the other three schemes is shown in Fig. 3-3. It's obvious that the longest completion time is 24 min and the completing time of the optimal solution—the second scheme—is 16 min among all 6 schemes. It shows the necessity of optimization.

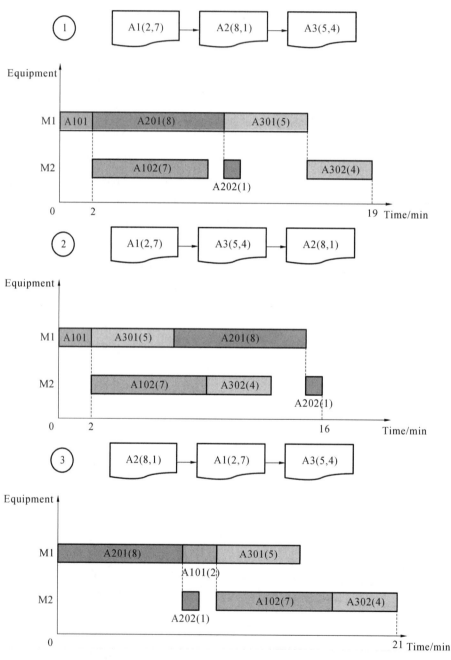

Fig. 3-2 Three Schemes and Corresponding Gantt Charts

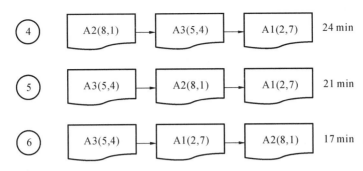

Fig. 3-3 Completion Time of the Other Three Schemes

The enumeration method can be used to find the optimal solution for only three jobs. But most of the scheduling problems are NPC problems. The number of solutions increases in geometric series as the scale increases. Under the same conditions, there are 5040 feasible solutions if the number of jobs increases to 7. The scale of the solution expands 840 times when there are only 4 more jobs. Therefore, it is difficult to solve with enumeration method when there are more jobs. After a profound study, Johnson concludes a feasible general algorithm, known as Johnson's Algorithm or Johnson's Rule.

The steps of Johnson's Algorithm are introduced by using a 7-job example. The processing time(unit:min) of two processes of all jobs is shown in Fig. 3-4.

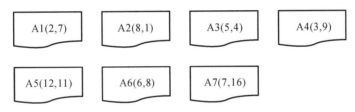

Fig. 3-4 Processing Time

Step 1: Establish a triple table. As shown in Table 3-1, the job number (No.) is taken as the first column of the table. The shorter processing time of two processes is taken as the second column of the table. And the corresponding equipment number is taken as the third column of the table.

Table 3-1 A Triple Table

Job No.	Processing time/min	Equipment No.
1	2	1
2	1	2
3	4	2
4	3	1
5	11	2
6	6	1
7	7	1

Step 2: Reordering the triple table. As shown in Table 3-2, reorder the rows of the

triple table according to the processing time from the small to the large.

Table 3-2 The Reordered Triple Table

Job No.	processing time/min	Equipment No.
2	1	2
1	2	1
4	2	1
3	4	2
6	6	1
7	7	1
5	11	2

Step 3: Fill the blanks from the two ends to the middle according to the equipment number. As shown in Fig. 3-5, when the equipment number is 1, use the job number to fill the blanks from the left to the middle, and when the equipment number is 2, use the job number to fill the blanks from the right to the middle. After that, the order obtained is the optimal solution.

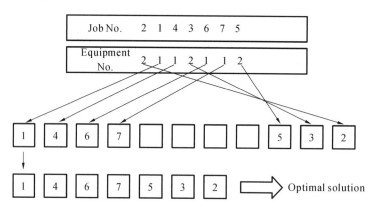

Fig. 3-5 Fill the Blanks from the Two Ends to the Middle

3.5 Job Shop Scheduling Problem

1. Basic Concepts of Job Shop Scheduling Problem

Job shop scheduling problem (JSSP) can be described as: n independent tasks are allocated to m equipments for processing. Each task may contain several processes that have a certain sequence. Each process can only be completed on the equipment with matched function. How to arrange them to make the system indexes optimal, such as the completion time, earliness or tardiness?

There is a set consisting of 4 independent tasks as shown in Fig. 3-6, and each task contains several parallel or serial processes, for instance, 106 and 107 are serial, and the parallel relations are formed between 108 and 106 and 107. There are three types of equipment in the system, A, B and C. The corresponding equipment type and processing time is on the top of the process in Fig. 3-8. For instance, process 101 can only be allocated to equipment A, and the processing time is 10 minutes. If there are 2, 3, 2 machines of A, B and C, which are numbered A1, A2, B1, B2, B3, C1, C2, respectively, then a job shop system consisting of 4 independent tasks with 33 related processes and 7 machines can be constructed. To solve this system is to distribute 33 processes to 7 machines reasonably with several constraints, and make system indexes optimal.

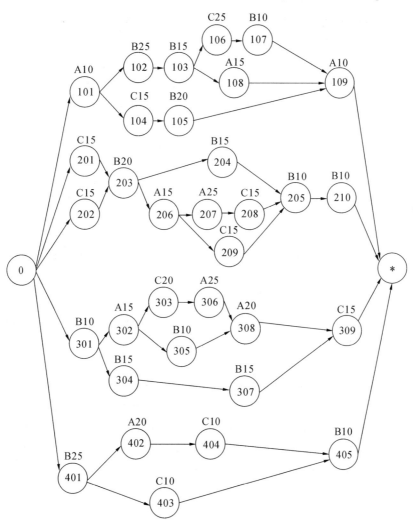

Fig. 3-6 Task Association in Job Shop System

For the job shop system, the following concepts are defined.

(1) Preorder process. There are several serial processes in a task. If a process can be initiated if and only if some definite processes are completed, these definite processes are called the preorder processes of this process. As shown in Fig. 3-6, 102 is the preorder of 103, 107 and 108 are the preorders of 109, but 106 is not the preorder of 109.

(2) Pre-process. When a series of processes are arranged to a certain equipment, the

processes will form a serial queue. In the queue order, a process that precedes a certain process is defined as the pre-process of this process.

(3) The serial constraint. A process has to be initiated after its pre-processes. This constraint is defined as the serial constraint. The solution must satisfy the serial constraint.

(4) The constraint of processing attributes. The function of a machine should match with the attributes of the processes assigned to that machine. For instance, process 201 must be assigned to a machine C for processing.

(5) The constraint of task exclusiveness. Two processes of one job can't be in progress at the same time because of the indivisibility of jobs, that is, for any task, at most one process can be in progress at one time.

(6) The constraint of equipment exclusiveness. Only one process can be in progress on one machine at one time because of the indivisibility of equipment, that is, overlap of time is not allowed during processing on one machine.

(7) Sorting mode. Referring to the sorting rules of process after the processes are assigned to a certain machine. Scheduling order and sorting mode determine the sequence of processes.

2. Relational Graph, Relational Table, Gantt Chart

The optimization model of JSSP will be introduced in detail in Chapter 4. Here are the introduction of the expression of relational graph, relational table and Gantt chart which can describe the attributes of JSSP.

Relational graph is a connection graph that expresses the attributes of job and the serial or parallel relationships between jobs. Fig. 3-6 is a typical relational graph. It can be concluded that a relational graph includes job number, attributes of job, the processing time, association of job, etc. As shown in Fig. 3-6, the process 109 needs to be completed on a machine A, which takes 10 minutes, and its preorders are 107, 108 and 105. Relational graph expresses the constraints of JSSP clearly.

Relational table is another way to express the attributes of JSSP, such as the job numbered 1, its relational table is Table 3-3. According to the relational table, the relation graph can be drawn and correspond to each other one by one.

Table 3-3 Relational Table

Job No.	Process No.	Machine	Processing time/min	Pre-process(es)
1	101	A	10	—
1	102	B	25	101
1	103	B	15	102
1	104	C	15	101
1	105	B	20	104
1	106	C	25	103

continued

Job No.	Process No.	Machine	Processing time/min	Pre-process(es)
1	107	B	10	106
1	108	A	15	103
1	109	A	10	107,108,105

Gantt chart is used to deliver scheduling schemes. Fig. 3-7 is a typical example. In a Gantt chart, the rectangular bars are used to express processes. The length of the rectangular bars means the processing time, and the two ends of the rectangular bars mean the start-stop time. It can be clearly seen from the Gantt chart that whether all constraints are satisfied, including the utilization rate of equipment, the completion time, the optimization degree of scheduling schemes, etc.

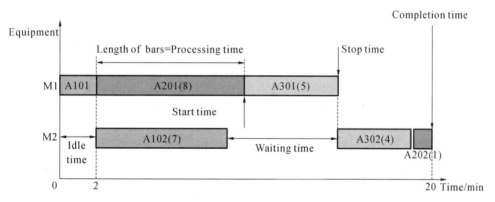

Fig. 3-7 A Gantt Chart

Job shop scheduling problem is a NP-Hard problem, which has always been a hotspot in the field of scheduling. At present, heuristic algorithm or meta-heuristic algorithm is often used to solve JSSP. However, it is mainly based on experience and practicality to find an acceptable solution in limited time. So far, there is no such method which is strictly proved by math as a standard tool to solve JSSP. In fact, any current method can't guarantee the optimal solution. The distance between the acceptable solution and the optimal solution can't even be measured. Although some research results have been obtained both at home and abroad, they mainly focus on the small-scale problems with simple correlation. The research is still in its infancy, and it has a long way to reach.

Chapter 4 The Analysis of Probability in Production System

4.1 Introduction to the Application of Probabilistic Analysis Method

Industrial engineering is a discipline that integrates design, improvement, and implementation of an integrated system of people, material, equipment, energy, and information. It combines the expertise and techniques of mathematics, physics, and social sciences, and combines the principles and methods of engineering analysis and design to validate, predict, and evaluate the system. The core goal of industrial engineering is to improve efficiency, and an important means to improve efficiency is the optimization method. Through the optimization method, efficient allocation of the resources can be realized, thereby it can improve efficiency. In the application process of the optimization method, there are some uncertain factors. These uncertain factors make the probability analysis necessary, and the probability analysis also provides a numerical basis for the application of the optimization method.

First, probability analysis optimizes cost allocation by predicting risk. Risk analysis is one of the important contents of probability analysis. It is an analysis method to judge the feasibility and risk of a project as well as the pros and cons of a project by studying the probability distribution of various uncertain factors and their influence on the economic benefit index of the project. Risk analysis is often used in the evaluation and decision making of large and medium-sized projects. For instance, by analyzing the failure probability of different parts of the product, the reasonable warranty period of different parts can be calculated. Another example is the risk analysis of each link of a large engineering project, so as to allocate different but more reasonable insurance amount for different links. These are all approaches to achieve optimal cost configuration through probability analysis.

Second, some potential problems can be found via probability analysis. For instance, if the accident rate of one equipment is much higher than that of other equipment, it is reasonable for us to question whether the equipment has design defects, then re-examine and re-identify the equipment instead of only strengthening safety training of workers. If the accident rate of a certain road section is very high, we have reasons to doubt whether there is a safety hazard in this road section. Therefore, we should conduct a detailed inspection of this road section instead of merely improving the driver's safe driving awareness. These probabilistic properties that deviate significantly from the normal probability category are called paranoid probabilities. Paranoid probability has important value for the discovery of potential problems.

Third, through probability analysis, the allocation of resources can be effectively optimized. The available number setting of supermarket checkout counters is a typical case. As the number of supermarket customers is dynamic, the number of customers is significantly different in various time periods. Therefore, if the number of available cashiers remains constant, human resources will be seriously idle in the period with fewer customers. Therefore, through the analysis of customers data in each period of a day, the expected number of customers in different time periods can be fitted, and then according to the expected number of customers and the expected length of cashier queue, the available number of cashiers in various time periods can be calculated, so as to optimize the allocation of human resources. In the design of a production system, this kind of optimal configuration based on probability analysis is also very common. For instance, config the number of maintenance personnel in accordance with the statistical data of the equipments; determine the amount of rotation for different time periods according to the statistics of the annual orders; determine the scale of expansion and reproduction according to the orders over the years.

Since probability theory itself is an important part of the mathematics discipline, it involves a lot of content and is very systematic. In this book, the mathematics discipline is not specifically discussed. This chapter introduces the basic concepts of probability theory, focusing on the probabilistic theories and methods used in the modeling and simulation of production systems, including central limit theorem, binomial distribution, normal distribution, queuing theory, etc.

4.2 Some Basic Concepts of Probability Theory with Applications

4.2.1 Probability Density Function

A random variable whose distribution function is a continuous function is called a continuous random variable. Continuous random variables are often visually described by their probability density function, which is defined as follows:

If $P\{a \leqslant x \leqslant b\} = \int_a^b f(x)\mathrm{d}x$, then $f(x)$ is the probability density of the continuous random variable X.

By definition, probability density $f(x)$ has following properties:
(1) Non-negative, $f(x) \geqslant 0, \forall x \in (-\infty, +\infty)$;
(2) Normative: $\int_{-\infty}^{+\infty} f(x)\mathrm{d}x = 1$;

(3) For any real number a, $b(a \leqslant b)$, $P\{a \leqslant x \leqslant b\} = \int_a^b f(x) \mathrm{d}x$;

(4) If $f(x)$ is continuous at x, then $F'(x) = f(x)$.

Normal distribution is one of the most common type of probability distribution, and its probability density is expressed as follows:

$$f(x) = \frac{1}{\sigma \sqrt{2\pi}} \mathrm{e}^{-\frac{(x-\mu)^2}{2\sigma^2}}, \quad -\infty < x < +\infty \tag{4-1}$$

The mathematical expectation μ of the normal distribution is equal to the positional parameter, which determines the position of the distribution; the standard deviation σ is equal to the scale parameter, which determines the magnitude of the distribution.

In manufacturing, we often adopt normal distribution to study the quality laws of some finished products, raw material and machines, etc., because the process quality fluctuation of each workstation and each production line has statistical regularity, so a production system can be estimated and evaluated by means of mathematical statistics.

Example 4-1 In this example, the number of unqualified products of the final products is taken as the quality index for a production process, adopting sampling survey method. Assuming that 8 samples with a sample size of 200 are taken for quality inspection, and the number of unqualified products in each sample is found to be 8, 3, 4, 1, 5, 0, 7, 6. It is known that the number of unqualified products allowed in the samples is 9. Try to analyze the process capability of this station.

Solution Average rate of unqualified products in each sample is

$$\bar{p} = \frac{8+3+4+1+5+0+6+7}{8 \times 200} = 0.02125 \text{(piece)}$$

The mathematical expectation of the number of nonconforming products of any sample with a capacity of 200 is

$$\mu = n\bar{p} = 200 \times 0.02125 = 4.25 \text{(piece)}$$

The process capability of the process is

$$C_p = \frac{TU - \mu}{3\sigma} = \frac{9 - 4.25}{3 \times \sqrt{4.25 \times (1 - 0.02125)}} = 0.754$$

where C_p represents the process capability of a process; TU represents the number of unqualified products allowed in the sample.

The determination standard of process capability is shown in Table 4-1.

Table 4-1 Procedure Capability Determination Standard

C_p	Process level	Conclusion
$C_p > 1.67$	special grade	Process capacity is too abundant
$1.67 \geqslant C_p > 1.33$	A-grade	Sufficient process capacity
$1.33 \geqslant C_p > 1.00$	B-grade	Process capability is qualified but not sufficient
$1.00 \geqslant C_p > 0.67$	C-grade	Insufficient process capacity
$C_p \leqslant 0.67$	D-grade	Process capacity is heavily inadequate

Therefore, the working procedure capacity of this station is insufficient.

4.2.2 Expectation and Variance

For some practical and theoretical problems, people are interested in certain constants that can describe a part of a random variable. For instance, the height of a basketball team's players is a random variable, and people often care about the average height of the players. The number of cars owned by a family in a city is a random variable. When investigating urban traffic conditions, people care about the number of cars owned by each household. When evaluating the quality of cotton, it is necessary to pay attention to the average length of the fiber and the deviation of the fiber length from the average length; the degree of deviation is smaller with the large average length, and then the quality is better. These constants describing a random variable are the expectation and variance.

In probability theory and statistics, the expected value of a discrete random variable is the sum of the probability of each possible outcome in the experiment multiplied by the result. In other words, the expected value is the average of the equivalent "expectations" calculated by the results of a random trial repeated many times over the same opportunity. Or the expected value is the average of the possible outcomes of a random trial, not necessarily any of the outcomes of a random trial.

For example, when purchasing some parts, a company wants to purchase as few unqualified products as possible or none. It is now known that the qualified products rate of the three manufacturers is 95.7%, 99%, and 97% respectively for each of the 1000 parts. Therefore, according to the definition of expectation, it can be calculated that the number of qualified products for each of the three manufacturers is 957, 990, 970. Therefore, the company can make decisions and choose to buy products from the second company.

The variance is the average of the square of the difference between each data and the mean, and it is used to measure the degree of deviation between the random variable and its mathematical expectation. For many practical problems, it is important to study the degree of deviation between random variables and the mean. It is not difficult to find that $E(|X-E(X)|)$ can effectively measure the degree of deviation of random variables from their mean $E(X)$. However, the above formula has an absolute value, the operation is inconvenient, and the numerical characteristic of the amount $E((X-E(X))^2)$ is usually used, that is, the variance. Generally, the calculation is performed by the following formula:

$$D(X) = E(X^2) - (E(X))^2$$

Variance of normal distribution:

$$D(X) = \sigma^2$$

Variance of binomial distribution:

$$D(X) = np(1-p)$$

wherein n is the number of times that a certain event (a random variable) occurs and p is the probability of the occurrence of this event.

For instance, in the workshop production of various manufacturing enterprises, the quality control adopted for the products produced is 6σ management; that is, using the definition and principle of variance, the quality of the final product is controlled in $\pm 3\sigma$.

Example 4-2 A quality inspection department of a manufacturer adopts a sample survey on the product parts produced by the manufacturers. The parts that do not conform to the standard are collectively considered as defective products. After a comprehensive inspection, the number of defects is counted for each product. Mark the results, as shown in the Table 4-2 and find the upper and lower boundaries of the defect number control chart.

Table 4-2 Defect Number Control Chart Data Sheet

Sample number	1	2	3	4	5	6	7	8	9	10	Total
Number of defects	5	7	4	6	9	8	3	6	4	3	55

Solution Average number of defects per sample is

$$\bar{c} = \frac{\sum c}{k} = \frac{55}{10} = 5.5 \text{(piece)}$$

The upper and lower boundaries of the defect number control chart are

$$\text{UCL} = \bar{c} + 3\sqrt{\bar{c}} = 5.5 + 3\sqrt{5.5} = 12.53 \text{(piece)}$$
$$\text{CL} = \bar{c} = 5.5 \text{(piece)}$$
$$\text{LCL} = \bar{c} - 3\sqrt{\bar{c}} = 5.5 - 3\sqrt{5.5} = -1.53 = 0 \text{(Replace negative values with 0)}$$

where UCL represents the upper boundary, CL represents the center line, and LCL represents the lower boundary.

4.2.3 Distribution Function

For a non-discrete random variable X, the values cannot be enumerated one by one, so we can't describe it like a discrete random variable with a distribution law. In addition, the probability that a non-discrete random variable we usually encounter takes a specified real value is equal to 0, so we are not concerned with the probability that it takes a certain value. For instance, the measurement error is 0.05 mm, the life-span of the component is 1251.3 h or the time of queuing for service, etc. We are interested in the probability that the value of such a random variable fall within a certain interval, namely $P\{x_1 \leqslant X \leqslant x_2\}$.

Definition: Let X be a random variable, x be any real number, and the function $F(x) = P\{X \leqslant x\}$ is called the distribution function of X.

The implications are as follows.

(1) If X is regarded as the coordinates of a random point on the number axis, the value of the distribution function $F(X)$ represents the probability that X falls within the interval $(-\infty, x]$.

(2) For any real number x_1, x_2 ($x_1 < x_2$), the probability that random points fall within the interval (x_1, x_2) is $P\{x_1 \leqslant X \leqslant x_2\} = P\{X \leqslant x_2\} - P\{X \leqslant x_1\} = F(x_2) - F(x_1)$.

(3) The distribution function of random variables is an ordinary function, which completely describes the statistical regularity of random variables. People can use the method of mathematical analysis to study the random variables comprehensively by that.

The distribution function has the following properties:
(1) Non-negative and bounded, $0 \leqslant F(x) \leqslant 1$;
(2) Monotonicity and undiminished, for any $x_1 < x_2$, there is $F(x_1) \leqslant F(x_2)$;
(3) The right continuity, $F(x+0) = F(x)$.

For instance, if the points on the number line $[a, b]$ are uniformly bounded, mark X as the position of the falling point (the coordinates on the number line), and then calculate the distribution function of the random variable X, then there are following cases.

(1) When $x < a$, $\{X \leqslant x\}$ is an impossible event, then $F(x) = P\{X \leqslant x\} = 0$.

(2) When $a \leqslant x \leqslant b$, because of $\{X \leqslant x\} = \{a \leqslant X \leqslant x\}$ and $[a, x] \subset [a, b]$, it is known by geometric probability that

$$F(x) = P(X \leqslant x) = P(a \leqslant X \leqslant x) = \frac{x-a}{b-a}$$

(3) When $x > b$, due to $\{X \leqslant x\} = \{a \leqslant X \leqslant b\}$, so $F(x) = P\{X \leqslant x\} = P\{a \leqslant X \leqslant b\} = \frac{b-a}{b-a} = 1$.

In summary, the distribution function of X is

$$F(x) = \begin{cases} 0, & x < a \\ \dfrac{x-a}{b-a}, & a \leqslant x \leqslant b \\ 1, & x > b \end{cases}$$

For a normal distribution, since $X \sim N(\mu, \sigma^2)$, $f(x) = \dfrac{1}{\sigma \sqrt{2\pi}} e^{-\frac{(x-\mu)^2}{2\sigma^2}}$, so

$$F(x) = \frac{1}{\sigma \sqrt{2\pi}} \int_{-\infty}^{x} e^{-\frac{(x-\mu)^2}{2\sigma^2}}, \quad -\infty < x < +\infty$$

Among them, the normal distribution of $\mu = 0, \sigma = 1$ is called the standard normal distribution, and the expression is as follows:

$$\Phi(x) = \frac{1}{\sqrt{2\pi}} \int_{-\infty}^{x} e^{-\frac{t^2}{2}} dt$$

$\Phi(x)$ has following important properties:

$$\Phi(x) = 1 - \Phi(-x)$$

The application of this type in the production system is to calculate the rate of unqualified products based on the yield of the product.

Example 4-3 A grinding machine workshop processes a shaft part, and the required outer diameter is $\phi\, 20_{0}^{+0.05}$ mm. After sampling a batch of parts, $\bar{d} = 20.025$ mm is obtained. The process capability is known as $C_p = 0.8$ and try to calculate the unqualified rate.

Solution   Because the distribution center of the part size produced coincides with the standard center, the qualified rate is calculated first:

$$P\{TL \leqslant X \leqslant TU\} = \Phi\left(\frac{T}{2\sigma}\right) - \Phi\left(-\frac{T}{2\sigma}\right)$$
$$= \Phi(3 C_p) - \Phi(-3 C_p)$$
$$= 1 - 2\Phi(-3 C_p)$$
$$= 1 - 2\Phi(-2.4)$$

(TL indicates the lower limit of the tolerance zone, and TU indicates the upper limit of the tolerance zone.)

Therefore, the rate of unqualified products is

$$P = 1 - P\{TL \leqslant X \leqslant TU\} = 2\Phi(-2.4)$$

Check the normal distribution table, we can know:

$$\Phi(-2.4) = 0.008198$$

So the rate of unqualified products is

$$P = 2 \times 0.008198 \times 100\% = 1.640\%$$

4.3 Central Limit Theorem with Applications

4.3.1 Bernoulli Experiment and Binomial Distribution

For an event in a random trial, the possible outcomes of the trial are only two opposites. This test with only two possible outcomes is called the Bernoulli experiment. For example, the result of a coin toss can only be one of heads or tails. Rolling a six-sided dice with a result greater than or equal to "5" means "success" and other results are "failure"; then the dice rolling means either "success" or "failure".

The Bernoulli experiment has two characteristics:

(1) Contrariety, the result of each trial can only be one of the opposite events, either A or non-A;

(2) Independence, the results of each test do not affect each other. The probability of occurrence of the event A in each test is equal and mark it as p; and the probability of occurrence of the non-A event is set as $q = 1 - p$.

In reality, statistical significance is often more worthy of attention. For example, for a supermarket, it won't concern whether a person comes to shopping in a certain period, but how many people come to shopping in a certain period, so as to optimize the number of available checkout counters in different periods. Therefore, the Bernoulli experiment is performed several times, and the sum of the number of occurrences of a certain result is a more worthy value. Repeated n times of the Bernoulli experiment formed a Bernoulli process, also known as n-fold Bernoulli experiment. For example, tossing a coin 100 times is a 100-fold Bernoulli experiment. Assume that the probability of event A occurring in one trial is $p(0<p<1)$, then the probability that event A happens exactly k times in the n-fold Bernoulli experiment is $P_n(k)=C_n^k p^k q^{n-k}, q=1-p, (k=0,1,2,\cdots,n)$.

Binomial distribution: the probability distribution formed by the occurrence times of a certain result in an n-fold Bernoulli experiment.

Example 4-4 In a workshop, there are 4 sets of equipment to process the same parts, and the processing of each equipment is independent from each other. The probability of shutdown in any period is 0.3. Try to calculate the probability of shutdown of two devices in one observation.

Solution Because the workshop has 4 sets of equipment, it is a 4-fold Bernoulli experiment, wherein $n=4$, $p=0.3$, then

$$P\{X=2\}=C_4^2 \times 0.3^2 \times 0.7^2 = \frac{8}{27}$$

Example 4-5 In the finished product warehouse, the quality inspection of 100 parts is carried out. It is known that 30 pieces of waste products and 70 pieces of qualified products are found in these 100 parts. Now, put back 5 times and only one piece of product is taken out at a time. Try to calculate: (1) the probability of 2 waste products out of 5 products; (2) the probability that at least 2 out of 5 products are wasted.

Solution The probability of getting the wasted products is 0.3, 5 times of drawing are independent of each other, so it is a 5-fold Bernoulli experiment.

Suppose x is the number of times the wasted products is taken out, then

$$P\{x=k\} = C_5^k \times 0.3^k \times 0.7^{5-k}, k=0,1,2,3,4,5$$

(1) $P\{x=2\} = C_5^2 \times 0.3^2 \times 0.7^3 = 0.3087$

(2) $P\{x \geq 2\} = 1 - P\{x<2\} = 1 - P\{x=0\} - P\{x=1\}$
$= 1 - C_5^0 \times 0.3^0 \times 0.7^5 - C_5^1 \times 0.3^1 \times 0.7^4 \approx 0.4718$

According to the above definition and examples, most of the real cases are subject to the binomial distribution, such as the total number of customers in a supermarket during a certain period, the total number of rainy days in a certain season, etc.

4.3.2 Normal Distribution

The normal distribution is first obtained in the asymptotic formula of the binomial distribution, which is the limit distribution of the binomial distribution. The normal distribution, also known as the Gaussian distribution, is a probability distribution that is very important in mathematics, physics, engineering and other fields and has a significant impact on many aspects of statistics. If the random variable X obeys the Gaussian distribution with a mathematical expectation of μ and a standard deviation of σ^2, it is recorded as $N(\mu, \sigma^2)$, and its probability density function is the normal distribution, and the expected value μ determines its position and the standard deviation σ determines the magnitude of the distribution. Because the curve is bell-shaped, people often call it the bell curve. The standard normal distribution commonly said is a normal distribution of $\mu=0$ and $\sigma=1$.

The probability density $f(x)$ of the normal distribution $N(\mu, \sigma^2)$ is shown in Fig. 4-1.

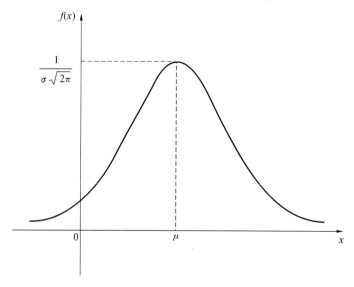

Fig. 4-1 Normal Distribution Probability Density Curve

The characteristics of the distribution curve are shown in Fig. 4-2 and described as follows:

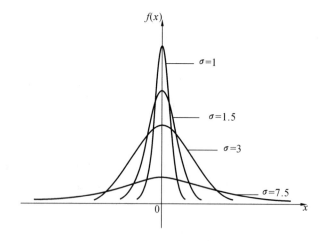

Fig. 4-2 Characteristics of a Normal Distribution Curve

(1) Symmetric about the line $x=\mu$;
(2) Maximize at $x=\mu$;
(3) There is an inflection point at $x=\mu\pm\sigma$;
(4) When $x\to\infty$, the curve is asymptotic with the x-axis;
(5) Fix σ, change μ, then the image is translated along the x-axis without changing its shape;

(6) Fix μ, change σ, then when σ decreases, the shape of the curve is like a minaret; when σ increases, the curve will tend to be flat.

4.3.3 Central Limit Theorem

Central Limit Theorem: If a random variable is the sum of a number of random variables, each of which has a small effect on the sum value, then the sum is approximately subject to normal distribution within the range of independent variables.

The central limit theorem is a theorem used in probability theory to describe the limit of the probability distribution of the sum of a series of random variables fulfilling certain conditions. This theorem is the theoretical basis of mathematical statistics and error analysis. In nature and production, some phenomena are affected by many independent random factors. If the influence of each factor is tiny, the total influence can be regarded as approximately obeying the normal distribution. The central limit theorem is the mathematical proof of this theory.

4.3.4 Applications

Example 4-6 There are 200 devices in a workshop. It is assumed that the probability of each device reporting a maintenance request is 0.6. At least how many maintenance personnel are on duty, and then the probability that all requests can be responded in time is 99.9%?

Solution Mathematical model:

This problem can be converted to the Bernoulli experiment of $n=200$, which follows the binomial distribution of $p=0.6$, that is, $X \sim B(200, 0.6)$ approximately follows the normal distribution.

Solution strategy:

Assuming that there are a maintenance staff on duty, when the number of reported requests is less than or equal to a, all requests can be processed in a timely manner, and the probability that the number of requests is less than or equal to a is

$$F(a) - F(0) = \Phi\left(\frac{a-\mu}{\sigma}\right) - \Phi\left(\frac{0-\mu}{\sigma}\right)$$

$$\mu = E(X) = 200 \times 0.6 = 120$$

$$\sigma = \sqrt{D(X)} = \sqrt{np(1-p)} = \sqrt{200 \times 0.6 \times 0.4} = \sqrt{48}$$

So

$$\Phi\left(\frac{a-120}{\sqrt{48}}\right) - \Phi\left(\frac{-120}{\sqrt{48}}\right) = 0.999$$

Lookup the normal distribution table, $a = 142$, therefore when 142 maintenance personnel are on duty, the response requirements can be met.

4.4 Queuing Characteristics Analysis

4.4.1 Basic Concepts of Queuing Systems

The queuing system contains following basic elements.

1) Input process

This is the process that service requests arrive at the queuing system on a regular basis.

(1) The total number of requests, it is also called input sources. Input sources can be finite or infinite.

(2) The form in which the request arrives. This describes how requests come to the system, individually or not.

(3) The probability distribution of the request, or the time interval distribution of the successive arrival of the request.

2) Service stations

The service stations can be described from the following three aspects.

(1) Number and composition of service stations: in terms of quantity, there are single and multiple service stations. From the formation type, there are one queue with single service station, one queue with multiple service stations parallel, multiple queues with multiple service stations parallel, one queue with multiple service stations cascade and so on.

(2) Service mode: refers to the number of customers receiving service at a certain time, including one for one service and mass service.

(3) Distribution of service time: in most cases, the service time of a customer is a random variable, and the distribution of service time is the same as the distribution of the time interval of customer arrival. The distribution of service time includes fixed length distribution, negative exponential distribution, Erlang distribution and etc.

In accordance with the above basic elements, the queuing systems can be divided into three types for queue characteristics: one queue with single service station, one queue with multiple service stations and multiple queues with multiple service stations, as shown in Fig. 4-3. According to service characteristics, it can be divided into equal service time queue and random service time queue. Therefore, there are six types of queuing systems: one queue with single service station in time manner, one queue with single service station in a random way, one queue with multiple service stations in time manner, one queue with multiple service stations in a random way, multiple queues with multiple service stations in time manner and multiple queues with multiple service stations in a random way.

Common concepts involved in analyzing queuing systems are as follows.

L: Average length, the expected value of the number of requests for the steady state

Chapter 4 The Analysis of Probability in Production System · 153 ·

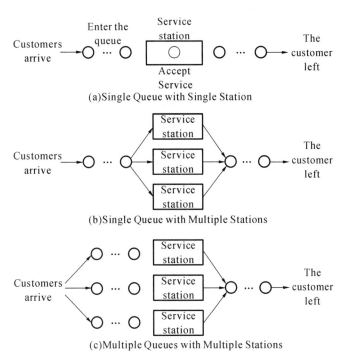

Fig. 4-3 Classification of Queuing Systems According to Queue Characteristics

system at any time.

L_q: Average waiting length, the expected value of the number of requests waiting for service at any time in the stable system.

W: Average staying time, the expected value of the requested staying time to enter the stable system at any time.

W_q: Average waiting time, the expected value of the request waiting time to enter the stable system at any time.

λ: The average rate of request arrival, the average number of requests arriving per unit time.

$1/\lambda$: Average time to arrival.

μ: Average service rate, the number of requests completed per unit time.

$1/\mu$: Average service hours.

s: The number of service stations in the system.

ρ: Service intensity, the average service time per unit time of each service station, generally $\rho = \lambda/(s \times \mu)$.

N: The state of the stable system at any time (the number of requests in the system).

U: The duration of any request in the stable system.

Q: The waiting time of any request in the stable system.

$P_n = P\{N=n\}$: State probability, the probability that there are n tasks in the system; especially when $n=0$, $P_n = P_0$, that is, the probability that all service station of the stable system are all idle.

λ_e: The effective average arrival rate, which refers to the probability of requests reaching the service system per unit of time (including not entering the system).

4.4.2 Characteristics Analysis of Equal Service Time Queue

In the equal service time queue, the service station's service time for each request is equal or approximately equal, such as subway card check-in system, similar product packaging system, and etc. The characteristics of the equal service time are calculated as follows:

Queue length expectation = the expected value of the reporting service — the number of people on the job;

Task waiting time expectation value = queue length expectation value × per unit service time;

Service idle rate = the expectation value of service staff idling/the total number of service staff;

Service utilization = 1 − service idle rate.

4.4.3 Analysis of Random Service Time Queue

1. Queue Factor

In the random service time queue, the service time of different requests may be quite different, such as supermarket cash register system queue. Because the number of goods purchased by customers is various, the service time is also quite different. The bank service queue has a large difference in service time due to the different services applied by customers. The following factors affect the characteristics of a random service time queue.

(1) Task factor.

① Average arrival interval: $T_0 = \dfrac{T}{n}$.

② Average speed of arrival: $\lambda = \dfrac{1}{T_0} = \dfrac{n}{T}$.

③ Distribution function of arrival time interval: $A_0(t) = 1 - F(t)$.

(2) Service factor.

① Average service time: $T_S = \dfrac{T}{n_S}$.

② Average service speed: $\mu = \dfrac{1}{T_S} = \dfrac{n_S}{T}$.

③ Service time distribution function: $A_S(t) = 1 - F_S(t)$.

④ Traffic intensity: $u = \dfrac{\lambda}{\mu} = \dfrac{n}{n_S}$.

⑤ Service intensity: $\rho = \dfrac{\lambda}{\mu}$.

where the subscript S is the initial letter of the word system, representing the system.

2. Characteristics Analysis

(1) State probability. The probability of n tasks in the system is $P_n = (1-\rho)\rho^n$.

Chapter 4 The Analysis of Probability in Production System

(2) Expectation value of the tasks.

$$L_S = \sum_{n=0}^{\infty} n P_n = \sum_{n=0}^{\infty} n(1-\rho)\rho^n = \frac{\rho}{1-\rho} = \frac{\lambda}{\mu-\lambda}$$

(3) Average number of waiting tasks.

$$L_q = \frac{\rho\lambda}{\mu-\lambda}$$

(4) Expectation value of task waiting time.

$$W_q = \frac{\rho}{\mu-\lambda}$$

Example 4-7 A processing center provides service for the task queue. The average arrival speed of tasks is 2.1 per hour, and the average time to complete tasks is 0.4 per hour. Try to analyze the performance indexex of the system.

Solution (1) The basic factors:

$$\lambda = 2.1(\text{unit/h}), T_S = 0.4(\text{h}), \mu = \frac{1}{4} = 2.5(\text{unit/h})$$

(2) Service intensity:

$$\rho = \frac{\lambda}{\mu} = 0.84$$

(3) System expectation:

$$L_S = \frac{2.1}{2.5 - 2.1} = 5.25$$

(4) Average waiting length:

$$L_q = \rho L_S = 0.84 \times 5.25 = 4.41$$

(5) Average waiting time:

$$W_q = \frac{0.84}{2.5 - 2.1} = 2.1(\text{h})$$

Example 4-8 In a production line, semi-finished products are transported and conveyed by a transmission chain. It is known that the supply system serves a processing equipment. The processing equipment is equipped with an operator. Try to calculate: (1) utilization rate of the operator; (2) average number of semi-finished products waiting; (3) the average number of semi-finished products processed by the operator; (4) average waiting time of semi-finished products; (5) average residence time of semi-finished products in the system.

Solution (1) Operator utilization:

$$\rho = \frac{\lambda}{\mu} = \frac{15}{20} = 75\%$$

(2) Average number of semi-finished products waiting:

$$\bar{n}_1 = \frac{\lambda^2}{\mu(\mu-\lambda)} = \frac{15^2}{20 \times (20-15)} = 2.25(\text{piece})$$

(3) The average number of semi-finished products processed by the operator:
$$\bar{n}_S = \frac{\lambda}{\mu - \lambda} = \frac{15}{20 - 15} = 3(\text{piece})$$

(4) Average wait time of semi-finished products:
$$\bar{t}_l = \frac{\lambda}{\mu(\mu - \lambda)} = \frac{15}{20 \times (20 - 15)} = 0.15(\text{h})$$

(5) Average residence time of semi-finished products in the system:
$$\bar{t}_S = \frac{1}{\mu - \lambda} = \frac{1}{20 - 15} = 0.2(\text{h})$$

4.5 Summary

Probabilistic analysis is one of the important means of modeling and simulation of a production system due to the uncertainty of the production system. This chapter first introduces some basic concepts of probability theory; then introduces the principles of Bernoulli experiment, binomial distribution, normal distribution, central limit theorem, etc. in detail. Through typical examples, the application of these theories in production system analysis is explained. At last, some concepts and basic theories of queuing theory are presented, and the general solution method of random service time queue is illustrated by examples.

Chapter 5   Production System Solution Based on Complex Method

5.1   Basic Idea and General Steps of Complex Method

Complex method is one of direct methods for solving constrained optimization problems whose basic idea is to construct an initial complex with n_1 vertexes in the feasible region and find the vertex with the maximum of objective function, i.e. the worst point is found by comparing objective function values of each vertex; then a feasible new vertex with the lowest value of objective function can be found through a series of calculations, which can be used to replace the original worst point to form a new complex. Consequently, it can converge to the optimum solution through the above iteration.

Aiming at the general optimization problems with only inequation constraints, the main steps of the complex method are shown in Fig. 5-1.

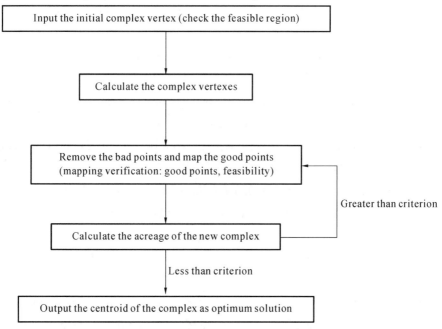

Fig. 5-1   General Steps of the Complex Method

(1) Initialization means to construct n_1 vertexes of the complex in the feasible region. If the number of variables in the optimization problem is n, the following values are generally taken:

$$n+1 \leqslant n_1 \leqslant 2n \qquad (5\text{-}1)$$

Initial vertex can be determined by designers or generated by random functions. First, input a feasible initial point X_1 (each vertex contains n variables); then generate the other n_1-1 points, where the point $X_{(k+1),i}$ can be generated according to Eq. (5-2):

$$X_{(k+1),i} = a_i + r_i(b_i - a_i), i = 1, 2, \cdots, n \qquad (5\text{-}2)$$

where $X_{(k+1),i}$ is the ith component of X_{k+1}, a_i and b_i is the lower and upper limits respectively, and r_i is a random number uniformly distributed in the interval $(0,1)$. The n_1-1 random points which are calculated from the formula above may not be in the feasible region, so the infeasible points should be moved into the feasible region. If X_{k+1} can conform to the conditions, the next vertex will be generated; otherwise, the centroid X_C of the first k vertexes should be found first.

$$X_C = \frac{1}{k} \sum_{j=1}^{k} X_j \qquad (5\text{-}3)$$

Then move X_{k+1} in the direction of the centroid X_C to the half of X_{k+1} to X_C.

$$X_{k+1} = X_C + 0.5(X_{k+1} - X_C) \qquad (5\text{-}4)$$

If the X_{k+1} is still infeasible, then calculate and make it continue to move to the centroid until the X_{k+1} is feasible according to Eq. (5-4). Obviously, the X_{k+1} can be moved to the feasible region as long as the centroid is feasible. After that, all n_1-1 generated points become feasible and an initial complex is formed.

This method is totally applicable to the case where the feasible region is convex. If the feasible region is non-convex and the centroid may not be in it, the method mentioned above may fail. At this time, vertexes should be regenerated by changing the lower and upper limits of variables.

(2) Calculating the function value of all vertexes of the complex.

$$f_j = f(X_j), j = 1, 2, \cdots, n_1 \qquad (5\text{-}5)$$

(3) By comparing them, the worst point X_H, the best point X_B and the second worst point X_G can be seen. The worst point is a point that maximizes the value of objective function, and the best point is a point that minimizes the value of objective function.

$$X_H : F(X_H) = \max(f_j \mid j = 1, 2, \cdots, n_1)$$
$$X_B : F(X_B) = \min(f_j \mid j = 1, 2, \cdots, n_1)$$
$$X_G : F(X_G) = \max(f_j \mid j = 1, 2, \cdots, n_1, j \neq H)$$

where H represents the j for the worst point.

(4) Judge the termination condition of the iteration. When the convergence accuracy of terminating the iteration ε is given and the standard deviation of objective function value is considered as criterion, the iteration is completed if the standard deviation is less than or

equal to ε and the optimal solution is as follows:
$$X^* = X_B, \quad f(X^*) = f(X_B)$$
If the standard deviation is greater than ε, then turn to step (5). The formula is
$$\sigma = \left[\frac{1}{n_1 - 1}\sum_{j=1}^{n_1}(f_j - \bar{f})^2\right]^{\frac{1}{2}} \leqslant \varepsilon \tag{5-6}$$
where $\bar{f}$ is the average value of objective function of n_1 points, i.e.
$$\bar{f} = \frac{1}{n_1}\sum_{j=1}^{n_1} f_j \tag{5-7}$$

(5) Find the centroid X_C of all points except the worst point X_H.
$$X_C = \frac{1}{n_1 - 1}\sum_{j=1, j \neq H}^{n_1} X_j \tag{5-8}$$
And judge whether the centroid X_C is feasible. If it is feasible, then turn to step (6); if not, the lower and upper limits of the variables should be reset, i.e. set
$$a = X_B, \, b = X_C$$
Then turn to step (1) and rebuild the initial complex.

(6) Finding the mapping point X^R. Generally, towards the direction of the connection between the worst point X_H and the centroid X_C, objective function would probably on the decrease. Map the worst point X_H in a certain proportion with the centroid X_C as the center, it is highly possible to find a new point X^R whose value is less than the value of the worst point X_H, so the X^R is called mapping point.
$$X^R = X_C + \alpha(X_C - X_H) \tag{5-9}$$
where $\alpha(\alpha > 0)$ is the mapping coefficient which generally is 1.2~1.5.

(7) Verify whether the mapping point X^R is a feasible point. Set $\alpha = \alpha/2$ and turn to step (6) to calculate the mapping point X^R until it is feasible if the mapping point X^R is not a feasible point.

(8) Calculate the value of objective function of the mapping point X^R. If $f(X^R) < f(X_H)$, replace the worst point X_H with the mapping point X^R to finish the iteration. Then a new complex will be formed and turn to step (3). If $f(X^R) \geqslant f(X_H)$, turn to step (9).

(9) If $\alpha \geqslant \mu$ (μ is a small positive number which is given in advance), then set $\alpha = \alpha/2$ and turn to step (6) to recalculate the mapping point X^R. The worst point X_H should be replaced by the second worst point X_G and turn to step (5) if $\alpha < \mu$.

The flow chart of the complex method is shown in Fig. 5-2.

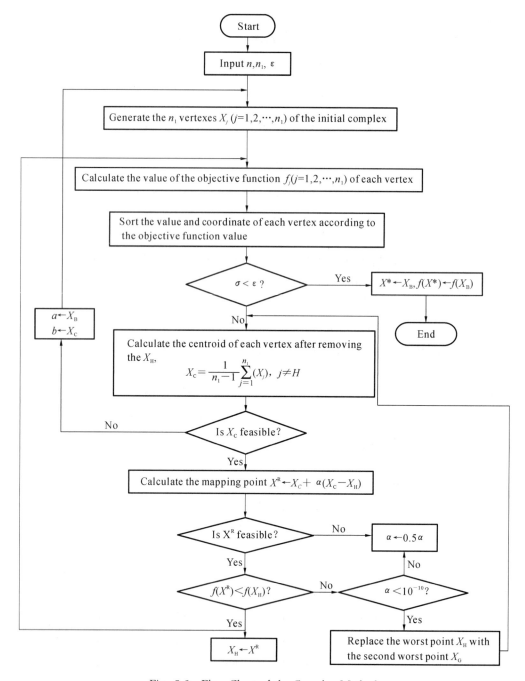

Fig. 5-2 Flow Chart of the Complex Method

5.2 Examples of the Complex Method

Example 5-1 Try to calculate x_1, x_2.

$$\min f(X) = 4x_1 - x_2^2 - 12$$

Chapter 5 Production System Solution Based on Complex Method

s. t.
$$D: g_1(X) = 25 - x_1^2 - x_2^2 \geqslant 0$$
$$x \in D \subset R^n$$
$$g_2(X) = x_1 \geqslant 0$$
$$g_3(X) = x_2 \geqslant 0$$

Two new complexes are required. Three vertexes of the initial complex are as follows:
$$X_1 = [2 \ \ 1]^T, \ X_2 = [4 \ \ 1]^T, \ X_3 = [3 \ \ 3]^T$$

Solution (1) Verify the feasibility of each vertex of the initial complex.

For X_1, there are
$$g_1(X_1) = 25 - 2^2 - 1^2 = 20 > 0$$
$$g_2(X_1) = 2 > 0$$
$$g_3(X_1) = 1 > 0$$

So the X_1 is feasible; similarly, the feasibility of the X_2, X_3 can be verified.

(2) Calculate the value of objective function of each vertex of the complex.
$$f(X_1) = 4 \times 2 - 1^2 - 12 = -5$$
$$f(X_2) = 4 \times 4 - 1^2 - 12 = 3$$
$$f(X_3) = 4 \times 3 - 3^2 - 12 = -9$$

So, the bad point $X_H = X_2$, the good point $X_B = X_3$.

(3) Calculate the centroid X_C of the other vertexes after removing the bad point X_H.

$$X_C = \frac{1}{n_1 - 1} \sum_{j=1, j \neq H}^{n_1} X_j$$
$$= \frac{1}{3-1} \times ([2 \ \ 1]^T + [3 \ \ 3]^T)$$
$$= [2.5 \ \ 2]^T, \ j \neq 2$$

(4) The centroid X_C should be put into the constraints to verify its feasibility.
$$g_1(X_C) = 25 - 2.5^2 - 2^2 = 14.75 > 0$$
$$g_2(X_C) = 2.5 > 0$$
$$g_3(X_C) = 2 > 0$$

Apparently, X_C is a feasible point.

(5) Set the mapping coefficient $\alpha = 1.3$ and calculate the mapping point X^R.
$$X^R = X_C + \alpha(X_C - X_H)$$
$$= [2.5 \ \ 2]^T + 1.3 \times ([2.5 \ \ 2]^T - [4 \ \ 1]^T)$$
$$= [0.55 \ \ 3.3]^T$$

(6) The mapping point X^R should be put into the constraints to verify its feasibility.
$$g_1(X^R) = 25 - 0.55^2 - 3.3^2 = 13.8075 > 0$$
$$g_2(X^R) = 0.55 > 0$$
$$g_3(X^R) = 3.3 > 0$$

Apparently, X^R is a feasible point.

(7) Calculate the value of objective function $f(X^R)$ of the mapping point X^R.
$$f(X^R) = 4 \times 0.55 - 3.3^2 - 12 = -20.69 < f(X_H) = f(X_2) = 3$$

So, replace the bad point X_H with the mapping point X^R to form the first new complex; and its three vertexes are as follows:
$$X_1 = [2 \quad 1]^T, X_2 = [0.55 \quad 3.3]^T, X_3 = [3 \quad 3]^T$$

(8) Calculate the value of objective function of each vertex of the first new complex.
$$f(X_1) = 4 \times 2 - 1^2 - 12 = -5$$
$$f(X_2) = 4 \times 0.55 - 3.3^2 - 12 = -20.69$$
$$f(X_3) = 4 \times 3 - 3^2 - 12 = -9$$

So, the bad point $X_H = X_1$, the good point $X_B = X_2$.

(9) Calculate the centroid X_C of the other vertexes after removing the bad point X_H.
$$X_C = \frac{1}{n_1 - 1} \sum_{j=1, j \neq H}^{n_1} X_j$$
$$= \frac{1}{3-1} \times ([0.55 \quad 3.3]^T + [3 \quad 3]^T)$$
$$= [1.775 \quad 3.15]^T, j \neq 1$$

(10) The centroid X_C should be put into the constraints to verify its feasibility.
$$g_1(X_C) = 25 - 1.775^2 - 3.15^2 = 11.926875 > 0$$
$$g_2(X_C) = 1.775 > 0$$
$$g_3(X_C) = 3.15 > 0$$

Apparently, X_C is a feasible point.

(11) Set the mapping coefficient $\alpha = 1.3$ and calculate the mapping point X^R.
$$X^R = X_C + \alpha(X_C - X_H)$$
$$= [1.775 \quad 3.15]^T + 1.3 \times ([1.775 \quad 3.15]^T - [2 \quad 1]^T)$$
$$= [1.4825 \quad 5.945]^T$$

(12) The mapping point X^R should be put into the constraints to verify its feasibility.
$$g_1(X^R) = 25 - 1.4825^2 - 5.945^2 = -12.540831 < 0$$
$$g_2(X^R) = 1.4825 > 0$$
$$g_3(X^R) = 5.945 > 0$$

Apparently, X^R is not a feasible point; then halve the mapping coefficient i. e. $\alpha = 0.65$ and recalculate the mapping point X^R.
$$X^R = X_C + \alpha(X_C - X_H)$$
$$= [1.775 \quad 3.15]^T + 0.65 \times ([1.775 \quad 3.15]^T - [2 \quad 1]^T)$$
$$= [1.6287 \quad 4.5475]^T$$

(13) The mapping point X^R should be put into the constraints to verify its feasibility again.
$$g_1(X^R) = 25 - 1.62875^2 - 4.5475^2 = 1.667413 > 0$$
$$g_2(X^R) = 1.62875 > 0$$
$$g_3(X^R) = 4.5475 > 0$$

Apparently, X^R is a feasible point.

(14) Calculate the value of objective function $f(X^R)$ of the mapping point X^R.

$$f(X^R) = 4 \times 1.62875 - 4.5475^2 - 12 = -26.1648 < f(X_H) = f(X_1) = -5$$

So, replace the bad point X_H with the mapping point X^R to form the second new complex; and its three vertexes are as follows:

$$X_1 = [1.62875 \quad 4.5475]^T, \quad X_2 = [0.55 \quad 3.3]^T, \quad X_3 = [3 \quad 3]^T$$

(15) Calculate the value of objective function of each vertex of the second new complex.

$$f(X_1) = 4 \times 1.62875 - 4.5475^2 - 12 = -26.163392$$
$$f(X_2) = 4 \times 0.55 - 3.3^2 - 12 = -20.69$$
$$f(X_3) = 4 \times 3 - 3^2 - 12 = -9$$

So, the bad point $X_H = X_3$, the good point $X_B = X_1$.

(16) The optimal solution is $X^* = X_1 = [1.62875 \quad 4.5475]^T$ after two iterations, and $f(X^*) = f(X_1) = -26.163392$.

Example 5-2 Try to calculate x_1, x_2.

$$\min f(X) = 60 - 10x_1 - 4x_2 + x_1^2 + x_2^2 - x_1 x_2$$

s. t.
$$D: g(X) = -x_1 - x_2 + 11 \geqslant 0$$
$$x \in D \subset R^n$$
$$0 \leqslant x_1 \leqslant 6$$
$$0 \leqslant x_2 \leqslant 8$$

Solution (1) Generate the vertexes of the initial complex. This example is a non-linear programming problem with two variables. Set the number of complex vertexes $n_1 = 2n = 2 \times 2 = 4$; all vertexes of the initial complex can be selected by artificial way. The following four points are selected as the initial complex vertexes:

$$X_1 = [1 \quad 5.5]^T, \quad X_2 = [1 \quad 4]^T, \quad X_3 = [2 \quad 6.4]^T, \quad X_4 = [3 \quad 3.5]^T$$

(2) The initial complex is formed to find the value of objective function of each vertex, and find out the value of the worst point X_H, the best point X_B and each vertex.

$$f(X_1) = 53.75, \quad f(X_2) = 47, \quad f(X_3) = 46.56, \quad f(X_4) = 26.75$$

Thus, the bad point $X_H = X_1$, the good point $X_B = X_4$.

(3) Calculate the centroid X_C of the remaining vertexes after removing the bad point X_H.

$$X_C = \frac{1}{n_1 - 1} \sum_{j=1, j \neq H}^{n_1} X_j$$
$$= \frac{1}{4-1} \times \left([1 \quad 4]^T + [2 \quad 6.4]^T + [3 \quad 3.5]^T \right)$$
$$= [2 \quad 4.63]^T, \quad j \neq 1$$

(4) The centroid X_C should be put into the constraints to verify its feasibility. The X_C is a feasible point with $g(X_C) = 4.37 > 0$ and $0 < 2 < 6, 0 < 4.63 < 8$.

(5) Set the mapping coefficient $\alpha = 1.3$, and calculate the mapping point X^R.

$$X^R = X_C + \alpha(X_C - X_H)$$
$$= [2 \quad 4.63]^T + 1.3 \times \left([2 \quad 4.63]^T - [1 \quad 5.5]^T \right)$$

$$= [3.3 \quad 3.499]^T$$

(6) The mapping point X^R should be put into the constraints to verify its feasibility. The X^R is a feasible point with $g(X^R)=4.201>0$ and $0<3.3<6, 0<3.499<8$.

(7) Calculate the value of objective function $f(X^R)$ of the mapping point X^R.

$$f(X^R) = 24.590301 < f(X_H) = f(X_1) = 53.57$$

So, replace the bad point X_H with the mapping point X^R to form the first new complex; and its four vertexes are as follows:

$$X_1 = [3.3 \quad 3.499]^T, \ X_2 = [1 \quad 4]^T, \ X_3 = [2 \quad 6.4]^T, \ X_4 = [3 \quad 3.5]^T$$

(8) Calculate the value of objective function of each vertex of the first new complex.

$$f(X_1) = 24.590301, \ f(X_2) = 47, \ f(X_3) = 46.56, \ f(X_4) = 26.75$$

Thus, we can see that the bad point $X_H = X_2$, the good point $X_B = X_1$.

(9) Calculate the centroid X_C of the remaining vertexes after removing the bad point X_H.

$$X_C = \frac{1}{n_1 - 1} \sum_{j=1, j \neq H}^{n_1} X_j$$

$$= \frac{1}{4-1} \times \left([3.3 \quad 3.499]^T + [2 \quad 6.4]^T + [3 \quad 3.5]^T \right)$$

$$= [2.77 \quad 4.46]^T, \ j \neq 2$$

(10) The centroid X_C should be put into the constraints to verify its feasibility. The X^R is a feasible point with $g(X_C) = 3.77 > 0$ and $0 < 2.77 < 6, 0 < 4.46 < 8$.

(11) Set the mapping coefficient $\alpha = 1.3$ and calculate the mapping point X^R.

$$X^R = X_C + \alpha (X_C - X_H)$$

$$= [2.77 \quad 4.46]^T + 1.3 \times \left([2.77 \quad 4.46]^T - [1 \quad 4]^T \right)$$

$$= [5.071 \quad 5.058]^T$$

(12) The mapping point X^R should be put into the constraints to verify its feasibility. The X^R is a feasible point with $g(X^R) = 0.871 > 0$ and $0 < 5.071 < 6, 0 < 5.058 < 8$.

(13) Calculate the value of objective function $f(X^R)$ of the mapping point X^R.

$$f(X^R) = 14.71 < f(X_H) = f(X_2) = 47$$

So, replace the bad point X_H with the mapping point X^R to form the second new complex and proceed the third iteration calculation; its four vertexes are as follows:

$$X_1 = [3.3 \quad 3.499]^T, \ X_2 = [5.071 \quad 5.058]^T, \ X_3 = [2 \quad 6.4]^T, \ X_4 = [3 \quad 3.5]^T$$

(14) It is necessary to check whether it meets the accuracy requirements when forming a new complex. The new complex gradually comes to the optimum point and the complex shrinks continuously as iteration keeps going above. When reaching the accuracy requirement ε which is set according to the stop calculation criterion, the best point X_B and its value are output, and then stop calculation. The optimal solution with the stop calculation criterion for this case is $X^* = [6 \quad 5]^T, f(X^*) = 11$.

5.3 Application of Complex Method in Job Shop Scheduling Problem

5.3.1 Model Analysis of Job Shop Scheduling Problem

1. Basic Assumption

The essence of job shop scheduling problem is allocating the limited resources of the system reasonably and effectively to meet the requirements of specific objectives. It can be described as follows: n tasks are processed in m machines; each task contains k processes (for each task, k can be different) and there is corresponding equipment for each process. In order to achieve the optimization of certain objectives, equipment should be allocated for all processes and start time should be determined according to some constraints.

Generally, there are several assumptions for job shop scheduling problem:

(1) There is no priority between tasks which are all independent of each other;

(2) There is a certain sequence between the process of each task;

(3) One machine can only process one workpiece at the same time and a process should be processed continuously;

(4) Only one process can be proceeded in each task at the same moment;

(5) Only one machine is required for each process;

(6) Each machine has only one specific processing function;

(7) There is more than one machine for each function;

(8) The manufacturing procedure of each task may not be unique and there are various feasible procedures on the premise of meeting the constraints between processes.

As a typical combination optimization problem, job shop scheduling problem is complex in both solving and constraint. The number of solutions will increase exponentially when the problem amount and constraints increase and the mutual constraints between processes become more complex, which makes it more difficult to solve job shop scheduling problem.

2. Objective Function of Job Shop Scheduling Problem

There are several optimization objectives of job shop scheduling problem.

(1) Minimum completion time. If the completion time of task i is C_i and the total number of tasks is n, then the objective function is

$$\min\left(\max\{C_i\}\right) \tag{5-10}$$

The objective is to minimize the maximum completion time of tasks.

(2) Minimum total tardiness. If the completion time of task i is C_i and the delivery time is d_i, then the tardiness of task i is $\max\{0, C_i - d_i\}$ and the objective function is

$$\min\left(\sum_{i=1}^{n}\max\{0, C_i - d_i\}\right) \tag{5-11}$$

The objective is to minimize the maximum tardiness of tasks.

(3) Minimum penalty cost of ahead of time/delay. Inventory cost will increase and unnecessary priority time resources will be occupied if it is completed ahead of schedule, while tardiness will lead to default of delivery time, so earliness or tardiness is not the ideal scheduling results.

Assuming the completion time of task i is C_i, the delivery time is $[D_{ei}, D_{li}]$, D_{ei} is the earliest delivery time of task i, D_{li} is the latest delivery time of task i. The penalty coefficient for earliness is λ_i and the penalty coefficient for tardiness is μ_i. Then the penalty cost of task i is

$$\lambda_i \times (\max\{0, D_{ei} - C_i\}) + \mu_i \times (\max\{0, C_i - D_{li}\}) \qquad (5-12)$$

Thus, the objective function is

$$\min\left[\sum_{i=1}^{n} (\lambda_i \times (\max\{0, D_{ei} - C_i\}) + \mu_i \times (\max\{0, C_i - D_{li}\}))\right] \qquad (5-13)$$

The objective is to minimize the total penalty cost of earliness/tardiness of tasks.

3. Constraints of Job Shop Scheduling Problem

Job shop scheduling is an activity of allocating equipment and formulating processing time for each process. A feasible scheme should be bound by the following constraints.

(1) The constraint of manufacturing procedure. Each task has its own manufacturing procedure which determines the processing sequence, including serial constraints and parallel constraints.

(2) The constraint of equipment exclusiveness. Processing time of processes allocated on the same equipment cannot overlap.

(3) The constraint of processing consistency. The function of equipment must be consistent with the required processing type.

(4) The constraint of task exclusiveness. Each task represents one workpiece, so two processes of a task cannot be processed at the same time.

(5) The constraint of processing continuity. Each process must be completed at one time.

These are the basic constraints of job shop scheduling problem. Other constraints should be considered in model-establishing and problem-solving if there are other conditions in the given problem which must meet, such as the tasks-switching time and the production inventory and so on.

4. Optimization Model of Job Shop Scheduling Problem

The symbols contained in the model of job shop scheduling problem and their meanings are as follows:

$O_{i,j}$ ——the jth process of task i;

$O_{i,j-1}$ ——the former process of the jth process of task i;

E^k ——the kth machine;

$BT_{i,j}$ ——the starting time of the jth process of task i;

$PT_{i,j}$ ——the processing time of the jth process of task i;

C_i——the completion time of task i;

$\mathrm{CT}_{i,j}$——the completion time of the jth process of task i;

$E_{i,j}^k$——the machine of the jth process of task i;

$F(O_{i,j})$——the processing type of the jth process of task i;

$F(E^k)$——the processing functions of machine k.

Considering the minimum completion time as the objective of the job shop scheduling problem, then a model with n tasks and m machines can be established as follows:

$$\min f = \max\{C_i\} \tag{5-14}$$

s. t.
$$\mathrm{BT}_{i,j} > \mathrm{BT}_{i,j-1} \tag{5-15}$$

$$(\mathrm{BT}_{i,j},\mathrm{CT}_{i,j}) \cap (\mathrm{BT}_{i,l},\mathrm{CT}_{i,l}) = \varnothing, j \neq l \tag{5-16}$$

$$(\mathrm{BT}_{i,j},\mathrm{CT}_{i,j}) \cap (\mathrm{BT}_{u,v},\mathrm{CT}_{u,v}) = \varnothing, E_{i,j}^k = E_{u,v}^k \tag{5-17}$$

$$\mathrm{BT}_{i,j} + \mathrm{PT}_{i,j} = \mathrm{CT}_{i,j} \tag{5-18}$$

$$F(O_{i,j}) = F(E_{i,j}^k) \tag{5-19}$$

In this model, Eq. (5-14) is the objective function and Eq. (5-15)~Eq. (5-19) are constraints of the objective. Eq. (5-15) represents the serial constraint of manufacturing procedure; Eq. (5-16) represents the constraint of task exclusiveness; Eq. (5-17) represents the constraint of equipment exclusiveness; Eq. (5-18) represents the constraint of processing continuity; Eq. (5-19) represents the constraint of processing consistence.

The completion time of each task is essentially the maximum completion time of the process contained in this task, which is shown in Eq. (5-20).

$$C_i = \max\{\mathrm{CT}_{i,j}\} \tag{5-20}$$

5. Representation and Analysis of the Solution of a Job Shop Scheduling Problem

The solution of a job shop scheduling problem includes the start time of all processes and the arrangement of equipment. Considering the scheduling situation of each process as an element in the solution, a set can be used to represent the solution. Assuming that the starting time is $\mathrm{BT}_{i,j}$ and the equipment of process $O_{i,j}$ is $E_{i,j}^k$, they can form a two-dimensional variable $[\mathrm{BT}_{i,j}, E_{i,j}^k]$ in the solution element; then the design variables of job shop scheduling problem can be expressed as a set S which contains all scheduling results.

$$S = \{[\mathrm{BT}_{i,j}, E_{i,j}^k]\}, i = 1, 2, \cdots, n; k = 1, 2, \cdots, m \tag{5-21}$$

The specific values of the design variables above correspond to a scheduling scheme.

5.3.2 Using Complex Method to Solve Job Shop Scheduling Problem

1. Feasibility-Proving of the Centroid

Complex method is one of the solutions of the traditional optimization problems, which is mainly used to solve continuous optimization problems. Common optimization problem can be solved directly by establishing mathematical models and steps of complex method. However, job shop scheduling problem varies from common optimization problem:

① Job shop scheduling problem has more constraints than common optimization problem and its constraints are more complicated;

② Job shop scheduling problem is a discrete optimization problem.

Above all, job shop scheduling problem is difficult to be solved directly by complex method. Therefore, it is necessary to improve complex method to apply the idea of complex method to job shop scheduling problem.

The probability of finding the feasible solution is relatively high if it can be sure that centroid variables have the characteristics of feasible solution. According to the solving process of centroid variables, the following conclusion can be drawn: the value of centroid variables does not change the serial constraints between processes, i. e. the feasible manufacturing procedure of each task can be found by sorting the start time of processes in centroid variables from the small to the large.

Prove: assuming that there are N processes in task i, process $O_{i,j}$ is the former process of the process $O_{i,j+1}$, the starting time of $O_{i,j}$ and $O_{i,j+1}$ are $BT_{i,j}$ and $BT_{i,j+1}$ in feasible solutions, the number of the initial feasible solutions is n_1, the lth solution is the worst one among all schemes, the starting time of $O_{i,j}$ and $O_{i,j+1}$ are $BT_{i,j}^{(k)}$ and $BT_{i,j+1}^{(k)}$ in the kth feasible solution and the processing time of $O_{i,j}$ is $PT_{i,j}$.

According to the characteristics of feasible solutions, for any $k \in n_1$, there is

$$BT_{i,j+1}^{(k)} \geqslant BT_{i,j}^{(k)} + PT_{i,j} \tag{5-22}$$

So

$$\sum_{k=1, k\neq l}^{n_1} (BT_{i,j+1}^{(k)} - BT_{i,j}^{(k)}) \geqslant (n_1 - 1) PT_{i,j} \tag{5-23}$$

According to the iteration process of complex method, the value of centroid after removing the bad point $O_{i,j}$ is

$$BT_{i,j}^{(0)} = \frac{1}{n_1 - 1} \sum_{k=1, k\neq l}^{n_1} BT_{i,j}^{(k)} \tag{5-24}$$

So, the starting time of centroid in all processes of task i is

$$BT^{(0)} = [BT_{i,1}^{(0)} \quad BT_{i,2}^{(0)} \quad \cdots \quad BT_{i,r}^{(0)} \quad \cdots \quad BT_{i,N}^{(0)}] \tag{5-25}$$

For any $O_{i,j}$, if its latter process $O_{i,j+1}$ exists, then it must be

$$BT_{i,j+1}^{(0)} - BT_{i,j}^{(0)} = \frac{1}{n_1 - 1} \sum_{k=1, k\neq l}^{n_1} \left(BT_{i,j+1}^{(k)} - BT_{i,j}^{(k)} \right) \geqslant PT_{i,j} \tag{5-26}$$

Therefore, the starting time of the latter process is greater than the amount of the starting time and processing time of the former process. Thus, centroid variables will not change the serial relation between processes, i. e. the centroid satisfies the serial relation between processes, which greatly reduces the complexity of feasibility checking in its iteration.

Although the serial relation between processes in centroid variables can be guaranteed, there may be time-overlapping zone between parallel processes of the same task and processes allocated in the same equipment. Thus, it is necessary to judge whether mapping point can meet these constraints or not; if not, it should be adjusted properly. The process of judgment and adjustment are as follows.

(1) The calculation of mapping point. In job shop scheduling problem, elements in

mapping point must be zero or positive integer after rounding, otherwise they need to be recalculated. The coordinate of centroid is considered as new point when the coefficient α is less than the given parameter.

(2) Feasibility-judging of the manufacturing procedure. All processes should be sequenced according to the starting time; the manufacturing procedure is feasible if every process can meet the former process constraints.

(3) A serial processing sequence can be found by sorting the processes in according to the starting time in mapping point; then judge whether there is processing time-overlapping and eliminate it if existing. The condition to judge overlapping is as follows:

$$BT_{i,j} + PT_{i,j} \leqslant BT_{i,j+1} \tag{5-27}$$

(4) Determine the set of processes to be distributed. The set contains all processes which are sorted from the small to the large according to the starting time, and then equipment can be allocated and the starting time can be adjusted. A solution can be found with all processes in the set scheduled.

(5) Equipment selection and the starting time adjustment in the same equipment. In order to find a complete solution with the manufacturing procedure constraints, it is necessary to allocate equipment to each process. Feasible equipment can be selected if it is available within the processing time, otherwise, calculate the processing time $ET^{(k)}$ when the equipment is able to be in effective operation, then allocate equipment to processes according to the value of $ET^{(k)}$. In order to ensure the serial constraints, it is necessary to reset the starting time of the unallocated processes in the same task and to reorder unallocated processes assembly according to the resource occupancy of the assigned processes.

2. Steps of the Algorithm

The specific steps of complex method in solving job shop scheduling problem are as follows. The flow chart of the algorithm is shown in Fig. 5-3.

(1) Initialization. The initial complex of job shop scheduling problem contains n_1 initial feasible scheme. The initial scheme can be seen by assigning equipment to each process and by determining the sequence of all tasks randomly. Meanwhile, set the number of iterations is Sum$=0$, $\alpha=1.3$; the termination condition parameter is ε, total iteration times is λ and the judging parameter of coefficient α is μ.

(2) Calculate the value of objective function $f^{(k)}$ of each scheme. Calculate the completion time C_i of each task and the maximum value is taken as the value of objective function.

(3) The termination condition parameter ε and total iteration times λ are given. According to Eqs. (5-28) and (5-29), the termination condition can be assessed. If the condition holds, then the iteration completes, and turn to step (12); if not, judge that whether the iteration times Sum$=\lambda$ is valid, if it is true, then the iteration completes, and turn to step (12), otherwise turn to step (4).

$$\left[\frac{1}{n_1-1}\sum_{i=1}^{n_1}(f^{(i)}-\bar{f})\right]^{1/2}<\varepsilon \qquad (5\text{-}28)$$

$$\text{Sum}=\lambda \qquad (5\text{-}29)$$

(4) Determine bad point X_H: take the point with maximum value of objective function as bad point.

(5) Calculate the centroid X_C and the starting time of the centroid of each process according to Eq. (5-24).

(6) The new point X^R can be found according to the bad point and centroid. Calculate the new point with the starting time $BT_{i,j}$ as a variable. Only the starting time of processes exists in X^R at present, judge whether the starting time is positive and the manufacturing procedure is feasible. If the value is feasible, turn to step (7), otherwise, turn to step (11).

(7) Judge and adjust the starting time of processes in the same task. The sequence of processes can be found according to the starting time. If $CT_{i,j}>BT_{i,j+1}$, then $CT_{i,j}=BT_{i,j+1}$.

(8) The set of processes to be allocated S_0 can be determined according to the starting time of the new points.

(9) Allocate equipment for processes and adjust the starting time according to the order in S_0. Select the process to be distributed $O_{i,j}$; determine the set of equipment to be allocated S_E; judge whether there is equipment which is available at the stating time $BT_{i,j}$ of $O_{i,j}$; if so, select equipment $E_{i,j}^k$ and remove $O_{i,j}$ from S_0; then reorder it until all processes are distributed. If not, calculate the starting time of equipment $ET^{(k)}$; if none equipment is available at the time of $BT_{i,j}$, choose the one which has minimum $ET^{(k)}$ for $O_{i,j}$, and make $BT_{i,j}=ET^{(k)}$. Meanwhile, adjust the starting time of the latter process of $O_{i,j}$ and remove $O_{i,j}$ from S_0 then reorder it until all processes are distributed.

(10) Calculate the value of objective function $f(X^R)$ of X^R. If $f(X^R)<f(X_H)$, replace X_H with X^R, set Sum=Sum+1 and turn to step (3); otherwise, if $X^R=X_C$, a randomly generated scheduling scheme $X^{(i)}$ can be found, then turn to step (3) until $f(X^{(i)})<f(X_H)$; if $X^R\neq X_C$, then turn to step (11).

(11) Judge whether α is less than μ. If $\alpha\geq\mu$, set $\alpha=\alpha/2$ and then turn to step (6) to recalculate the new point; if $\alpha<\mu$, then turn to step (7).

(12) After that, the scheme $X^{(b)}$ with minimum objective function value can be taken as the final solution.

3. Analysis of Problem-Solving Performance of the Algorithm

Complex method has a good astringency and global searching ability so that it's an appropriate way to solve job shop scheduling problem. It is known that the bad point will be replaced by the new point which makes the value of objective function better in iteration. Therefore, solutions can converge to the optimum one through the iteration. In addition, complex method is often used to solve optimization problems with few variables. For a large-scale JSSP, new methods still need to be explored.

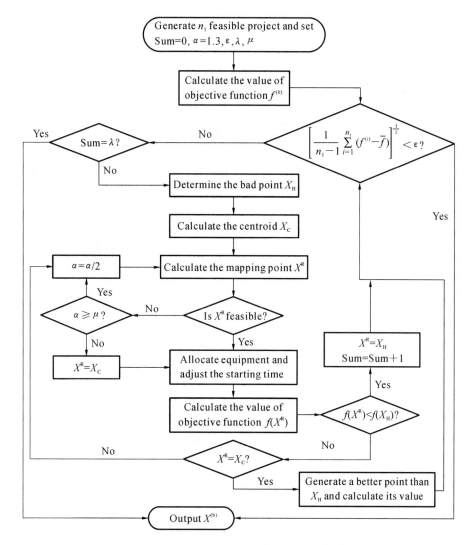

Fig. 5-3 Flow Chart of Complex Method

Chapter 6 Genetic Algorithm and Its Application in Production Scheduling

6.1 Formation and Development of Genetic Algorithm

Genetic algorithm (GA) is a highly parallel, random and adaptive search algorithm, which uses natural selection and natural genetic mechanism for reference. It is a multi-parameter, multi-population optimization method, which imitates the principle of "natural selection, survival of the fittest" in the evolution of natural organisms. After more than 20 years of development, genetic algorithm has been successfully applied in the field of data mining, production scheduling, machine learning, image processing and so on.

Genetic algorithm originated from computer simulation of biological systems. In the early 1960s, Professor J. Holland of the University of Michigan began to study it by bio-simulation technology. He applied genetic algorithm to search the parameter set of chess game evaluation function, and put forward the term genetic algorithm for the first time. In 1965, Holland published the classic book of genetic algorithm—*Adaptation Natural and Artificial Systems*, which systematically expounded the basic theory and method of genetic algorithm. In the same year, De Jong completed his doctoral thesis, *Analysis of the Behavior of a Class of Genetic Adaptive Systems*, combining Holland's model theory with his computational experiments to further improve selection, crossover, and mutation operations. Some new genetic manipulation methods are proposed. After entering 1980s, genetic algorithm has been developed rapidly and has been applied in more areas. In 1983, Goldberg, a student of Holland, applied genetic algorithm to the optimization of pipeline gas system, which solved this very complicated problem. In the aspect of machine learning, since Holland proposed the basic theory of genetic algorithm, he has devoted himself to the research of classifier system. Holland hopes that the system can classify the external stimuli and send it to the place that needs it, so it is named classifier system. After that, Holland, in cooperation with other researchers, simulated some economic phenomena with the classifier system, and satisfactory results were obtained. In 1991, L. Davis published the book *Handbook of Genetic Algorithm*, which introduced many application examples of genetic algorithm in scientific computing, engineering technology and social economy. In 1992, John R. Koza applied genetic algorithm to the optimization design and automatic generation of computer programs, and put forward the concept of genetic programming (GP).

Genetic algorithm has the characteristics of strong robustness, and its ability to solve NP-Hard problem has attracted extensive attention of scholars both at home and abroad. In recent years, the application of genetic algorithm to solving the optimization problem of production system has become a hot spot.

6.2 Genetic Algorithm Foundation

6.2.1 Introduction to the Principle of Genetic Algorithm

The basic idea of genetic algorithm comes from Darwin's theory of evolution and Mendel's theory of genetics. The most important point of Darwin's theory of evolution is the principle of survival of the fittest. It is believed that each species adapts to the environment more and more in the process of development, and the basic characteristics of each one of the species are inherited by the progeny, but the offspring will make some new changes different from the parent generation. When the environment changes, only those individual characteristics that adapt to the environment can be preserved.

The most important point of Mendel's theory of genetics is the principle of genetic inheritance. It believes that heredity exists in the cell in the form of code and is contained in the chromosome in the form of gene; each gene has a special location, and controls some particular nature; therefore, the individuals produced by each gene have some kind of adaptability to the environment. Gene mutation and chromosome hybridization can produce offspring with different characteristics. By the process of survival of the fittest, the structure of gene with high adaptability can be preserved.

Because genetic algorithm is a direct search optimization method inspired by evolution theory and genetic mechanism, various concepts of evolution and genetics are used in genetic algorithm, such as genes, loci, alleles, chromosomes, genetics and etc. Different from the traditional search algorithm, genetic algorithm starts the search process from a set of random initial solutions, called "population". Individual in the population is a solution to the problem, called "chromosome". These chromosomes continue to evolve over subsequent iterations and are selectively preserved, known as inheritance. In each generation, the fitness is used to measure the quality of chromosomes. The next generation of chromosomes that are generated is called offspring. The offspring are formed by crossover or mutation operation on the previous generation of chromosomes.

Genetic algorithm does not require much knowledge of the problem itself. It only evaluates each chromosome according to the problem solved, and selects the chromosome through the fitness, giving high fitness chromosomes more chances to survive. In genetic algorithm, several numerical codes, namely chromosomes, are generated randomly to form the initial population. The fitness function gives individual a numerical evaluation to eliminate a number of individuals with low fitness, select a number of individuals with high fitness to participate in genetic operation, and form the next generation of new population through the collection of individuals after genetic operation. The next round of new population evolves repeatedly, which is the basic principle of genetic algorithm.

Genetic algorithm abstracts from the evolution process of biological population. Through random selection crossover and mutation operation in the evolution process, the genetic algorithm uses historical information to infer a set of advantages for the improvement of the expected performance of the next generation. By the continuous evolution, it finally converges to an individual who is most adaptative to the environment, and then the optimal solution of the problem can be obtained. The general genetic algorithm is called basic genetic algorithm (or standard genetic algorithm). In various engineering practice, combined with the characteristics and knowledge of problems in different areas, researchers have made many improvements to the basic genetic algorithm and formed various specific genetic algorithm, so that they can solve different types of optimization problems.

The application of basic genetic algorithm includes five elements: problem parameter coding, initial population setting, fitness function design, genetic operation method and control parameter setting. As shown in Fig. 6-1, the basic genetic algorithm calculation process is an iterative process, and the basic steps are as follows.

Step 1: select the encoding policy; mark the parameter assembly X of the actual problem as the bit string.

Step 2: according to the optimization objective of the actual problem, define the function of fitness value.

Step 3: determine genetic strategy, including population size n, selection, crossover, mutation operation method, crossover probability p_c, mutation probability p_m and other parameters.

Step 4: generating the initial population P.

Step 5: calculate the fitness value of all individuals in the population.

Step 6: in accordance with the genetic strategy, individuals in the population are selected to replicate, cross, and mutate to form the next generation of population.

Step 7: determine whether the population performance meets the termination condition. If not, return to step 6 and proceed to the next iteration; if the condition is met, the calculation will be completed and the result will be output.

The main concepts in genetic operation along with its significance are as follows.

(1) Gene: a basic unit that expresses the design variable , also the element that determines the trait of the design variable.

(2) Selection: pass down the gene in whole or in part to the next generation.

(3) Crossover: a certain point of the gene string is cut off and exchanged with another

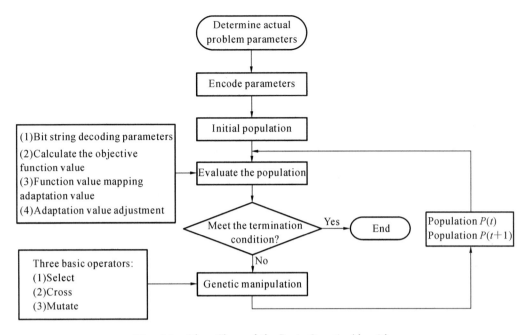

Fig. 6-1 Flow Chart of the Basic Genetic Algorithm

string that is cut at the same position.

(4) Mutation: during the process of replication, some genes make replication errors, resulting in new traits. The probability of mutation in minimal.

(5) Population: a group of individuals that can produce crossover.

(6) Individual: a single design variable value containing integrity information.

(7) Fitness: the degree of individual optimization.

6.2.2 Genetic Algorithm Encoding and Decoding Method

Since the genetic algorithm is solved by translating the problem into genetic coding, there are problems with encoding and decoding.

1) Encoding accuracy

Assuming that the value range of a parameter is $[U_{min}, U_{max}]$, and use a binary coded symbol string of length L to represent this parameter, as shown in Table 6-1.

Table 6-1 Binary Encoding Step Size and Accuracy

Binary encoding	Parameters
$000\cdots000=0$	U_{min}
$000\cdots001=1$	$U_{min}+\sigma$
$000\cdots010=2$	$U_{min}+2\sigma$
$\cdots$	$\cdots$
$111\cdots111=2^L-1$	U_{max}

The encoding accuracy is

$$\sigma = \frac{U_{max} - U_{min}}{2^L - 1} \tag{6-1}$$

2) Decoding method

$$X = U_{min} + \left[\sum_{i=1}^{L} (b_i \cdot 2^{i-1}) \right] \frac{U_{max} - U_{min}}{2^L - 1} \tag{6-2}$$

where X is the decimal numeral which is transformed by binary system, L is the length of binary numeral, b_i is 0 or 1 in binary numeral.

The encoding and decoding methods are explained by an example.

Example 6-1 Assuming that $-3.0 \leqslant x \leqslant 12.1$, accuracy requirement $\sigma = 1/10000$. Question: How many bits of binary are needed to achieve coding accuracy? How to decode the result of the solution?

Solution Since

$$\sigma = \frac{U_{max} - U_{min}}{2^L - 1} = \frac{12.1 + 3.0}{2^L - 1} = \frac{1}{10000}$$

Then

$$2^L = 151001, \text{ i. e. } 2^{17} < 2^L < 2^{18}$$

So 18 bits binary encoding is required.

The decoding of the result can be brought into the Eq. (6-2), such as 010001001011010000 is decoded into

$$X = -3.0 + 70352 \times \frac{12.1 + 3.0}{2^L - 1} = 1.052426$$

6.2.3 The Characteristics and Application of Genetic Algorithm

As can be seen from the basic principles of the above genetic algorithm, the genetic algorithm has following unique advantages compared with traditional optimization calculation method.

(1) The genetic algorithm starts with a collection of problem solutions rather than a single solution. This is the biggest difference between genetic algorithm and traditional optimization algorithm. The traditional optimization algorithm finds the optimal solution from a single initial value iteration, and it is easy to fall into a partial optimal solution. The genetic algorithm starts from the collection of solutions, and the coverage is large, which is more conducive to comprehensive optimization.

(2) The genetic algorithm uses less information of a specific problem, so it is easy to form a general algorithm process. Since the genetic algorithm adopts the information of the fitness value, it does not need to solve the information directly related to the problem such as the derivative of the objective function. Genetic algorithm only needs general information such as fitness value and bit string encoding, therefore it can be applied in most of the engineering problems.

(3) Genetic algorithm has strong fault tolerance. The initial bit string assembly of genetic algorithm itself has a large amount of information far from the optimal solution. The selection, crossover, and mutation operation can quickly eliminate the bit string that greatly differs from the optimal solution. This is a strong filtering process. Therefore, the genetic algorithm has a high fault tolerance.

(4) Genetic algorithm has implicit parallelism. The genetic algorithm has parallelism from the set of previous generation solutions to the next, which is very suitable for parallel computing.

Genetic algorithm is a relatively general algorithm framework for system optimization, combinatorial optimization and other issues. It does not depend on specific problems, and has strong robustness, parallelism and comprehensive optimization for solving various types of problems, so it is widely used in many disciplines.

6.3 Genetic Algorithm Application Case—Workshop Equipment Layout Optimization

6.3.1 Mathematical Model of Workshop Equipment Layout

1. Constraints on Workshop Equipment Layout

As a two-dimensional engineering layout problem, the workshop equipment layout problem belongs to the two-dimensional layout problem with performance constraints. In addition to the overall performance constraints, there are many other layout requirements in the layout process. These requirements have an important impact on solving layout problems.

Layout constraints can be divided into hard constraints and soft constraints. A hard constraint is a constraint that must be met in a layout, such as a non-interference constraint between layout objects, that is, two objects cannot overlap. If the hard constraints are violated, the layout scheme fails. A soft constraint is a constraint that should be satisfied to a certain extent. Usually the objective function in a mathematical model is a soft constraint. The constraints of the workshop equipment layout scheme mainly include the constraints of target constraint, mode constraint, shape position constraint, etc.

(1) Target constraint: the goal of workshop equipment layout is to maximize logistics efficiency. This constraint is a soft constraint and a heuristic rule.

(2) Mode constraint: including the relation between equipment and workshop in the middle of the layout scheme, such as multiple machines with same function must be arranged in groups, etc. This constraint is a hard constraint and must be satisfied first in the layout design.

(3) Shape position constraint: including the relative positional relation between each equipment and workshop in the layout scheme, mainly the equipment cannot interfere with each other, and there must be a certain safety distance among the relative position of every

equipment. The location of all layout equipment must be set within the workshop, and there is a certain safety distance among the equipment and the workshop wall. There are obstacles and prohibited areas (such as pillars, pools or workshop areas).

2. Evaluation Criteria for Workshop Equipment Layout Plan

Logistics efficiency is the main evaluation index in workshop equipment layout plan. The logistics efficiency analysis includes the flow order of material between the various processing equipment and the intensity of the flow per unit time. The flow order of material between the various processing equipment should be a sequential flow until all processes are completed without too much reentry or backflow.

Since the processing and assembly process of each part has determined the type of machine tools and equipment used and the number of times which one equipment is used. So, the analysis of the logistics efficiency is transformed into the analysis of the logistics strength and the layout scheme, and met the needs of the production process. The analysis and calculation of logistics intensity can be expressed by quantitative means by mathematical modeling, such as Eq. (6-3):

$$F = \sum_{i=1}^{n} \sum_{j=1}^{n} f_{ij} \cdot d_{ij} \cdot c_{ij} \tag{6-3}$$

where F is logistics intensity. f is the logistics frequency matrix between equipment and its elements are f_{ij}; d is the distance matrix between equipment and its elements are d_{ij}; c is the logistics unit cost matrix between equipment and its elements are c_{ij}; i and j are the numbers of equipment.

3. Mathematical Model of Workshop Equipment Layout

The actual workshop and equipment are simplified as follows to establish a mathematical model of the equipment layout. The layout container is a workshop, and the objects to be arranged are various machine tools. Simplify the workshop and machine tools into a rectangle of a certain area. The length and width of the workshop are L and W respectively, and the length and width of the machine tools are S and Q respectively. Next, establish the Cartesian coordinate system of the workshop as shown in Fig. 6-2.

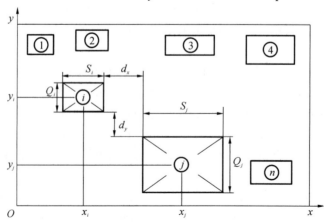

Fig. 6-2 Schematic Diagram of the Layout Constraints of the Workshop

The position of the equipment is directly determined by the Cartesian coordinate values of the equipment center (x_i, y_i), (x_j, y_j). There are n processing equipments in the workshop to participate in the layout. The mutual material transfer times between the n equipments are represented by matrix f, the distance between equipments is represented by matrix d, the logistics cost per unit distance between equipments can be represented by matrix c.

$$f = \begin{bmatrix} f_{11} & f_{12} & \cdots & f_{1n} \\ f_{21} & f_{22} & \cdots & f_{2n} \\ \vdots & \vdots & \ddots & \vdots \\ f_{n1} & f_{n2} & \cdots & f_{nn} \end{bmatrix} \tag{6-4}$$

$$d = \begin{bmatrix} d_{11} & d_{12} & \cdots & d_{1n} \\ d_{21} & d_{22} & \cdots & d_{2n} \\ \vdots & \vdots & \ddots & \vdots \\ d_{n1} & d_{n2} & \cdots & d_{nn} \end{bmatrix} \tag{6-5}$$

$$c = \begin{bmatrix} c_{11} & c_{12} & \cdots & c_{1n} \\ c_{21} & c_{22} & \cdots & c_{2n} \\ \vdots & \vdots & \ddots & \vdots \\ c_{n1} & c_{n2} & \cdots & c_{nn} \end{bmatrix} \tag{6-6}$$

The evaluation goal of the layout is the highest logistics efficiency, that is, the logistics cost is minimized, and the calculation formula is given by Eq. (6-3).

$$F_{\min} = \min \sum_{i=1}^{n} \sum_{j=1}^{n} f_{ij} \cdot d_{ij} \cdot c_{ij} \tag{6-7}$$

The problem contains the following hard constraints.

(1) The constraints of the layout container, that is, the layout cannot exceed the limit of the length L and the width W of the workshop, and the Eq. (6-8) should be satisfied.

(2) The non-interference between the objects to be arranged, that is, the layout position of the machine tools cannot intersect and either the Eq. (6-9) or Eq. (6-10) must be satisfied.

$$\begin{cases} x_{ri} - x_{li} + \dfrac{S_{ri} + S_{li}}{2} \leqslant L \\ y_{nj} - y_{lj} + \dfrac{Q_{nj} + Q_{lj}}{2} \leqslant W \end{cases} \tag{6-8}$$

$$|x_i - x_j| \geqslant \frac{S_i + S_j}{2} + d_x \tag{6-9}$$

$$|y_i - y_j| \geqslant \frac{Q_i + Q_j}{2} + d_y \tag{6-10}$$

where x_{ri}, x_{li} represent the abscissa of the leftmost and rightmost equipment in the layout, and y_{nj}, y_{lj} represent the ordinate of the top and bottom equipment.

6.3.2 Solving Workshop Equipment Layout Problem by GA

According to the requirements of the equipment layout optimization design, design two sets of chromosomes, namely X (the abscissa of the equipment, $x_1, x_2, \cdots, x_n$), Y (the ordinate of the equipment, $y_1, y_2, \cdots, y_n$). The (x, y) indicates the coordinate position of the equipment center in the workshop.

Design a workshop layout case comparison experiment and the specific layout parameters are: workshop length 22 m, workshop width 16 m, workshop contains 6 equipments. Its length and width matrix s, unit distance logistics cost matrix c and equipment mutual material flow matrix f respectively are

$$s = [L \quad W] = \begin{bmatrix} 4 & 3 & 6 & 2.5 & 2 & 5 \\ 4 & 1.5 & 3.5 & 2 & 2 & 3 \end{bmatrix}^T \quad (6\text{-}11)$$

$$c = \begin{bmatrix} 0 & & & & & \\ 2 & 0 & & & & \\ 4 & 2.5 & 0 & & & \\ 1.5 & 1.5 & 2.5 & 0 & & \\ 1.5 & 1 & 2.5 & 1 & 0 & \\ 2.5 & 2 & 3 & 2 & 2 & 0 \end{bmatrix} \quad (6\text{-}12)$$

$$f = \begin{bmatrix} 0 & & & & & \\ 31 & 0 & & & & \\ 12 & 21 & 0 & & & \\ 9 & 41 & 14 & 0 & & \\ 28 & 24 & 12 & 72 & 0 & \\ 90 & 62 & 21 & 80 & 40 & 0 \end{bmatrix} \quad (6\text{-}13)$$

The minimum safety distance between the equipments is 2 m, and the minimum distance between the machine and the boundary is 2 m. It is required to solve the optimal layout scheme.

According to the above analysis, the defined fitness value function is

$$f(x) = \max - (Z_{\min} + \lambda_1 F_1(x) + \lambda_2 F_2(x)) \quad (6\text{-}14)$$

$$F_1(x) = (L - \frac{S_{ni} + S_{li}}{2} - (x_{ni} - x_{li}))^2 + (W - \frac{Q_{nj} + Q_{lj}}{2} - (y_{nj} - y_{lj}))^2 \quad (6\text{-}15)$$

$$F_2(x) = (|x_i - x_j| - \frac{S_i + S_j}{2} - d_x)^2 + (|y_i - y_j| - \frac{Q_i + Q_j}{2} - d_y)^2 \quad (6\text{-}16)$$

In Eq. (6-14), the $f(x)$ is the fit function, max is the initial limit value. The Eq. (6-15) is the constraint of Eq. (6-8), Eq. (6-16) is the constraint of Eq. (6-9) or Eq. (6-10).

In the operation of genetic operators, the selection operator is simplified. The crossover and mutation operators use standard operations. When 150 iterations are used, the optimal individuals are obtained in the 111th generation, namely $X=$ (6.45,12.82,10.44,4.62,18.46,6.68,1.26,5.69,12.54,9.64,4.45,1.80), and the optimal target value is 1.8022×10^4. The cost convergence diagram and the final layout diagram are Fig. 6-3 and Fig. 6-4.

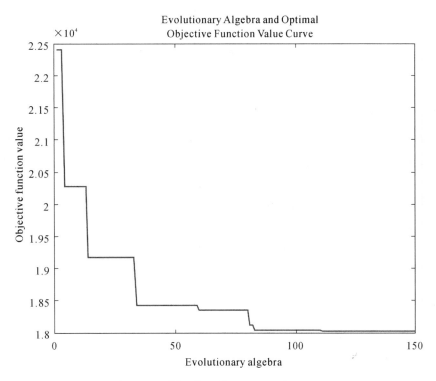

Fig. 6-3 The Cost Convergence Diagram

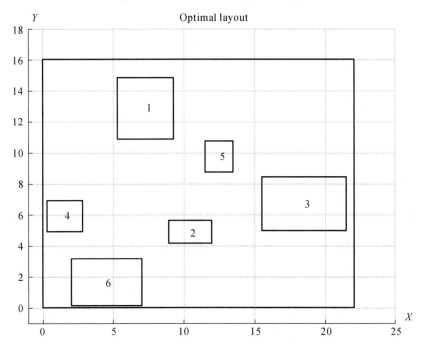

Fig. 6-4 The Final Layout Diagram

6.4 Genetic Algorithm Application Case—Packing Problem

6.4.1 Packing Problem Model

Like the backpack problem, the packing problem requires that several items from n items should be loaded into one box. Each item has a volume ($V_i > 0$) and a value (p_i), and each box has a volume limit ($V_0 > 0$). The goal is to find the optimal solution for assigning items to the box so that the sum of the volume of the items in each box does not exceed its limit and the value is the greatest.

The mathematical representation of the packing problem is as follows:

$$\max z(x) = \sum_{i=1}^{n} p_i(x_i) \tag{6-17}$$

s. t.
$$\sum_{i=1}^{n} V_i x_i \leqslant V_0 \tag{6-18}$$

$x_i \geqslant 0$ and x_i is an integer ($i \in N = \{1, 2, \cdots, n\}$)

where $x_i = 1$ means that item i is loaded into the box, and $x_i = 0$ means that item i is not selected.

6.4.2 Case Verification

Select some items from Table 6-2 to maximize the total value and the total volume cannot exceed 1000.

Table 6-2 Volume and Value of the Items

Number	1	2	3	4	5	6	7	8	9	10
Volume/L	80	82	85	70	72	70	66	50	55	25
Value/yuan	220	208	198	192	180	180	165	162	160	158
Number	11	12	13	14	15	16	17	18	19	20
Volume/L	50	55	40	48	50	32	22	60	30	32
Value/yuan	155	130	125	122	120	118	115	110	105	101
Number	21	22	23	24	25	26	27	28	29	30
Volume/L	40	38	35	32	25	28	30	22	50	30
Value/yuan	100	100	98	96	95	90	88	82	80	77
Number	31	32	33	34	35	36	37	38	39	40
Volume/L	45	30	60	50	20	65	20	25	30	10
Value/yuan	75	73	72	70	69	66	65	63	60	58

continued

Number	41	42	43	44	45	46	47	48	49	50
Volume/L	20	25	15	10	10	10	4	4	2	1
Value/yuan	56	50	30	20	15	10	8	5	3	1

The results of genetic algorithm are shown in Fig. 6-5.

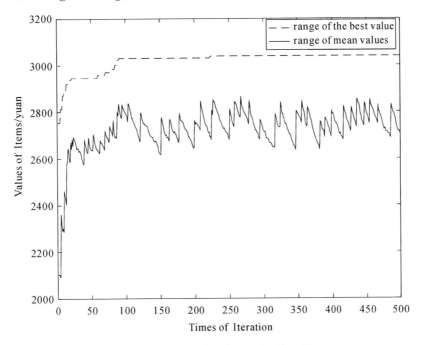

Fig. 6-5 The Results of Genetic Algorithm

The best combination numbers are 1, 2, 4, 5, 8, 9, 10, 11, 13, 14, 16, 17, 19, 20, 21, 22, 24, 25, 26, 27, 28, 35, 37, 40, 41, 43, 44, 49.

The total volume of these items just meets the maximum volume constraint, with a total value of 3073 yuan.

6.5 Solving Job Shop Scheduling Problems by GA

As shown in Fig. 6-6, the workpiece 1 and the workpiece 2 have 5 and 3 processes respectively. Among them, 101 is the preorder process of 102 and 104, and 103 and 104 are the preorder processes of 105. Both process 101 and process 105 can be processed on equipment 1 or equipment 2; both process 102 and process 104 can be processed on equipment 3 or equipment 4; process 103 can be processed on equipment 5 or equipment 6. Processes 201, 202, and 203 are serial processes, the process 201 can be processed on equipment 1 or equipment 2; the process 202 can be processed on equipment 3 or equipment 4; the process 203 can be processed on equipment 5 or equipment 6. The number above the processes is the processing time(s).

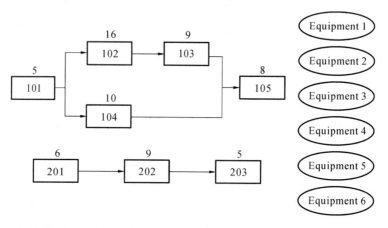

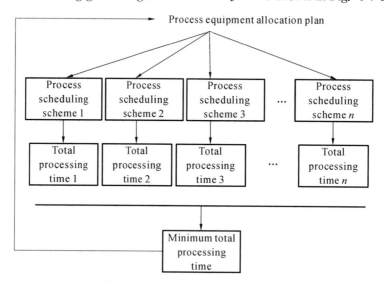

Fig. 6-6 Correspondent Relation Between Each Process and Optional Equipment

The basic idea of using genetic algorithm to solve JSSP is shown in Fig. 6-7 and Fig. 6-8.

Fig. 6-7 Processing Time Calculation and Equipment Allocation Idea

(1) Order of sequence: the order in which equipment is assigned to the process. The constraint of order of sequence is to satisfy the serial constraint of the process, and the order of sequence that satisfies this constraint is the effective sequence of the order. Such as 101—102—104—103—105—201—202—203 is an effective scheduling sequence, and 101—103—102—104—105—201—202—203 is an invalid scheduling sequence.

(2) Sorting mode: according to the process order, the process is sequentially arranged on the equipment by a certain rule, thereby obtaining a certain process sequence.

(3) The order is only the order of the process, and the serial constraints are satisfied on the same equipment only. On different equipment, the first process is not necessarily processed first. For instance, in the following order of the process 101—201—202—104—102—203—103—105, the process 202 arranges the equipment prior to the process 104.

(4) Chromosome design: the same coding method is adopted for the serial process problem. Due to the existence of the parallel process, the process selection rule is

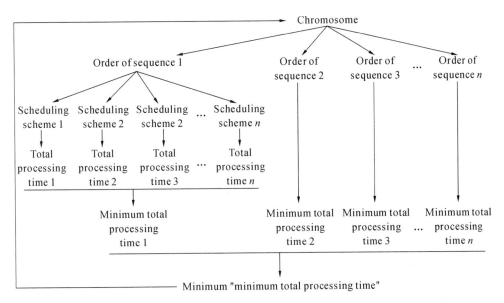

Fig. 6-8 Chromosome Design and Its Correspondent Relation with Scheduling Method

randomly selected in the latter process or the parallel process of the previous process. The chromosome is designed into two gene segments, the front segment representing the equipment selection and the latter representing the process.

Mark the equipment: equipments 1, 3, 5 are numbered 1, equipments 2, 4, 6 are numbered 2. Randomly generated chromosomes such as [1 1 1 2 2 1 2 1 2 1 1 1 2 1 1 2] in which the last eight numbers indicate the processes, the first eight numbers indicate the equipments. The chromosome indicates that the processes 201, 101, 102, 103, 202, 104, 105, 203 respectively select the 1st, 1st, 1st, 1st, 2nd, 1st, 2nd, 1st equipments, namely equipment 1, equipment 1, equipment 3, equipment 5, equipment 4, equipment 3, equipment 2, equipment 5.

(5) Population initialization, the process is similar to the serial process.

(6) Calculate the conversion of the target value and the fitness value.

(7) Select replicate, cross, mutate, and produce offspring. During this operation, the inferior solutions outside the optimal individual are cross-mutated, and the crossover only happens in the second half of the chromosome.

(8) Calculate the fitness of the offspring, select the excellent offspring and the father to compare, determine to keep or replace and proceed to the next round of selection.

(9) Update the population back to step(3) or output the results.

Experimental result is as follows.

The program is designed according to the genetic algorithm process. The optimal solution is: the shortest completion time is 38 s, and the optimal ranking is 201—101—102—202—103—104—105—203, and the corresponding processing equipments are equipment 1, equipment 1, equipment 4, equipment 3, equipment 5, equipment 3, equipment 2, equipment 6. The Gantt chart of the optimal solution is shown in Fig. 6-9.

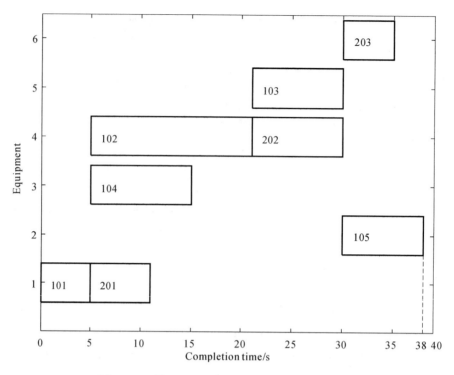

Fig. 6-9 The Gantt Chart of the Optimal Solution

6.6 Summary

This chapter first introduces the formation and development of genetic algorithm, and then illustrates the basic principle and method of genetic algorithm. Taking workshop machine layout problem, packing problem and job shop scheduling problem as examples, the application of genetic algorithm in a production system is expounded.

Chapter 7   Ant Colony Algorithm and Its Application in Production System Optimization

7.1   An Overview of Ant Colony Algorithm

1. The Origin of the Algorithm

In the 1990s, Italian scholars M. Dorigo, V. Maniezzo, A. Colorni and others were inspired by the mechanism of biological evolution and proposed a new simulated evolutionary algorithm—ant colony algorithm, one of the main algorithms in the field of colony intelligence theory—by simulating the search path behavior of ants in nature. This algorithm is used to solve traveling salesman problem (TSP), assignment problem and job shop scheduling problem, and good experimental results are obtained. Preliminary research shows that ant colony algorithm has some advantages in solving complex optimization problem, especially discrete optimization problem. It shows that ant colony algorithm is a promising algorithm.

2. Background

Bionics was founded in the mid-1950s and inspired by the mechanism of biological evolution. Many new methods are proposed to solve complex optimization problems, such as evolutionary programming, evolutionary strategy, genetic algorithm and etc. These algorithms have successfully solved some practical problem.

Unlike most gradient-based optimization algorithm, colony intelligence relies on probabilistic search algorithm. Although the probabilistic search algorithm usually uses more evaluation functions, compared with gradient-based algorithm and traditional evolutionary algorithm, its advantages are still remarkable, mainly in the following aspects:

(1) Without centralized control constraints, the solution of the whole problem will not be affected by the malfunction of individual, which ensures that the system has stronger robustness;

(2) Ensure the expansibility of the system by means of non-direct information exchange;

(3) Parallel distributed algorithm model can make full use of multi-processor;

(4) No special requirement for the continuity of the problem definition;

(5) Simple algorithm.

There are two main algorithms in the field of colony intelligence: ACO (ant colony optimization) and PSO (particle swarm optimization). The former is a simulation of food collection process in ant community and has been successfully applied to many discrete optimization items. The latter is derived from the simulation of a simple social system, initially simulating the process of birds foraging, but later found that it is a good optimization tool.

7.2 The Basic Principle of Ant Colony Algorithm

7.2.1 Foraging Behavior

Ants are social insects with simple communication and information transmission. Ant colony can perform complex tasks far beyond the individual ability of ants in many cases, which shows a high level of intelligence.

Ants can find the shortest path from the nest to the food source without any visible indication, and can dynamically search for new paths even with the change of environment (such as obstacles); and find new shortest path. The secret lies in the fact that each ant secretes a chemical—pheromone on the path it walks, and the other ants sense the presence and concentration of the substance in motion, thus guiding its course of action and move towards the direction of high pheromone concentration and eventually form the shortest path that almost all ants will choose. In the selection process, ants also have a certain small probability of "error", like towards the direction with low pheromone concentration to avoid the problem that most ants choose a relatively short path instead of the shortest path. Thus, ants do not transmit and communicate directly with each other, they only interact with the surrounding environment, indirectly affect others through the surrounding environment, then transmit and update information.

Regarding the foraging behavior of ants under constrained conditions, a well-known equal length double bridge experiment was carried out by Deneguourg etc., and then a pheromone model was put forward according to the experimental results. In this model, the probability that an ant selects a branch at a certain time depends on the number of ants that have passed the branch, the more the number of ants choose, the higher the probability of selection is. The equal length double bridge experiment and its results are shown in Fig. 7-1.

In the experiment, the ants arrive at the food source through two branches of equal length from the ant nest, and there is no pheromone in the two branches at first. The experiment recorded the percentage of ants passing through both branches in 30 minutes, as shown in Fig. 7-1 (b). At first, the percentage of ants choosing two branches was equal. After an initial short period of turbulence, the ants began to tend to move along to

Chapter 7   Ant Colony Algorithm and Its Application in Production System Optimization

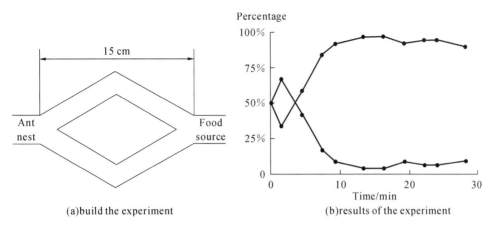

(a) build the experiment   (b) results of the experiment

Fig. 7-1   The Tow-Branch Bridge Experiment of Equal Length

one branch, and finally most (more than 90%) ants chose the same path.

The equal length double bridge experiment can also be extended to the case of unequal branch length. The result of the experiment is that after initial fluctuation, ants gradually tend to select short branches. And the probability of final selection of short branches is on the increase with the climb of the ratio of the two branches.

As for the foraging behavior of ants, the following Fig. 7-2 is given.

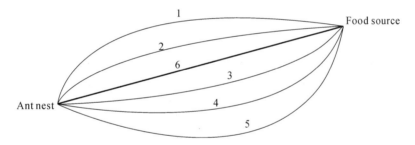

Fig. 7-2   The Foraging Behavior of Ants

The first five ants (1, 2, 3, 4, 5) go out for food, dropping pheromones along the way. There are five paths (1, 2, 3, 4, 5) in the picture, and obviously ant 2 takes the shortest path and returns to the nest first, hence ant 2 sets out again with the largest number of pheromones on path 2 (since other ants have not yet returned, and the number of ants passing through this path is 2). It still follows the original path (path 2), and when other ants return to carry food, there are the most pheromones on path 2, so they also choose path 2 to move in the direction of path 2, thus path 2 becomes the current shortest path. But the shortest path in the graph is not path 2, but path 6, so the discovery of path 6 is based on a small probability "error" that occurs when the ants choose the path. For instance, ant 1 "mistakenly" chose path 6 when choosing the path, then found the shortest path. As more and more "errors" and pheromone accumulate, and according to the rules of choosing the path, path 6 is determined to be the final optimal path.

7.2.2　Introduction of Artificial Ant

In ant colony algorithm, the concept of artificial ant is proposed. On the one hand, artificial ant is an abstract of the behavior characteristics of real ants, and it retains the most important part of the foraging behavior of ant colony. On the other hand, it also has some characteristics that real ants do not have. For instance, artificial ants live in discrete states, have certain memory ability and update pheromones relying on specific problems and etc. Before introducing the principle of ant colony algorithm, the following concepts are introduced.

(1) Information square: information square refers to the range of distances that ants observe and move. Generally, it is a 3 cm×3 cm information square.

(2) Environment: the environment in which ants are located contains obstacles, other ants, pheromones, etc. Each ant can only sense the environmental information within its scope. The environment makes the pheromone disappear at a certain rate (to avoid partial optimization and stagnation due to excessive partial pheromone concentration).

(3) Pheromone: pheromone is a kind of chemical that ants sprinkle along the way while searching for food and nests, which can be perceived by other ants passing through this path and guide their direction of movement. The greater the concentration of the pheromones on the path, the greater the probability of ants moving beyond this path. Pheromones disappear at a certain rate.

(4) Foraging rules: ants search for food within the perceived scope, and if it has, ants move in the direction of food; if not, move in the direction of the most pheromones and make mistakes with a small probability (not necessarily in the direction of the most pheromones). Ant's small probability error can also effectively avoid partial optimization, make "innovation" and find a new optimal solution.

(5) Moving rule: moving in the direction of the most pheromones. If there is no guidance of pheromones, ants select the direction of movement according to inertia or random choice, accompanied by random small disturbances. Ants remember the points they have passed as they move, and try to avoid repeating the points they have already passed.

(6) Obstacle avoidance rule: the direction of movement is selected randomly when the obstacle is encountered; but if there is pheromone guidance, the path is chosen according to the foraging rule. Ants can dynamically find the new shortest path according to the rules of movement.

(7) Spreading pheromones: ants spread pheromones on the path they pass, and the pheromones disappear with a certain probability.

There is no direct relation between ants, but each ant interacts with the environment, and through the pheromone link, the ants are connected to each other. For instance, when an ant finds food, it does not directly tell the other ants that there is food, but rather spreads pheromones into the environment, and when other ants pass around it, they can feel the presence of pheromones. The food is found in accordance with the guidance of pheromones.

7.2.3 The Process and Characteristics of Ant Colony Algorithm

Ants release pheromones on the path during the cycle and choose the next direction or target in a probabilistic manner. This probability is a function of the concentration of the pheromones and heuristic factors. Ants are not allowed to access targets that have already been visited in a loop. At the beginning, all ants are initialized (such as the number of ants, the maximum number of pheromones, heuristic factor coefficients and pheromone volatilization coefficients, etc.), and the search process is carried out; then the fitness of each ant is calculated; next determine whether to meet the termination condition. If satisfied, the project would be ended; if not, the timer increases a unit of time to update pheromones.

The flow of a simple ant colony algorithm is shown in Fig. 7-3.

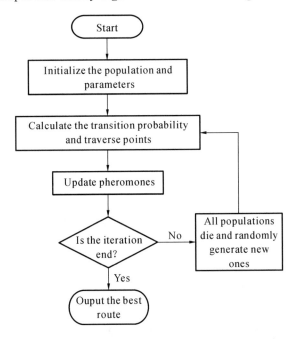

Fig. 7-3 Flow Chart of Simple Ant Colony Algorithm

According to the different algorithm and the problem to be solved, the flow of the algorithm also has some differences and changes. The parameters and the formula of the algorithm should also be determined according to the specific problem.

Ant colony algorithm has the following characteristics.

(1) Positive feedback. When ants spread pheromones on the path, the more ants pass through, the higher the concentration of pheromones are, the higher the probability of choosing the path is, thus increasing the concentration of pheromones in the path and forming an autocatalytic process. By using the pheromones as positive feedback, the stronger solution of the system is self-enhanced, and the solution of the problem evolves in the direction of comprehensive optimization. Finally, the relatively optimal solution is obtained effectively.

(2) Concurrency. The search process is not from a point, but from multiple points at the same time, and constructs multiple solutions in the problem space at the same time.

(3) Strong robustness. It makes it easy to be fused with other approaches. The behavior of a single ant does not affect the optimal solution to the system, and the ant colony can find the optimal solution when the environment changes. The improved algorithm can also be applied to other kinds of problems, and it can be combined with genetic algorithm and immune algorithm.

(4) Probabilistic comprehensive search. This uncertainty enables the algorithm to have more opportunities to solve the comprehensive optimal solution.

(5) Independent of strict mathematical properties such as continuity and derivability of functions as well as exact mathematical description of objective function and constraint function.

(6) The search time is long, and the stagnation phenomenon is easy to occur. When the colony size is large, it is difficult to converge to the optimal solution in a short time. It takes a long time to get a good solution. When the search goes to a certain extent, partial optimization may occur. The evaporation of pheromone and the "error" of small probability can prevent the partial optimization and stagnation to some extent.

7.2.4 Development and Present Situation

Dorigo first proposed ant colony optimization algorithm—ant system (AS) and applied it to solve the classical traveling salesman problem (TSP) in computer science. From the beginning of the ant system, the basic ant colony algorithm has been developed and perfected, and is further verified in the TSP and many practical optimization problems. One of the common features of these improved versions of AS is to enhance the ability of searching for optimal solution in ant search process. The difference between them lies only in the aspect of search control strategy. Moreover, the ACO with the best results is realized by introducing the partial search algorithm, which is a hybrid probabilistic search algorithm combined with the standard partial search algorithm. It is beneficial to improve the solution quality of ant colony system in optimization problem.

There are three versions of AS originally when proposed: ant-density, ant-quantity, and ant-cycle. In ant-density and ant-quantity, the ant updates the pheromone after each move between the two location nodes, while in ant-cycle, the pheromone is updated when all ants have completed their journey, and the pheromone released by each ant is expressed as a function reflecting the quality of the corresponding journey. Compared with other general heuristic algorithms, the solving ability of these three algorithms is ideal in TSP with no more than 75 cities, but when the problem scale expands, the problem-solving ability of them decreases greatly.

Therefore, the later research work of ACO is mainly focused on the improvement of AS performance.

1. Standard Ant Colony Algorithm

The original ant colony algorithm was called ant system (AS). In the AS, the probability of state transition $p_{ij}^k(t)$ and formula of updating pheromone are shown as Eq. (7-1) and Eq. (7-2).

$$p_{ij}^k(t) = \begin{cases} \dfrac{[\tau_{ij}(t)]^\alpha [\eta_{ij}(t)]^\beta}{\sum_{s \in J_k(i)} [\tau_{is}(t)]^\alpha [\eta_{is}(t)]^\beta}, & j \in J_k(i) \\ 0, & \text{otherwise} \end{cases} \quad (7\text{-}1)$$

where p_{ij}^k is the transfer probability of ant k from city i to city j; α and β are the relative importance of pheromones and heuristic factors; τ_{ij} is the information element quantity of the edge (i,j); η_{ij} is the heuristic factor; $J_k(i)$ is the next permit cities of ant k.

$$\begin{cases} \tau_{ij}(t+n) = (1-\rho)\tau_{ij}(t) + \Delta\tau_{ij} \\ \Delta\tau_{ij} = \sum_{k=1}^{m} \Delta\tau_{ij}^k \\ \Delta\tau_{ij}^k = \begin{cases} \dfrac{Q}{L_k}, & \text{if ant } k \text{ passes through the edge}(i,j) \\ 0, & \text{otherwise} \end{cases} \end{cases} \quad (7\text{-}2)$$

where ρ is the pheromone evaporation coefficient, $0 < \rho < 1$; $\Delta\tau_{ij}$ is the amount of information left by the ant k on the edge (i, j) in this iteration; Q is a positive constant; L_k is the path length that ant k passes in this round.

M. Dorigo proposed three models: ant-cycle, ant-quantity and ant-density. The difference among them is to calculate the amount of information left on the edge (i, j) of the ant k in the iteration.

Ant-cycle:
$$\Delta\tau_{ij}^k = \begin{cases} \dfrac{Q}{L_k}, & \text{if ant } k \text{ passes through the edge}(i,j) \\ 0, & \text{otherwise} \end{cases} \quad (7\text{-}3)$$

Ant-quantity:
$$\Delta\tau_{ij}^k = \begin{cases} \dfrac{Q}{L_k}, & \text{if ant } k \text{ passes through the edge}(i,j) \\ 0, & \text{otherwise} \end{cases} \quad (7\text{-}4)$$

Ant-density:
$$\Delta\tau_{ij}^k = \begin{cases} Q, & \text{if ant } k \text{ passes through the edge}(i,j) \\ 0, & \text{otherwise} \end{cases} \quad (7\text{-}5)$$

The AS algorithm in fact is a combination of positive feedback and heuristic algorithm because it uses not only the pheromone on the path but also the reciprocal of the distance between cities as the heuristic factor. The experimental results show that the ant-cycle algorithm has better performance than the other two algorithms, because it is updated by comprehensive pheromone but ant-quantity and ant-density algorithms is updated by partial pheromone. When M. Dorigo solved the TSP of 30 cities, he found that if $\alpha = \{0.5, 1\}$ and $\beta = \{1,2,3,4,5\}$, AS algorithm can always converge to the optimal solution and when the number m of ants is close to the number n of cities, the algorithm has better performance.

2. Improving ACO Algorithm

In view of the deficiency of ACO algorithm (such as complexity is high, stagnation is easy to appear and etc.), many scholars have done a lot of work around how to improve the ACO algorithm and improve the performance of algorithm. Among them, an ant system with elitist strategy, a rank-based version of ant system, an ant colony system and a max-min ant system are wildly used and representative. The improved ant colony algorithms mainly enhance the strategy and state transfer rule of pheromone updating.

(1) Ant system with elitist strategy is also called optimal solution retention strategy ant system. It was the first to improve the ant system given similar elitist strategy adopted in genetic algorithm. Given ant system with elitist is similar to elitist strategy in genetic algorithm, it is also named ant system with elite strategy.

The quality of solution in ant system can be improved by using optimal ants. After each iteration, the comprehensive optimal solution is further utilized, that is, when updating the pheromone trajectory, it is assumed that many ants have chosen the path. Compared with the AS algorithm, the algorithm enhances the utilization of the comprehensive optimal solution when the pheromone is updated, and then its pheromone update strategy is

$$\begin{cases} \tau_{ij}(t+1) = (1-\rho)\tau_{ij}(t) + \Delta\tau_{ij} + \Delta\tau_{ij}^* \\ \Delta\tau_{ij} = \sum_{k=1}^{m} \Delta\tau_{ij}^k \\ \Delta\tau_{ij}^k = \begin{cases} \dfrac{Q}{L_k}, & \text{if ant } k \text{ passes through the edge}(i,j) \\ 0, & \text{otherwise} \end{cases} \\ \Delta\tau_{ij}^* = \begin{cases} \sigma \dfrac{Q}{L^{gb}}, & \text{if edge}(i,j) \in \text{Route}_{best} \\ 0, & \text{otherwise} \end{cases} \end{cases} \quad (7\text{-}6)$$

where $\Delta\tau_{ij}^*$ is the amount of information added by ants on the edge (i, j); σ is the optimal ant number; L^{gb} is the comprehensive best solution.

The experimental results show that the optimal ant number has a certain range, when the optimal ant number is less than this range, with the increase of the optimal ant number, the ability of the algorithm to find the better solution increases, and the time of finding the better solution is shortened. However, when the number of ants exceeds a certain range, the performance of the algorithm will decrease with the increase of the number of ants.

(2) Rank-based version of ant system (ASrank). It is obtained by applying the concept extension of ranking in the genetic algorithm to the AS. The basic idea is: first, the colony is classified according to the fitness, and then the probability of being selected depends on the ranking of the individual. The higher the fitness, the greater the probability of the selection of the individual in the colony. Or after each iteration, the path of ants is arranged from small to large, and given different volume according to the path length, the shorter the path length is, the greater the volume is. The volume of the comprehensive optimal solution is w, and the volume of the rth optimal solution is max $\{0, w-r\}$. The updating strategy for pheromones on each path is as follows:

$$\begin{cases} \tau_{ij}(t+1) = (1-\rho)\tau_{ij}(t) + \sum_{r=1}^{w-1}(w-r)\Delta\tau_{ij}^r(t) + w\Delta\tau_{ij}^{gb}(t) \\ \Delta\tau_{ij}^r(t) = 1/L^r(t), \quad \Delta\tau_{ij}^{gb}(t) = 1/L^{gb} \end{cases} \quad (7\text{-}7)$$

(3) Ant colony system (ACS). It is an improved version of the AS algorithm, which is mainly distinguished from AS algorithm as follows: ① when choosing the next city, the ACS algorithm makes more use of the current better solution; ② ACS algorithm adds pheromone only on the edge of the comprehensive optimal solution; ③ when ants crawl from city m to city n, the pheromone on edge (m, n) will decrease appropriately.

In the ACS algorithm, ants use the pseudo-random ratio selection rule to select the next city, that is, for ant k located in the city i, the ant k moves to the city with probability q_0. In the sentence, i is the city which makes $\tau_{iu}(t) \times [\eta_{iu}]^\beta$ the largest. This selection allows the ant to select the most likely city by probability q_0 into the solution constructed by the ant. In addition, the ant chooses the next city j with the probability of $1-q_0$. The state transition formula is

$$j = \begin{cases} \arg\max_{u \in \text{allowed}_k} [\tau_{iu}(t)][\eta_{iu}]^\beta, & \text{if } q \leqslant q_0 \\ s, & \text{otherwise} \end{cases} \tag{7-8}$$

Generate q randomly before selecting the next city; if the value of q is less than or equal to the constant q_0, find the city in allowed cities which would make the $\tau_{iu}(t) \times [\eta_{iu}]^\beta$ largest and make it become the next selected city. If the random number q is greater than q_0, the formula for selecting the next city is

$$p_k(i,j) = \begin{cases} \dfrac{[\tau_{ij}(t)][\eta_{ij}]^\beta}{\sum_{s \in J_k(i)} [\tau_{is}(t)][\eta_{is}]^\beta}, & j \in J_k(i) \\ 0, & \text{otherwise} \end{cases} \tag{7-9}$$

The partial pheromone update formula is

$$\tau_{ij} = (1-\xi)\tau_{ij} + \xi\tau_0 \tag{7-10}$$

The comprehensive pheromone updating formula is

$$\begin{cases} \tau_{ij}(t+1) = (1-\rho)\tau_{ij}(t) + \rho\Delta\tau_{ij}^{gb} \\ \Delta\tau_{ij}^{gb} = \begin{cases} 1/L^{gb}, & \text{if edge}(i,j) \in \text{Route}_{\text{best}} \\ 0, & \text{otherwise} \end{cases} \end{cases} \tag{7-11}$$

where τ_0 is a constant; $\xi \in (0, 1)$ is an adjustable parameter.

In most cases, ACS algorithm is superior to or equivalent to AS algorithm, simulated annealing, evolutionary programming, genetic algorithm and analog-genetic algorithm. In solving asymmetric TSP, ACS algorithm has more advantages.

(4) Max-min ant system (MMAS). At present, it is the best ant colony algorithm for solving TSP and quadratic assignment problem (QAP). Compared with other optimization algorithms, MMAS is still the best one. It comes directly from ACO algorithm. Three major improvements have been made: ① after each iteration, only the information on the path where the optimal solution belongs to is updated; ② limit the pheromone concentration of each path in $[\tau_{\min}, \tau_{\max}]$ and out-of-range ones would be forced setting as $\tau_{\min}$ or $\tau_{\max}$ which can effectively avoid the partial optimal solution too early; ③ at the initial moment, the pheromone concentration on each path is set as $\tau_{\max}$, ρ takes a smaller value. After all ants complete one iteration, update the pheromones on each path according to Eq. (7-12):

$$\begin{cases} \tau_{ij}(t+1) = (1-\rho)\tau_{ij}(t) + \Delta\tau_{ij}^{best}(t), \rho \in (0,1) \\ \Delta\tau_{ij}^{best} = \begin{cases} 1/L^{best}, & \text{if edge } (i,j) \in \text{Route}_{best} \\ 0, & \text{otherwise} \end{cases} \end{cases} \quad (7\text{-}12)$$

The updated path can be the comprehensive optimal solution or the optimal solution of this round of iteration. It has been proved that increasing the frequency of the comprehensive optimal solution gradually enable the algorithm to achieve better performance.

7.3 The Case of Ant Colony Algorithm

7.3.1 Job Shop Scheduling Problem

Scheduling problem, also called scheduling problem, refers to the process of processing some jobs on machines, arrange machines and jobs reasonably in order to make the objective function optimal.

Case description is as follows.

Known: there are n jobs $\{J_1, J_2, \cdots, J_n\}$ and they have two production processes need to be processed on two machines M1 and M2; different jobs are free from constraints of processing and the processing sequence on these two machines are the same.

Restrains of job: the two production processes need to be processed on these two machines once only; the processes start working without interval when the job reaches to the machine only.

Restraints of machine: each machine should only process one production at the same time; more importantly, the sequence is under the control; the machine is working.

Target: present the reasonable order which makes the completed time shortest.

Take 9 jobs as an example, and the processing time of the jobs is shown in Table 7-1.

Table 7-1　The Processing Time of the Jobs　　　　　　　　(Unit:s)

Job No.	1	2	3	4	5	6	7	8	9
Time of process 1	10	13	15	12	14	9	16	17	15
Time of process 2	14	17	13	12	10	13	17	9	6

$$\min f = \sum_{i=1}^{n} d_{i,2} + \max(0, d_{i-1,2} - d_{i,1}), i = 2,3,\cdots,9 \quad (7\text{-}13)$$

where d_{ij} is the processes jth of the job ith.

The steps of solving the job shop scheduling problem by ant colony algorithm is as follows.

Time matrix of job's process 1 is regarded as the distance matrix in general (the dimension is 9×1).

Initialization parameters α, β, ρ. The initial parameters are set before the iterative optimization, and the reasonable parameters are helpful to find better iterative results more quickly.

Iterative optimization. This step is the core of the whole algorithm. In popular language, it can be understood that each ant moves from one city to the next according to a certain probability, and generally has a greater probability of transfer to a closer city. When all cities are searched and returned to the origin, the optimization process of an ant is completed. After all ants complete their own search of the city path, they complete an iteration and update the pheromone.

After reaching the maximum number of iterations, analyze and determine whether the results meet the required accuracy, and then compare with other methods; evaluate the performance of the ant colony algorithm, or change the initial parameters to observe the impact on the results, and try to improve the optimization mechanism to find better results or speed up the iteration.

The steps of the ant colony algorithm program are shown in Fig. 7-4. Through the realization of the program, the results can be obtained: in the case of the maximum number of iterations $N=100$ and the initial number of 5 ants, the shortest processing time is 135 s and the shortest path is 1, 9, 6, 4, 3, 2, 5, 7, 8. Figs. 7-5 and 7-6 show the results of the program, from which the ant colony algorithm can quickly converge to the shortest waiting time when solving the job shop scheduling problem in this case.

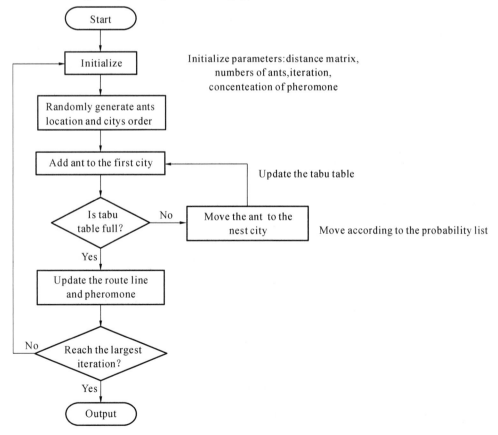

Fig. 7-4 Solving Steps for JSSP with ACO Algorithm

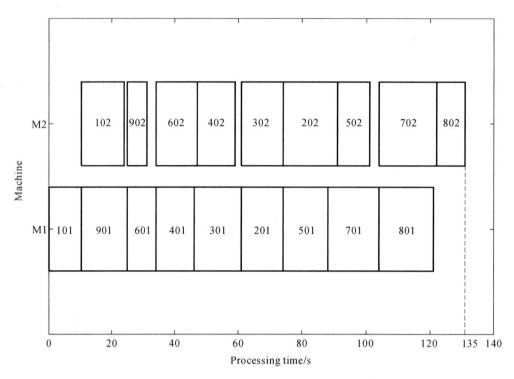

Fig. 7-5 Gantt Chart of Final Process Results (100 Times of Iteration)

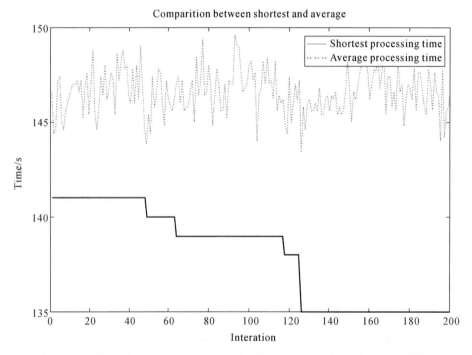

Fig. 7-6 Time Convergence Diagram of ACO Algorithm for Solving the JSSP
(200 Times of Iteration)

7.3.2 Path Planning of Parts Distribution

Path planning is one of the main research contents of motion planning. Motion planning is composed of path planning and trajectory planning. The sequence point or curve connecting the starting position and the end position is called path, and the strategy of forming the path is called path planning. The goal is to meet workstation's needs, and to get the shortest distance, the lowest cost and the shortest time under certain constraints. Path planning of parts distribution problem can be described as shown in Fig. 7-7.

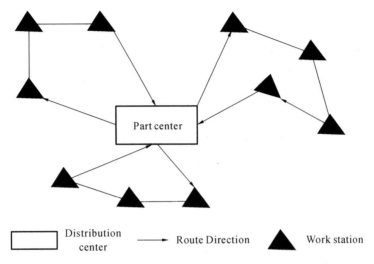

Fig. 7-7 Schematic Diagram of Path Planning of Parts Distribution Problem

The path problem is one of the most basic problems in the network optimization. Because of the wide and economic value of its application, it has been widely concerned by domestic and foreign scholars since the introduction in 1959. The vehicle routing problem (VRP) mainly includes the following elements: distribution center, vehicle, goods, customer, transportation network, constraint condition and objective function.

1. Basic Issues and Modelling

Assuming that there are 19 areas to be supplied around the distribution center of parts, the coordinates of which are arranged as shown in Table 7-2, and the path between the distribution point and the distribution center is the shortest in the case of meeting the distribution requirements.

Table 7-2 Distribution Center and Distribution Point Coordinates

Location	1	2	3	4	5	6	7	8	9	10
Abscissa	0	0	0	−2	−3	3	−4	−4	1	1
Ordinate	0	−1	3	−2	−3	−1	0	−1	−2	−1
Location	11	12	13	14	15	16	17	18	19	20
Abscissa	1	3	−3	2	1	2	2	1	−3	−1
Ordinate	3	4	0	0	−3	−1	1	−4	2	−1

Target function:
$$\min f(x) = \sum_{i=0}^{m}\sum_{j=0}^{m} c_{ij}\sqrt{(X_i-X_j)^2+(Y_i-Y_j)^2} \qquad (7\text{-}14)$$

Constraints:
$$c_{ij} = 0 \text{ or } 1(i,j \in I) \qquad (7\text{-}15)$$

Formula (7-14) is the target function, $f(x)$ is the distance of total path, (X_i,Y_i) and (X_j,Y_j) are the coordinate of two points. As the transportation cost of distribution center is related to the driving path, the longer the distance is, the higher the transportation cost is. Hence the target is to minimalize the distance of path.

Formula (7-15) is the decision variables, when i and j have path planning, c_{ij} equals 1, else 0.

2. Calculation Flow and Results of the Process

The calculation flow is shown in Fig. 7-8, and the results are shown in Figs. 7-9 and 7-10.

Path sequence: 1, 2, 15, 18, 9, 1, 20, 4, 5, 8, 13, 1, 3, 11, 12, 17, 14, 6, 16, 10, 1, 19, 7, 1. The shortest path: 43.6695.

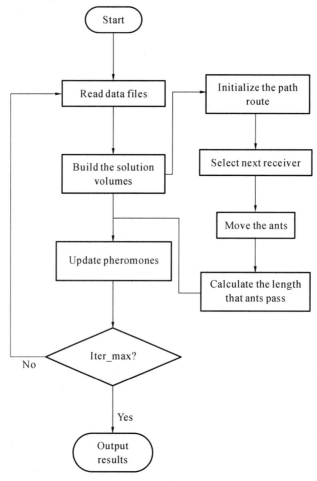

Fig. 7-8 Flow Chart of the Algorithm

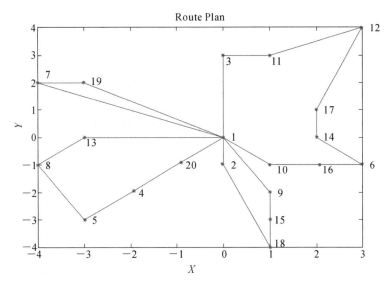

Fig. 7-9　Final Path Plan

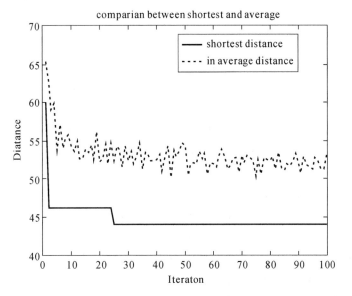

Fig. 7-10　Distance Range Diagram

7.4　Summary

This chapter describes the origin, development, basic principles and solution steps of ACO algorithm. Taking the job shop scheduling problem and path planning of parts distribution problem as cases, the steps and methods of ACO algorithm applied to optimize production system are illustrated.

Chapter 8   The Theory and Approach of Production Line Balance

8.1   Production and Assembly Line Optimization

8.1.1   Introduction to Production Line and Assembly Line

A production line is an operation line that aims at a certain production goal and operates according to a definite process, including elements such as personnel, equipment, material and etc. Assembly Line was first created in 1913 by Henry Ford's T-type vehicle assembly line. With the development of the industry, the assembly line has been given new contents and form. Production line with higher process degree and fast operation tempo can be called assemble line as well. From the perspective of load balancing, the optimization of the production system, whether it is a production line or an assembly line, adopts the same evaluation index and balance method. Therefore, in this chapter, the production line and the assembly line are regarded as the same concept.

Assembly line has following operating characteristics:

(1) The job produced is processed in different stations according to a certain order through the transport of the conveyor belt, and workers and production equipments in the station do not move synchronously;

(2) There will be more than one worker at each station, and each worker will work differently;

(3) Workers at each station need to complete the processing when the job leaves the station;

(4) There is no direct impact between each station, but the completion of the work content of the worker at the previous station will affect the work of the workers at the next station.

8.1.2   Standard of Scheduled Time and Quantity of Assembly Line

Standard of scheduled time and quantity, also known as the operating plan standard, refers to a series of standards about the quantity and time of production and processing products in the whole production and operation through scientific analysis and accurate calculation. Whether an assembly line can run efficiently depends on whether the schedule standard is reasonable.

The assembly line's standard of scheduled time and quantity criteria include work in process (WIP) occupancy, takt time, and visual management diagram.

1. WIP Occupancy

WIP is the object that needs to be processed and produced on the assembly line. Namely the general term for all products that have not completely finished processing technology from the beginning of the whole production to the end, in the form of raw material into the production and then in the form of finished products into the warehouse. Therefore, WIP occupation quota refers to the quantity standard required to ensure the continuity of the whole production process under the existing production conditions such as technical organization. Modern manufacturing industry mostly adopts the just in time(JIT) production mode, so in the production process, the trend of WIP is on the decrease.

2. Takt Time

The takt time, also known as the production time, refers to the time needed to produce a finished product on an assembly line, numerically equal to the total effective working time of a day divided by the qualified products produced in a day. The takt time is a kind of artificial target time, which changes according to the daily production plan, and the daily production plan depends on the market demand of the day. For instance, the takt time of a central air conditioner is 200 s on the assembly line, and a car is 160 s on the assembly line.

Because there will be some equipment downtime, unqualified products, and workers' operational errors during the process of the production, which will lead to the chaos of the assembly line, the calculation formula of the takt time is as follows:

$$\text{Takt time} = \frac{\text{Daily total effective production time} \times \text{Utilization rate of the procduction line}}{\text{Daily plan of total production quantity} \times \text{Passing rate}}$$

Among them, utilization rate of the production line refers to the total daily production time of the production line after leaving out the invalid production time of the production line caused by factors such as equipment, machine, staff and unqualified products, which would get the utilization time; then the ratio between utilization time and the total daily production processing time is called utilization rate.

Example 8-1 An automobile manufacturer plans to sell 30000 vehicles per year and needs additional 10% of the total production to cope with market changes. It is known that the workshop adopts a two-shift working mode with a working time of 8 hours per shift. The utilization rate of the production line is 95% and the rejection rate is 2%. The actual production days per year are 300 days. Try to calculate the takt time of the production line.

Solution The effective production time per year is

$$T = 300 \times 2 \times 8 \times 60 \times 95\% = 273600 (\text{min})$$

The number of qualified products actually to be produced each year is

$$Q = \frac{30000 + 30000 \times 10\%}{1 - 2\%} = 33674 \text{(unit)}$$

The takt time of the production line is

$$C = \frac{T}{Q} = \frac{273600}{33674} = 8.1 \text{(min)}$$

The takt time can also be used in the service industry to determine the number of waiters. If a bank has an average of 15 customers per hour to handle related business, then the bank's takt time is $60/15 = 4$(min), that is, for every 4 minutes, there will be one customer that requires service. If a bank clerk spends an average of 5 minutes on a customer, then we can be sure that the bank needs at least $5/4 = 1.25$ clerks, which means at least 2 clerks.

This gives us an idea of using takt time to identify bottlenecks. Bottleneck refers to the slowest production cycle in a production line and limits the production speed of the entire production line. Similar to the "barrel law", the maximum capacity (production efficiency) of a production line does not depend on the station with the shortest operation time, but the longest operation time. The greater the difference of two stations, the greater the production capacity loss of the production line. Therefore, bottleneck processing can be optimized to increase production line productivity.

Cycle time refers to the time required to produce a product on a production line. It can be manually measured. Its value reflects the production rate of the line. The cycle time can be unequal to the takt time. When the cycle time of production is greater than the takt time, it is necessary to work overtime or to make a plan on production in advance to meet the production tempo. However, both overtime working or advanced production will increase the production cost. Therefore, when arranging the production plan of the production line, we should try to keep the production cycle time consistent with the production pace, otherwise it will lead to the increase of production cost and the waste of production resources.

Pitch time can be adjusted according to the state of workers. It represents the time interval between two adjacent workstations. In the manufacturing process, pitch time is always equal to cycle time. However, when the worker does not enter the working state, the pitch time can be first increased and then slowly adjusted to equal the cycle time.

Cell line is realized on the basis of balance of production line. It is a practice way of lean thinking. Unitization refers to divide the whole manufacturing workshop into several units according to the order of production and processing. Arrangement is performed to minimize the handling of production material in each unit to complete part or all of the production process. By arranging the workshop, the process complexity of each station can be reduced, and the flexibility of the whole production line can be improved. Different types of products can be produced flexibly, and can adapt to the demand of the market quickly, so that the competitiveness of manufacturers can be enhanced. Each unit can have a shorter assembly line, and the production mode can be that the production stations are arranged in the order of processing process, or one station completes all process operations within the unit.

3. Visual Management

Visual management organizes the production by using a large amount of visual information. Because each station of the entire assembly line complete a lot of repetitive work in accordance with a certain number of takt time to meet the specified production requirements, it is necessary to strictly establish a relevant work standard system for each station. According to the takt time and the time of each process, some detailed work charts and work instruction charts are prepared. These charts have a significant effect on improving labor rate and equipment utilization, so they can be relied upon to ensure the realization of the production plan on the assembly line.

8.1.3 Assembly Line Classification

After more than one hundred years of evolution, the assembly line has become more diverse. The following three classification methods will be introduced in different forms.

1. Classification by Assembly Line Takt Time

(1) The rough takt line: the actual processing time of each process is very different from the established takt time of the assembly line. In order to ensure the continuity of production, only a reasonable period of time can be determined to arrange the production plan.

(2) Forced takt line: it must accurately comply with the required takt time, strict requirements for each component involved in production on the assembly line, and tolerates zero errors to ensure the realization of the production cycle of the assembly line.

(3) The free takt line: it is based on the proficiency of the processing workers to ensure the realization of the assembly line takt time, and is widely used in batches in production, machining workshops, assembly workshops, etc.

2. Classification by Whether the Object of Production or the Worker Moves

(1) A moving assembly line: in which the objects of production (WIP) move during production and the locations of workers, machines and tools used in production are fixed. It refers to the gradual transformation of the object of production from raw material to semi-finished product or finished product after each processing procedure, such as the assembly line of car and home appliance.

(2) The fixed assembly line: in contrast to the moving assembly line, the object of production is fixed. The worker carries the tools needed for processing according to the order of processing. Common ones are the assembly lines of the assembly of large heavy machinery and equipment, large parts processing, etc.

3. Classification by Whether the Production Process Is Continuously

(1) Continuous assembly line: the sum of processing time of all processes on an assembly line is equal to the integral multiple of the given takt time of the assembly line.

(2) Discontinuous assembly line, because the production capacity of each process does not match, there is a bottleneck process so that the number of finished products produced and processed in a certain time is different. Objects that need to be processed cannot be moved continuously on the assembly line and will have different waiting time at different stations.

8.1.4 Description and Balancing Method of Assembly Line Balance Problem

1. Description of Assembly Line Balance Problem

The core issue in planning and production in industrial manufacturing is the problem of assembly line balance. It refers to complete the production task in a certain station by using a given number of raw materials, parts and other production elements in accordance with the processing sequence under the given time constraints, machine labor, production planning and other conditions. That is to say, all working elements are reasonably arranged and then distributed to a limited number of workstations for processing and production, and the goal is to make the processing time of each workstation equal to an integral multiple of the cycle time.

Suppose there is an assembly line on which n (n is a positive integer) workstations are arranged. Each job goes through in turn along the conveyor belt; and then passes through all workstations sequentially into the finished product factory finally. The balance problem of assembly line refers to determine the minimum number of workstations required according to the order of processing, and then assign each process to different workstations and optimize balance to achieve the completion of each workstation.

The mathematical model of assembly line balance is

$$T_{N_k} = \sum_{i \in N_k} T_i \tag{8-1}$$

$$\text{IT}_k = \text{CT} - T_{N_k} \tag{8-2}$$

where N_k represents all job tasks assigned to the kth workstation; T_i indicates the time required to complete the ith job; IT_k indicates the idle time of the kth workstation, that is, when the kth workstation finishes processing, it needs to wait for other workstations to complete the processing task; CT represents the cycle time in seconds.

Example 8-2 A company is now producing A-type products on the assembly line. It is known that 20 kinds of processes need to be completed on the assembly line, wherein the longest operation time is 3 minutes and the sum of all process operations is 20 minutes. The assembly line works 480 minutes (T) per day. Try to calculate: (1) What is the maximum and minimum takt time (C) on this line? (2) What is the maximum output of this assembly line? How many workstations are needed to achieve this yield? (3) It is necessary to guarantee production every day, and the number (Q) of productions is 150. What is the takt time of the assembly line at this time?

Solution (1) The maximum takt time is the time when all the processes are in the same workstation, so the maximum takt time is 20 minutes; the minimum takt time is the longest operation time is independent of one workstation, so the minimum takt time is 3 minutes.

(2) Since $C=\frac{Q}{T}$, we know that $Q=\frac{T}{C}$, so the maximum output of the line is

$$Q = \frac{T}{C} = \frac{480}{3} = 160 \text{(piece)}$$

Minimum number of workstations required is

$$N_{min} = \lceil \frac{\sum T}{C} \rceil = \lceil \frac{20}{3} \rceil = 7 \text{(piece)}$$

where $\lceil \ \rceil$ means round up.

(3) When the production plan is 150, the takt time of the assembly line is

$$C' = \frac{T}{Q'} = \frac{480}{150} = 3.2 \text{(min)}$$

Example 8-3 There are 15 tasks to be balanced on an assembly line, among which the longest operation time(C_{max}) is 2.5 minutes and the total operation time (C_{sum}) is 14 minutes. The assembly line actually works for 350 minutes every day. Try to calculate: (1) What is daily production capacity of the assembly line on theory? (2) If the cycle time (C) is 8 minutes and 12 minutes respectively, what is the daily production capacity?

Solution (1) The minimum production capacity of the assembly line is

$$Q_{min} = \frac{\sum T}{C_{sum}} = \frac{350}{14} = 25 \text{(piece)}$$

The maximum capacity of the assembly line is

$$Q_{max} = \frac{\sum T}{C_{max}} = \frac{350}{2.5} = 140 \text{(piece)}$$

Therefore, the daily theoretical capacity of the assembly line is 25~140 pieces.

(2) When $C=8$ min, there is

$$Q = \frac{350}{8} = 43.75 \approx 43 \text{(pieces)}$$

When $C=12$ min, there is

$$Q = \frac{350}{12} = 29.17 \approx 29 \text{(pieces)}$$

The biggest problem to optimize the balance of the assembly line is how to match all the production factors with a given number of workstations through reasonable arrangement and combination under the constraints of the cycle condition, so that the production efficiency of the assembly line is the highest. It can be known that if we want to increase the production efficiency of the assembly line, we need to make the idle time of each workstation equal to zero, that is, the time for each workstation to complete the processing task is equal to the cycle time of the assembly line, and the balance rate is 100%. When the balance rate of the assembly line is not 100%, the working time of the workstation is less than the cycle time of the assembly line, then the non-productive idle time, i. e. the waiting time of the workers and the machine is generated. In other words, in order to increase the productivity of the entire assembly line, efforts should be made to reduce the idle time of each workstation to zero.

According to different objectives and constraints, the assembly line balance problem can be classified as follows. First, known the cycle time of the assembly line and the operation time of each process, the minimum number of workstations is required; second, known the number of workstations given by the assembly line and the operation time of each process, calculate the minimum cycle time matched; third, known the number of workstations and the cycle time of the assembly line, how to reasonably combine and allocate each process to obtain the allocation scheme with the highest efficiency (maximum balance rate). Because the constraint condition and objective function are different, each kind of problem has its own corresponding mathematical model. When facing the actual situation, we should first determine which kind of balance problem it is, and then use the relevant formulas to solve it.

2. Balance Method

As the assembly line balance problem is actually a combinatorial optimization problem, it is the NPC problem. In other words, the optimal solution can be obtained theoretically by some methods such as branch and bound method and dynamic programming. However, the time complexity of such problems increases exponentially with the increase of the number of tasks. Similar to the traveling salesman problem, with the explosion of the solution scale, the simple solution method is not fully applicable. If n jobs are sorted, $n!$ different permutations will be generated. When $n = 10$, there will be 3628800 permutations. Even if it is reduced by 90% according to the constraint of the sequence of procedures, there will still be more than 360000 permutations. This number is not helpful to find the optimal solution.

In fact, each approach to balance optimization of an assembly line requires some basic parameters on the line first, such as the minimum number of workstations and the production cycle time on the line. After grasping the data, we can arrange and combine the various processes reasonably and then assign them to different workstations.

The mathematical model established is as follows:

$$C = \frac{T}{Q} \tag{8-3}$$

$$N_{min} = \left\lceil \frac{t_{sum}}{C} \right\rceil \tag{8-4}$$

$$E = \frac{t_{sum}}{NC} \times 100\% \tag{8-5}$$

where C is cycle time on the assembly line; T is daily production time on the assembly line; Q is production tasks to be completed within the total production time T; N_{min} is the minimum number of workstations to be allocated; t_{sum} is the sum of the time required to complete the full production of a product in real work; $\lceil \ \rceil$ is round up to get the smallest integer greater than or equal to this number; N is the final number of workstations; E is the balance rate of the assembly line.

This mathematical model expresses the idea of calculating the cycle time of the entire assembly line, determining the minimum number of workstations based on the cycle time and the sum of all processes of a product. In fact, we determine that the final number of workstations is greater than or equal to the minimum number of workstations. After that, all workstations should be specifically assigned. According to the above mathematical model, it can be known that the optimal solution is that the number of workstations is equal to the minimum number of workstations, and when it is greater than the minimum number of workstations, the solution is sub-optimal or feasible. In the workstation, if the number of jobs is relatively small, a simple calculation can be used to find the balance and deduce the final result. However, when the number of tasks is too large, heuristic algorithm can be used to solve the problem.

The heuristic algorithm can often achieve high efficiency through direct observation or summarization of some simple rules when faced with a simple problem. However, when the problem becomes slightly complicated, its solution result is difficult to be satisfactory, let alone a large-scale problem.

Example 8-4 An assembly line needs to complete an air conditioner assembly. It is known that the number of daily production task is 520 and the assembly line's working time is 440 minutes a day. Fig. 8-1 is the network diagram of the air conditioner assembly, where A, B, ···, K represent the processing processes, and the corresponding number in bracket indicates the processing time in seconds. Try to calculate the required minimum number of workstations and the line balance rate according to the cycle time of the production process of order.

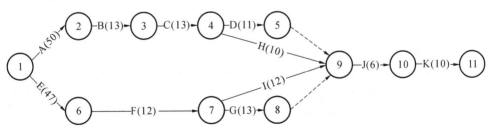

Fig. 8-1 Air Conditioner Assembly Network Diagram

Solution According to the production tasks and total working time per day to determine the takt time of the assembly line, the cycle time should be the same as the production takt time in order to maximize the balance rate; then through all processes of the sum of processing time and cycle time, calculate the minimum number of workstations needed; finally arrange and combine each process in no more than the production takt time under the premise of cycle time (workstations) and distribute all processes as far as possible to a minimum number of workstations.

$$C = \frac{T}{Q} = \frac{440 \times 60}{520} = 50.8(\text{s})$$

$$N_{\min} = \left\lceil \frac{50+47+13+12+12+13+13+11+10+6+10}{50.8} \right\rceil = \left\lceil \frac{197}{50.8} \right\rceil = 4(\text{piece})$$

All needed is to distribute all processes reasonably among workstations. In the process distribution, it should reduce the number of distribution randomness and the waiting time for the workstation to make processing time equal to cycle time as far as possible. Processing time can be prioritizing for processes with more working procedure or with a much longer time. In this way, invalid computation is reduced and the optimal solution is more convenient to get.

The final distribution plan is as follows:

Workstation 1: A (50);

Workstation2: E (47);

Workstation3: B(13), F(12), G(13), I(12);

Workstation4: C(13), D(11), H(10), J(6), K(10).

According to this distribution method, the balance rate of the assembly line is

$$E = \frac{197}{4 \times 50.8} \times 100\% = 96.9\%$$

At this point, the balance rate of this assembly line is already acceptable, and the task assignment of the above four workstations is our final choice.

Since the above problem is a parallel operation problem, the assignment can be made regardless of the order of the routes, But when faced with a single column probtem, the order of the processes must be considered first, and then obtain the optimal distribution plan.

Next, a solution to the complex distribution problem with a large number of processes is to be presented. Ranked positional weights, also called position weighting, is a solution proposed by Hungarian and Bernie in 1961. First of all, it calculates the order of each job position according to the order of the process. The value of the order is equal to the working time of the process, and then plus all working time after this point, and calculate the order value of each working element; and arrange them according to the position weight of each working element. Moreover, attention should be paid to the process with higher position weight in the process of distribution. This can greatly reduce the number of workstations to improve the efficiency of the assembly line.

Example 8-5 An assembly line is responsible for assembly automotive's chassis. It is known that the production task of this assembly line is 400 per day, and the effective working time is 520 mins per day. Table 8-1 lists working time and working order according to the production cycle time and the sequence of each process requirements. Try to calculate the minimum number of workstations needed and the line balance rate.

Chapter 8 The Theory and Approach of Production Line Balance

Table 8-1 Processing Procedure for Automotive's Chassis

Process	A	B	C	D	E	F	G	H	I
Working time/s	50	28	19	30	26	29	14	11	22
Immediate process(es)	—	A	B	B	C,D	E	F	F	G,H

Solution (1) First determine the production cycle time of the line and the minimum number of workstations required.

$$C = \frac{T}{Q} = \frac{520 \times 60}{400} = 78(s)$$

$$N_{min} = \left\lceil \frac{50+28+19+30+26+29+14+11+22}{78} \right\rceil = \left\lceil \frac{229}{78} \right\rceil = 3 \text{(piece)}$$

Thus, it can be known that at least 3 workstations are required.

(2) According to the data given in Table 8-1, sequence diagram of chassis processing and assembly is drawn as Fig. 8-2.

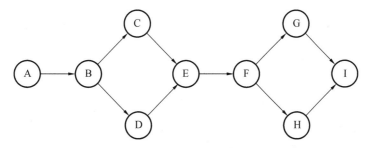

Fig. 8-2 Sequence Diagram of Chassis Processing and Assembly

(3) According to the working sequence of the chassis processing assembly, matric table of the working sequence is drawn as Table 8-2. The principle of the table is as follows: the task of each process is analyzed. If the ith process must be completed before the jth process, then "+1" is used in the sequence matrix table; the work tasks can be processed side by side, that is, there is no sequential processing order, which is represented by "0" in the table; when the ith process must be processed after the jth process, it is represented by "−1" in the sequence matrix table. Each task has no prioritization to itself, and "0" is used in the matrix table to represent it.

Table 8-2 The Sequence Matrix Table of Chassis Processing and Assembly

Process	A	B	C	D	E	F	G	H	I
A	0	+1	+1	+1	+1	+1	+1	+1	+1
B	−1	0	+1	+1	+1	+1	+1	+1	+1
C	−1	−1	0	+1	+1	+1	+1	+1	+1
D	−1	−1	−1	0	+1	+1	+1	+1	+1
E	−1	−1	−1	−1	0	+1	+1	+1	+1
F	−1	−1	−1	−1	−1	0	+1	+1	+1

continued

Process	A	B	C	D	E	F	G	H	I
G	−1	−1	−1	−1	−1	−1	0	+1	+1
H	−1	−1	−1	−1	−1	−1	−1	0	+1
I	−1	−1	−1	−1	−1	−1	−1	−1	0

(4) According to the working sequence matrix table of the chassis processing and assembly, the position weight calculation is performed for each operation. The calculation rule is: for any process x, find the row where the process x is located in the table; ignore "−1", and weight the position marked "+1", whose weight is equal to the working time ×1 of the corresponding process in the column. Then all columns marked with "+1" are summed up, and the time after the sum plus the working time of processes is the position weight of the process. The final calculation results are as follows:

Position weight of process A: 50+28+19+30+26+29+14+11+22=229;
Position weight of process B: 28+19+30+26+29+14+11+22=179;
Position weight of process C: 19+26+29+14+11+22=121;
Position weight of process D: 30+26+29+14+11+22=132;
Position weight of process E: 26+29+14+11+22=102;
Position weight of process F: 29+14+11+22=76;
Position weight of process G: 14+22=36;
Position weight of process H: 11+22=33;
Position weight of process I: 22.

(5) By calculating the position weight and the takt time of the workstation, the distribution of each workstation job task can be performed according to the time of the above two. The distribution rule is rearrange the processing steps according to the order of the position weight, and the result is A, B, D, C, E, F, G, H, I. Because the takt time of each workstation is 78 s, the workstation 1, 2 and 3 are sequentially filled according to the order of position weight. Note that the upper limit of the allowable processing time of the workstation is 78 s, which cannot be exceeded.

The final distribution results are as follows:
Workstation 1: A(50), B(28);
Workstation 2: D(30), C(19), E(26);
Workstation 3: F(29), G(14), H(11), I(22).

The non-productive time of each workstation is 0, 3 s and 2 s respectively.

(6) Finally, calculate the balance rate of the assembly line.

$$E = \frac{229}{3 \times 78} \times 100\% = 97.9\%$$

Example 8-6 It is known that a certain furniture manufacturer has put a batch of raw material into production. The flow chart on production line is shown in Fig. 8-3, where

1 (30) indicates the first processing step of job 1 and the processing time is 30 s. The production plan that needs to be completed is 1440 pieces per day, adopting two shifts. The working time is 8 hours per shift, regardless of the downtime. The specific information of workstations is shown in Fig. 8-4. Try to optimize the assembly line.

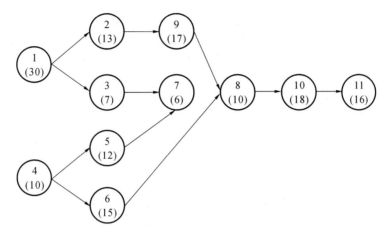

Fig. 8-3　Process Flow Chart of the Assembly Line

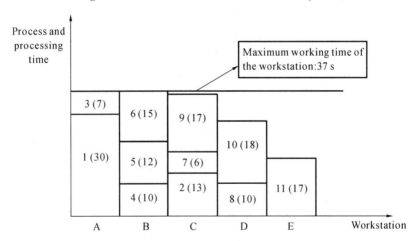

Fig. 8-4　Workstation Information of the Assembly Line

Solution　The production takt time of the assembly line is

$$C = \frac{\sum T}{Q} = \frac{2 \times 8 \times 60 \times 60}{1440} = 40(\text{s})$$

The balance rate before optimization of this assembly line is

$$E = \frac{\sum t}{N \times C} \times 100\% = \frac{30+13+7+10+12+15+6+10+17+18+16}{5 \times 40} \times 100\%$$

$$= \frac{154}{5 \times 40} \times 100\% = 77\%$$

The on-site assignment distribution allows each workstation to have a long non-productive idle time, and the balance rate of the assembly line is only 77%, so there is a lot of room for optimization. In the optimization, the minimum number of workstations required by the assembly line should be calculated first, and then the redistribution should be carried out according to the sequence of assignment. Optimization processes are as follows.

Minimum number of the workstations required for the assembly line is

$$N_{min} = \left\lceil \frac{\sum t}{C} \right\rceil = \left\lceil \frac{154}{40} \right\rceil = 4 \text{(piece)}$$

So, it needs to eliminate a workstation and redistribute assignments.

Assignment 1 and assignment 4 are in no particular order and have a high priority. The sum time of the two assignments is 40 s, which is equal to the takt time, and can be put into one workstation.

Assignments 2, 5 and 6 are of the same level, and there is no sequential processing. The sum of the working time is 40 s, which is equal to the takt time, and can be put into one workstation.

Assignment 7 can only be processed after the completion of assignment 3, and assignment 8 can only be processed after the completion of assignment 7. There is no sequence between assignment 9 and assignments 3, 7 and 8. The sum time of the four assignments is 40 s, which is equal to the takt time.

The remaining assignments 10 and 11, with a total time of 35 s, less than takt time, can be put into one workstation.

The optimization results are shown in Fig. 8-5.

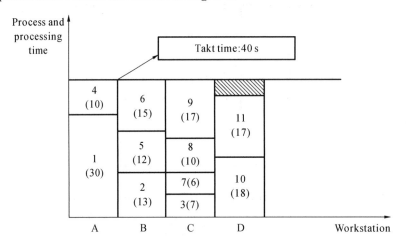

Fig. 8-5 Optimized Workstation Specific Information

Optimized line balance rate is

$$E = \frac{154}{4 \times 40} \times 100\% = 96.3\%$$

The optimized balance rate has increased form 77% to 96.3%, which is a highly satisfactory project.

8.2 Mixed Production Line Balance

8.2.1 Balance Problem of Mixed Production Line

The assembly line has experienced from one product assembly production to the present mixed assembly production of different products. In order to complete the given production task, a variety of products with similar structure and roughly the same working procedure but different specifications and models are put into the production line in a scientific and reasonable arrangement order to achieve continuous production with takt time in proportional manner. And the basic premise is a comprehensive balance of product varieties, worker and machines, the task plan, etc. The mixed production line has a high degree of flexibility and automation, and the corresponding scheduling can be made quickly according to the change of production tasks, which is suitable for multi-varieties and small batch production planning. This production mode is widely used in household appliances (air conditioner, refrigerator) and automobile production.

Similar to the single-variety assembly line, the core problem is how to arrange and combine multiple processes and assign them to the least number of workstations. The processing time of each workstation is as close as possible to the takt time of the production line, so that the working elements of the entire production line can be fully utilized, the sum of the production time of all workstations is the least, and the entire production line has the highest production efficiency.

Compared with the balance problem of a single variety production line, the production balance problem of a mixed production line is a combination problem of production balance of a different single varieties. It needs not only to consider the balance of each product, but also to analyze and consider different products according to the production capacity and processing time, which greatly increases the complexity of this problem.

As the mixed production line is an organic arrangement of each single production line, it is not simply piled up. Therefore, the goal of solving the mixed production line becomes more diverse, and its constraints are various. This type of problem belongs to the NPC problem and can't be solved at the polynomial level. Thus, it needs to be solved by software and algorithm. When faced with simple problems, Excel or VBA (visual basic for applications) is a tool for calculation. When faced with more complicated problems, WinQSB, COMSOAL, ASYBL and other softwares can be helpful. These softwares can handle thousands of process assignments.

The causes of the idle time of the mixed production line are as follows.

(1) As a result of the intermittent production caused by a worker's operational error or machine failure, the following worker needs to help this worker in the station to complete the production task, leaving the workers and machines in the follow-up workstation idle.

(2) Waiting in process caused by unreasonable production scheduling (process conflict). When the parts have been processed in the previous procedure and sent to the next workstation by the conveyor belt for processing, but the next workstation is in the working state, then the WIP needs to wait outside the workstation, which would waste time.

(3) Time wasted due to the lack of timely access to the auxiliary tools required for production. The auxiliary tools on production line are not in one-to-one correspondence with the production volume, but are recycled. For instance, work-in-process of different models and specifications needs to use different fixtures in different processes. When work-in-process has arrived at the workstation for production, but the fixture of the workstation has not returned to the workstation in time, the waiting time of work-in-process is generated.

8.2.2 Mathematical Model of Mixed Production Line Balance

The mathematical model of mixed production line balance is similar to the mathematical model of a single production line balance, it is necessary to first calculate the takt time of the production line, determine the minimum number of workstations required according to the takt time, and then arrange and combine the various assignments to fill the workstation, and finally calculate the balance rate of the production line. However, unlike a single production line, with the variety of models to be produced, and the amount of each kind of production is not necessarily the same per day, when calculating the takt time and the minimum number of workstations required, the original formula should make some changes. The specific changes are as follows:

$$C = \frac{\sum\limits_n t}{\sum\limits_{i=1}^{n} N_i} \tag{8-6}$$

$$N_{\min} = \left\lceil \frac{\sum\limits_{i=1}^{n} t_i N_i}{C \sum\limits_{i=1}^{n} N_i} \right\rceil \tag{8-7}$$

$$E = \frac{\sum\limits_{i=1}^{n} t_i N_i}{NC \sum\limits_{i=1}^{n} N_i} \tag{8-8}$$

where N_i is the number of the ith product produced per day; t_i is the production time required to produce an ith product; the rest of the variables are described above.

Example 8-7 A workshop plans to produce two different types of products. It is known that there are three different facilities in the workshop, and the production of the two models is the same each day. The processes of two different types of products are shown in Fig. 8-6, where 101 (11) indicates the first processing step of the job 1, and the processing time is 11 s. It is known that the production line has a production takt time of 30 s. Try to calculate the number of workstations that are ultimately needed and the balance rate of the production line.

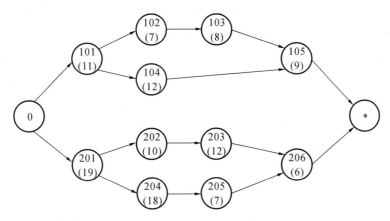

Fig. 8-6 Network Diagram of Processing for Two Models

Solution (1) First determine the minimum number of workstations required for this line. As the takt time of the line is known to be 30 s, so the minimum number of workstations required is

$$N_{\min} = \left\lceil \frac{\sum_{i=1}^{n} t_i}{C} \right\rceil = \left\lceil \frac{47+72}{30} \right\rceil = 4 \text{(piece)}$$

(2) According to the number of workstations and the takt time, the process assignments shall be distributed according to certain rules:

① Distributed according to the processing interval in which the processing task is located;

② When the processing time is relatively long, the assignment has a higher priority and should be distributed first;

③ When the sum of the process assignment time is greater than the production takt time, the process should be re-adjusted for distribution;

④ In the process of the distribution, the production line should be balanced at the same time.

First, the workstation 1 is allocated, and the number of process of workstation 1 is sequentially increased until the sum of the assignments' time is equal to the takt time or the processes of this workstation cannot be continued due to other reasons, such as time, sequence of processes, etc. By analogy, workstations followed are filled by assignments.

The final distribution results are as follows:

Workstation 1:201(19),202(10);

Workstation 2:101(11),102(7),104(12);

Workstation 3:203(12),204(18);

Workstation 4:103(8),105(9),205(7),206(6).

(3) Calculate the balance rate of the line:
$$E = \frac{47+72}{4 \times 30} \times 100\% = 99.2\%$$

In this way, the balance rate of the production line reaches 99.2%, so the satisfaction degree (acceptable degree) of assignments distribution is high.

Example 8-8 A mixed production line needs to produce 35, 25, and 20 pieces of A, B, and C products each day respectively. It adopts an 8-hour shift, regardless of the downtime, and the processing chart and the processing schedules of the three products are shown in Table 8-3, Figs. 8-7, 8-8, and 8-9, where 1 (4) indicates that the processing time of process 1 is 4 minutes. Try to calculate the balance rate of the mixed production line and optimize it with genetic algorithm.

Table 8-3 Processing Time for Each Process

Process number	1	2	3	4	5	6	7	8	9	10	11	12	13	14	15	16
Processing time/min	4	4	5	3	4	3	1	3	4	5	5	4	3	2	2	4

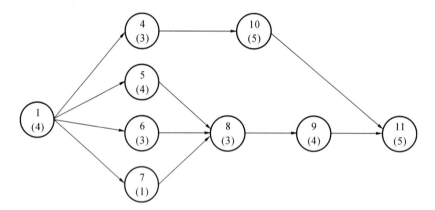

Fig. 8-7 Process Flow Chart of Product A

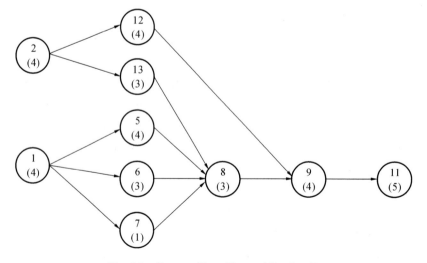

Fig. 8-8 Process Flow Chart of Product B

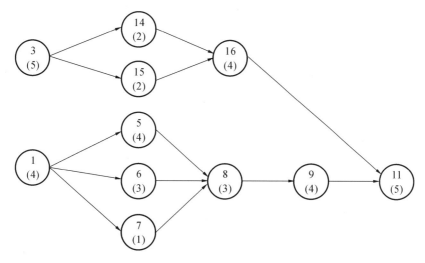

Fig. 8-9　Process Flow Chart of Product C

Solution　According to the diagrams above, it is known that product A has 9 processes and needs 32 minutes for assembly. Product B requires 10 processes with 35 minutes for assembly. Product C experiences 11 processes with 37 minutes. Due to the different quantities of product A, B and C produced each day, the total working time of producing product A, B and C per day is 1120 minutes, 875 minutes and 740 minutes respectively.

The production takt time of this mixed assembly line is

$$C = \frac{\sum T}{\sum_{i=1}^{n} N_i} = \frac{8 \times 60}{35 + 25 + 20} = 6(\min)$$

According to the takt time of the production line, the minimum number of workstations required by the production line is calculated as follows:

$$N_{\min} = \left\lceil \frac{\sum_{i=1}^{n} N_i t_i}{C \times \sum_{i=1}^{n} N_i} \right\rceil = \left\lceil \frac{35 \times 32 + 25 \times 35 + 20 \times 37}{6 \times (35 + 25 + 20)} \right\rceil = 6(\text{piece})$$

The workstations of the mixed assembly should be assigned. Three products all have common processes 1, 5, 6, 7, 8, 9, 11, the output of products A, B, C is 35, 25 and 20 pieces respectively; so process 1 needs $80 \times 4 = 320$ minutes per day. By analogy, the working time of each process can be calculated.

Then use genetic algorithm to solve the above case.

(1) Encoding. Encoding according to the sequence of each process, that is, each process(assignment element) that needs to be processed corresponds to the genetic position of one chromosome. After encoding, all elements on the chromosome must be arranged in descending order according to the position weight (set a priority). A feasible encoding method is shown in Fig. 8-10.

(2) Decoding. The individual assignment elements after the completion of the

Fig. 8-10 A feasible encoding method

encoding only express the order of processing in the real production. The decoding is based on the principle that the processing time of all assignment elements of each workstation is not greater than the production takt time, and the chromosome is sequentially distributed to each workstation.

The steps of decoding are as follows.

Step 1: tt =tt+time(x_i), if tt ⩽CT⩽tt+time(x_i), then $M=M+1$. If $i=N-1$, $M=M+1$, go to the step 2.

Step 2: $i=i+1$. If $i⩽N-1$, then go to the step 1. If $i=N$, the decoding ends.

where tt represents the sum of the working hours; the encoded chromosome sequence is x_i, which represents the serial number of each assignment, $i=1,2,\cdots,n$ ($n=16$), the initial value of i is 1; and the initial value of M is 0.

(3) Select the operator. In this case, the operator is selected by the optimal preservation method, that is, use the assignment with the smallest M value in all workstations directly to replace the one with the largest M value.

(4) Cross operator. According to the principle of the genetic algorithm, the result of the crossover of the 8th position as the crossover point is shown in Fig. 8-11.

Fig. 8-11 Crossover Result with the 8th Position as the Crossover Point

(5) Mutate operator. The result of mutation with the 6th position as the mutation point is shown in Fig. 8-12.

Fig. 8-12 Mutation Result with the 6th Position as the Mutation Point

The algorithm is programmed in software, the variable production takt time is set as 480 min, the population size is 100, the evolving algebra is 200, the optimal number of workstations is 6, the probability of crossover between chromosomes is 0.85, and the probability of mutation is 0.05. The calculated workstation information is shown in Fig. 8-13.

The optimized balance rate is

$$E = \frac{35 \times 32 + 25 \times 35 + 20 \times 37}{6 \times 6 \times (35 + 25 + 20)} \times 100\% = 95\%$$

With the optimization of the production line, the balance rate is greatly increased, and the distribution of working hours of each workstation is more balanced and reasonable, which improves the production efficiency.

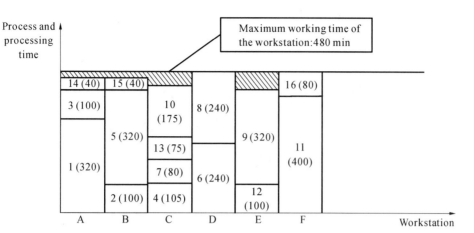

Fig. 8-13 Workstation Information

Chapter 9 Course Design of Production System Modeling and Simulation

9.1 Task Description of Course Design

The task, as described in section 3.5, is to solve different scale job shop scheduling problems with various constraints by using the optimization methods. Use traditional method (complex method), choosing or improving appropriate bionic algorithm (bionic algorithm for short) and manual scheduling method to solve the small-scale and medium-scale problems respectively and draw the Gantt charts; then analyze the main characteristics of these methods comparatively.

9.2 A Case of a Small-Scale Job Shop Scheduling Problem

There is a small-scale job shop scheduling problem involving only 3 jobs to be processed, as shown in Fig. 9-1. The processing types, the relations among each processing and the processing time are described in Fig. 9-1. The letter above the process represents the processing type, and the number next to it represents the processing time. For example, the type of process 101 is A, and the processing time is 16 mins. The equipment information is described in Table 9-1. It can be known that this job shop scheduling problem includes 3 jobs, 10 processes and 5 equipments from 5 types.

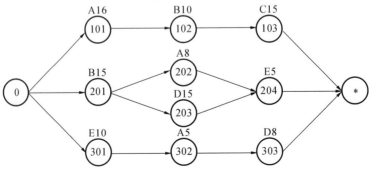

Fig. 9-1 Relations Between Processes and Equipments of Small-Scale JSSP

Table 9-1 Equipment Information of Small-Scale JSSP

Equipment No.	1	2	3	4	5
Equipment type	A	B	C	D	E

Complex method is used to seek the solution. The search process is shown in Fig. 9-2, the optimal solution is shown in Table 9-2, and the Gantt chart of the optimal solution is shown in Fig. 9-3.

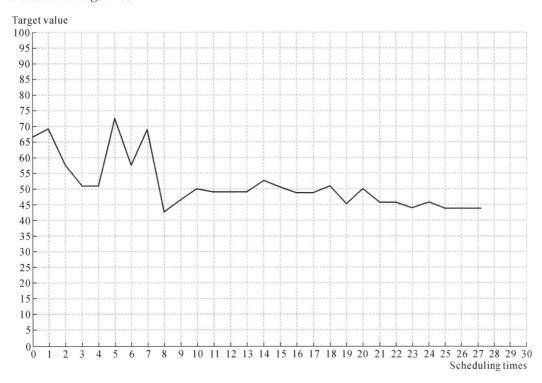

Fig. 9-2 Scheduling Curve of Small-Scale JSSP by Complex Method

Table 9-2 Scheduling Results of Small-Scale JSSP by Complex Method

Job No.	Equipment No.	Processing time/min	Start time/min	Completion time/min
101	1	16	0	16
102	2	10	16	26
103	3	15	26	41
201	2	15	0	15
202	1	8	31	39
203	4	15	16	31
204	5	5	39	44
301	5	10	0	10
302	1	5	19	24
303	4	8	32	40

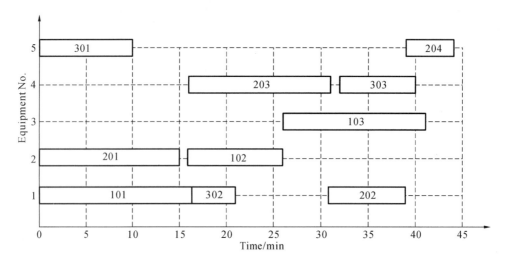

Fig. 9-3   Gantt Chart of Small-Scale JSSP by Complex Method

Bionic algorithm is used to seek the solution. The search process is shown in Fig. 9-4, the optimal solution is shown in Table 9-3, and Gantt chart of the optimal solution is shown in Fig. 9-5.

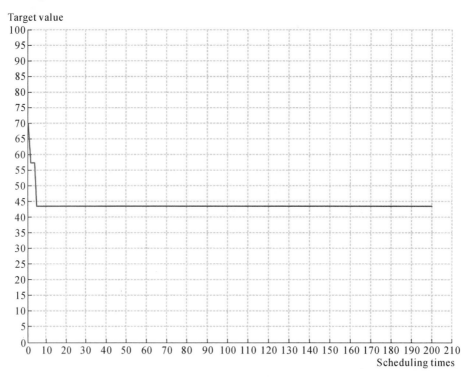

Fig. 9-4   Scheduling Curve of Small-Scale JSSP by Bionic Algorithm

Table 9-3   Scheduling Results of Small-Scale JSSP by Bionic Algorithm

Process No.	Equipment No.	Processing time/min	Start time/min	Completion time/min
101	1	16	0	16
102	2	10	16	26

continued

Process No.	Equipment No.	Processing time/min	Start time/min	Completion time/min
103	3	15	26	41
201	2	15	0	15
202	1	8	30	38
203	4	15	15	30
204	5	5	38	43
301	5	10	0	10
302	1	5	16	21
303	4	8	30	38

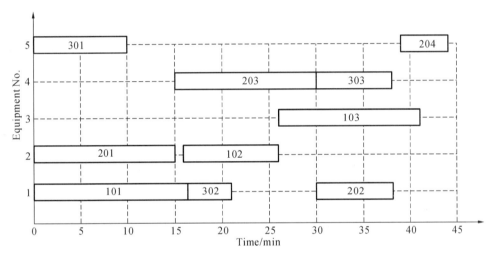

Fig. 9-5 Gantt Chart of Small-Scale JSSP by Bionic Algorithm

Manual scheduling method is used to seek the solution. The optimal solution is shown in Table 9-4, and the Gantt chart of the optimal solution is shown in Fig. 9-6.

Table 9-4 Scheduling Results of Small-Scale JSSP by Manual Scheduling Method

Equipment No.	Process No.	Start time/min	Completion time/min
1	101	0	16
1	202	30	38
1	302	16	21
2	102	16	15
2	201	0	26
3	103	26	41
4	203	15	30
4	303	30	38
5	204	38	43
5	301	0	10

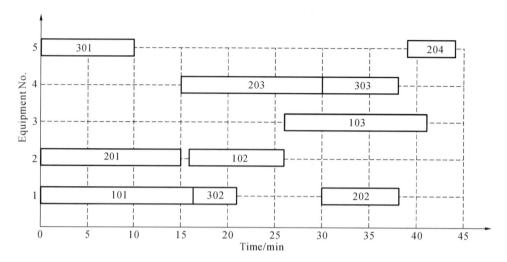

Fig. 9-6 Gantt Chart of Small-Scale JSSP by Manual Scheduling Method

According to the scheduling results above, three key parameters of the three scheduling methods are calculated: the total completion time, the idle time of equipment and the utilization ratio of working hours, as shown in Table 9-5.

Table 9-5 Comparison of Key Parameters

Key parameter	Complex method	Bionic algorithm	Manual scheduling method
The total completion time/min	44	43	43
The idle time of equipment/min	42	41	41
The utilization ratio of working hours	28.4%	28.1%	28.1%

From the table above, it can be found that different methods have pretty good reliability in solving small-scale JSSP. Moreover, the small-scale JSSP can be solved only by manual scheduling, and the difference is small between the solution obtained by complex method and that obtained by manual scheduling method.

9.3 A Case of a Medium-Scale Job Shop Scheduling Problem

There is a medium-scale job shop scheduling problem involving 4 jobs to be processed, as shown in Fig. 9-7. This job shop scheduling problem includes 4 jobs, 32 processes and 7 equipents of 5 categories. The equipment information is described in Table 9-6.

Table 9-6 Equipment Information of Medium-Scale JSSP

Equipment No.	1	2	3	4	5	6	7
Equipment type	A	A	B	B	C	D	E

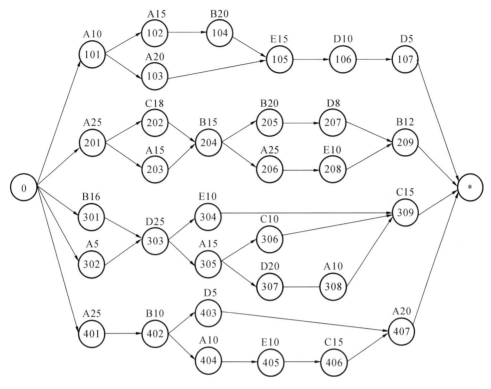

Fig. 9-7 Relations Between Processes and Equipments of Medium-Scale JSSP

Complex method is used to seek the solution. The search process is shown in Fig. 9-8, the optimal solution is shown in Table 9-7, and the Gantt chart of the optimal solution is shown in Fig. 9-9.

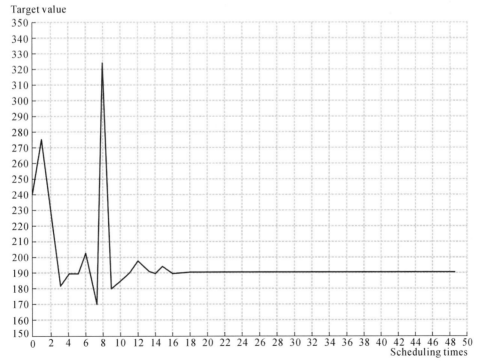

Fig. 9-8 Scheduling Curve of Medium-Scale JSSP by Complex Method

Table 9-7 Scheduling Results of Medium-Scale JSSP by Complex Method

Process No.	Equipment No.	Processing time/min	Start time/min	Completion time/min
101	1	10	16	26
102	1	15	62	77
103	1	20	42	62
104	3	20	77	97
105	7	15	97	112
106	6	10	118	128
107	5	5	141	146
201	2	25	13	38
202	5	18	55	73
203	2	15	40	55
204	4	15	73	88
205	4	20	93	113
206	1	25	113	138
207	6	8	138	146
208	7	10	146	156
209	3	12	160	172
301	3	16	8	24
302	1	5	3	8
303	6	25	28	53
304	7	10	85	95
305	2	15	70	85
306	5	10	95	105
307	6	20	146	166
308	1	10	166	176
309	5	15	176	191
401	1	25	62	87
402	3	10	97	107
403	6	5	128	133
404	2	10	107	117
405	7	10	133	143
406	5	15	146	161
407	2	20	161	181

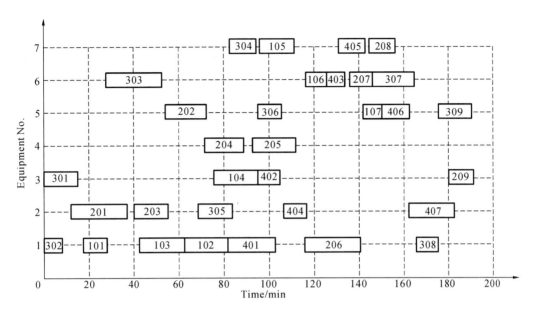

Fig. 9-9 Gantt Chart of Medium-Scale JSSP by Complex Method

Bionic algorithm is used to seek the solution. The search process is shown in Fig. 9-10, the optimal solution is shown in Table 9-8, and the Gantt chart of the optimal solution is shown in Fig. 9-11.

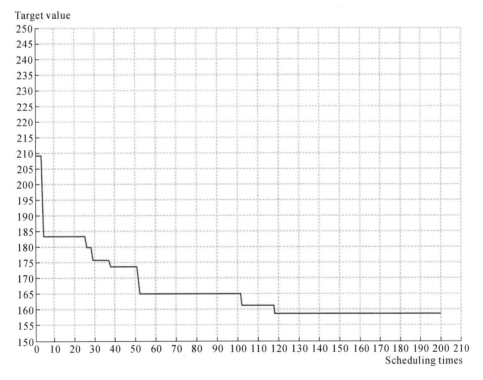

Fig. 9-10 Scheduling Curve of Medium-Scale JSSP by Bionic Algorithm

Table 9-8 Scheduling Results of Medium-Scale JSSP by Bionic Algorithm

Process No.	Equipment No.	Processing time/min	Start time/min	Completion time/min
101	2	10	25	35
102	2	15	55	70
103	1	20	35	55
104	3	20	83	103
105	7	15	103	118
106	6	10	120	130
107	5	5	143	148
201	2	25	0	25
202	5	18	50	68
203	2	15	35	50
204	3	15	68	83
205	4	20	83	103
206	2	25	111	136
207	6	8	103	111
208	7	10	136	146
209	3	12	146	158
301	3	16	0	16
302	1	5	25	30
303	6	25	30	55
304	7	10	118	128
305	1	15	55	70
306	5	10	90	100
307	6	20	70	90
308	2	10	100	110
309	5	15	128	143
401	1	25	0	25
402	4	10	25	35
403	6	5	115	120
404	1	10	70	80
405	7	10	80	90
406	5	15	100	115
407	1	20	120	140

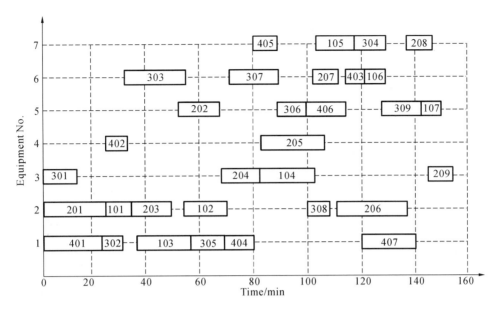

Fig. 9-11 Gantt Chart of Medium-Scale JSSP by Bionic Algorithm

Manual scheduling method is used to seek the solution. The optimal solution is shown in Table 9-9, and the Gantt chart of the optimal solution is shown in Fig. 9-12.

Table 9-9 Scheduling Results of Medium-Scale JSSP by Manual Scheduling Method

Equipment No.	Process No.	Start time/min	Completion time/min
1	103	35	55
1	302	25	30
1	305	55	70
1	401	0	25
1	404	70	80
1	407	120	140
2	101	25	35
2	102	55	70
2	201	0	25
2	203	35	50
2	206	111	136
2	308	100	110
3	104	83	103
3	204	68	83
3	209	146	158
3	301	0	16
4	205	83	103

continued

Equipment No.	Process No.	Start time/min	Completion time/min
4	402	25	35
5	107	143	148
5	202	50	68
5	306	90	100
5	309	128	143
5	406	100	115
6	106	120	130
6	207	103	111
6	303	30	55
6	307	70	90
6	403	115	120
7	105	103	118
7	208	136	146
7	304	118	128
7	405	80	90

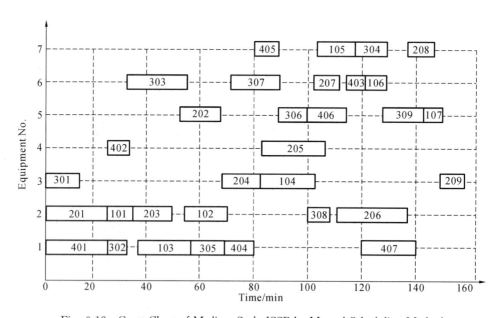

Fig. 9-12 Gantt Chart of Medium-Scale JSSP by Manual Scheduling Method

According to the results, three key parameters of these three scheduling methods are calculated: the total completion time, the idle time of equipment and the utilization ratio of working hours, as shown in Table 9-10.

Table 9-10 Comparison of Key Parameters

Key parameters	Complex method	Bionic algorithm	Manual scheduling method
The total completion time/min	191	158	158
The idle time of equipment/min	265	185	185
The utilization ratio of working hours	52.3%	60.2%	59.8%

It can be seen that bionic algorithm and manual scheduling method are significantly better than complex method for medium-scale problems in accordance with key parameters comparison. And bionic algorithm is slightly better than manual scheduling method. However, manual scheduling method is more cumbersome and requires more man power resources compared with bionic algorithm. Therefore, bionic algorithm is a better choice for medium-scale JSSP.

9.4 Summary

Job shop scheduling problem can be solved by traditional method (complex method), bionic algorithm and manual scheduling method. Their characteristics are as follows.

(1) Current methods have decent reliability in solving small-scale and medium-scale problems, but there is still no effective method for large-scale problems.

(2) Traditional method, bionic algorithm and manual scheduling method can be used to solve small-scale and medium-scale problems. Solution solved by manual scheduling method is more satisfying, but it needs lots of manual work. So, for small-scale and medium-scale problems, solutions solved by bionic algorithm and manual scheduling method are more optimized.

(3) Each method has different dependence on initial solution and parameters. Both manual scheduling method and traditional method have strong dependence on initial solution and parameters. For instance, the superiority of the initial solution, the termination condition and the mapping coefficient have significant influence on convergence, solving efficiency and optimization degree when using complex method. Bionic algorithm and manual scheduling method have better stability.

As the job shop scheduling problem is NP-Hard problem, there is no generally accepted mathematical method proved to be absolutely feasible so far. Based on experience, manual scheduling method or traditional method can be used to solve small-scale JSSP. And bionic algorithm can be used to solve medium-scale JSSP. However, there is still no effective and reliable method for large-scale JSSP. The related research is in its infancy, and there is still a long way to reach.

References

[1] REEVES C R, ROWE J E. Genetic algorithms—principles and perspectives: a guide to GA theory[M]. Boston:Kluwer Academic Publishers, 2003.

[2] CORMEN T H. Introduction to algorithms[M]. Cambridge, MA:MIT Press, 2005.

[3] GIORDANO F R , FOX W P, HORTON S B. A first course in mathematical modeling [M]. 5th edition. Boston:Brooks-Cole, 2013.

[4] HILLIER F S, LIEBERMAN G J. Introduction to operations research[M]. 10th edition. New York:McGraw-Hill, 2014.

[5] TAHA H A. Operations research—an introduction[M]. 10th edition. New York: Pearson Education Limited, 2017.

[6] HOLLAND J H. Adaptation in natural and artificial systems[M]. Ann Arbour: The University of Michigan Press, 1975.

[7] HOLLAND J H. Studying complex adaptive systems[J]. Journal of Systems Science and Complexity, 2006, 19(1):1-8.

[8] JOHNSON S M. On the representations of an integer as the sum of products of integers[J]. Transactions of the American Mathematical Society,1954, 76(2): 177-189.

[9] KOMAKI G M, SHEIKH S, MALAKOOTI B. Flow shop scheduling problems with assembly operations: a review and new trends[J]. International Journal of Production Research, 2019,57(10):2926-2955.

[10] DORIGO M, GAMBARDELLA L M. Ant colonies for the travelling salesman problem[J]. Biosystems, 1997, 43(2):73-81.

[11] MIKELL P G. Automation, production systems, and computer-integrated manufacturing [M]. 4th edition. New Jersey:Prentice Hall,2011.

[12] SHELDON M R. Stochastic process [M]. 2nd edition. New York:John Wiley & Sons,1996.

[13] STEFAN H. Mathematical modeling[M]. Berlin:Springer-Verlag, 2011.

[14] VITAL-SOTO A,AZAB A,BAKI M F. Mathematical modeling and a hybridized bacterial foraging optimization algorithm for the flexible job-shop scheduling problem with sequencing flexibility[J]. Journal of Manufacturing Systems, 2020, 54: 74-93.

[15] LUO Y B. Nested optimization method combining complex method and ant colony optimization to solve JSSP with complex associated processes [J]. Journal of Intelligent Manufacturing, 2017,28:1801-1815.